The Hemmings Motor News Book of

STUDEBAKERS

ISBN 0-917808-56-8
Library of Congress Card Number: 00-106571

One of a series of Hemmings Motor News Collector-Car Books. Other books in the series include:
The Hemmings Motor News Book of Cadillacs; The Hemmings Motor News Book of Corvettes; The Hemmings
Motor News Book of Chrysler Performance Cars; The Hemmings Motor News Book of Mustangs; The Hemmings
Motor News Book of Postwar Fords

Hemmings Motor News
Collector Car Publications and Marketplaces
1-800-CAR-HERE (227-4373)
www.hemmings.com

The Hemmings Motor News Book of
STUDEBAKERS

Editor-In-Chief
Terry Ehrich

Editor
Richard A. Lentinello

Designer
Nancy Bianco

Cover photo by Fred Fox

This book compiles driveReports which have appeared in Hemmings Motor News's Special Interest Autos magazine (SIA) over the past 30 years. The editors at Hemmings Motor News express their gratitude to the following writers, photographers, and artists who made this book possible through their many fine contributions to Special Interest Autos magazine:

Bob Bourke	Ken Gross	Moreford Pidgeon
Arch Brown	John F. Katz	Connie Stanton
Dave Brown	Bud Juneau	John Stanton
Jean Constantine	George Krem, Jr.	Brooks Stevens
Mike Cook	George Krem, Sr.	Denis Tanney
Lynn Eyerly	Michael Lamm	Rich Taylor
Fred K. Fox	Duncan McRae	Russ von Sauers
Jeff Godshall	Darryl Norenberg	Josiah Work
		Vince Wright

We are also grateful to David Brownell, Michael Lamm, and Rich Taylor, the editors under whose guidance these driveReports were written and published. We thank Car and Driver, Fototecnica, Raymond Loewy, Strother MacMinn, Motor Trend, Richard Quinn, E.T. Reynolds, John Shanahan, Brooks Stevens Collection, Studebaker Drivers Club, and Jonathan Thompson, who have graciously contributed photographs to Special Interest Autos magazine and this book.

CONTENTS

Special Interest Autos (SIA) magazine's back issues are referred to in this book by issue number. If in stock, copies may be purchased directly from Hemmings Motor News at 800-227-4373 or at www.hemmings.com.

RIDES FOR RENT

EVER since 1858, when John Mohler Studebaker returned to South Bend from the California gold fields with an $8,000 poke — his savings from five years' work building wheelbarrows for the miners in old Hangtown — Studebaker had been a pioneer in the transportation industry, and a builder of high-quality vehicles.

Studebaker wagons had already established a solid reputation for themselves before young John, third of five Studebaker brothers, became a part of the organization. But John was the aggressive member of the family, and besides, his savings supplied the capital that enabled the brothers to expand their business.

The Civil War broke out a couple of years later, and the Studebaker brothers were able to make a small fortune building freight wagons for the Union army. Then in the years following the war the business expanded until, by 1881, the company's annual sales came to more than two million dollars. A full line of vehicles was offered, including freight wagons, farm wagons, formal broughams, hearses and a pert little buggy called the "Izzer."

A story goes with it. According to family legend, at a local horse

1926 STUDEBAKER TAXI

by Josiah Work
photos by Bud Juneau

auction, Peter Studebaker, the salesman in the family, overheard a seller extolling the virtues of his nags by reciting a litany of their past performances, blue ribbons won, and the like. A bystander listened for a time, then exclaimed in disgust, "Has-beens! They're all has-beens! I don't want no 'Wuzzer.' I want an 'Izzer'!" And so the "Izzer" buggy was brought to market. For many years it was a Studebaker best-seller.

By 1902, four of the five Studebaker brothers had died. Only John remained, aided in the operation of the company by his son-in-law, Fred Fish, a prominent corporation lawyer and former lieutenant governor of New Jersey. Happily, Fish had the foresight to see what was about to happen to the transportation industry; and at his instigation Studebaker undertook to build electric runabouts, one of which was sold to Thomas Edison.

Two years later, Fish wanted to build gasoline-powered automobiles. Now, John Mohler Studebaker had his own opinion of the gas-buggies of the day, and John was never reluctant to express his views. He declared, "To me, the gasoline automobile is a clumsy, dangerous, noisy brute of a vehicle. They're going to catch fire. They're not safe. They blow up. Accidents will happen. A lot of people are going to be killed. The damned things stink to high heaven, they shake your liver to pieces, they always break down at the worst moment, and in short they are a public nuisance, and even worse, a public menace!"

Having got that off his chest, John Studebaker gave his reluctant blessing to Fred Fish's plan to build gasoline-powered motorcars. The first one, a 16-horsepower, two-cylinder machine, was sold that year — 1904 — to another Studebaker son-in-law, H. D. Johnson. And by the following year, John himself was using a new Studebaker-Garford automobile.

By 1911, Studebaker's volume came to twenty-eight and a half million dollars, an astronomical figure by the standards of the time; and Studebaker was America's second-largest producer of motorcars, with the year's output totalling 26,827 cars. John Studebaker, 78 years old by then, turned the presidency of the company over to Fred Fish, though he remained as chairman of the board and continued to take a lively interest in company affairs until his death in 1917.

In 1915, upon Fred Fish's retirement, Albert Russel Erskine took the helm at Studebaker. Over the next eight years, Erskine tripled the company's gross sales, doubled the net profits and delighted the stockholders with his practice of paying generous dividends. Ultimately Erskine's open-handed fiscal policies led to receivership for Studebaker and suicide for its genial but ill-starred president. But in the meanwhile, there were several more good years — and thousands of fine automobiles.

By 1920, Studebaker was building six-cylinder cars exclusively. They came in three series, the Light Six, Special Six

Above: Cowl-mounted headlamps allow taxi to be seen, but not to see terribly well. **Below:** And you thought side marker lights first appeared in the sixties. **Bottom:** In terms of salaries back then a taxi ride was a pricey way to travel.

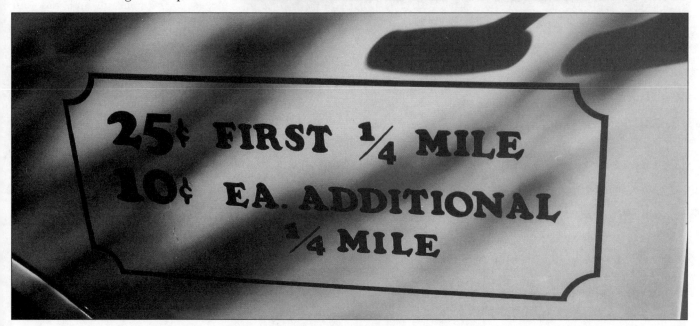

STUDEBAKER

and Big Six, with engine displacements of 207.1, 288.6 and 353.8 cubic inches, respectively. Prices ranged from $1,435 to $2,135 in the popular "touring car" body style. All three models carried one of the strongest guarantees in the industry. They were developed by Studebaker's own engineering department, and reflected the thinking of Fred Zeder, who would later play a leading role in the creation of the first Chrysler automobile.

By 1925 the Light Six had been re-titled the Standard Six, otherwise known as the Model ER. Its wheelbase had been stretched from 112 to 113 inches and weight was increased by a couple of hundred pounds. Engine displacement had grown to 241.6 cubic inches, from which 50 honest horsepower and an unspecified but generous amount of torque was developed. The price, in the popular phaeton style, had been cut to $1,145 by that time, $30 less than the 190.8-c.i.d. Buick Standard Six. At that figure it surely must have been one of the best buys, possibly *the* best buy, in the lower-medium-price field. (It must be admitted, however, that Studebaker's closed cars were not as competitively priced, at that time, as the open models.)

If the Studebakers of this era had one drawback, it had to do with their brakes. Buick and Chrysler had both adopted four-wheel binders in 1924, mechanicals in the Buick, hydraulics for the Chrysler. Studebaker, however, resisted, noting what they called the "admitted danger" of locking the front wheels. "The regular brake equipment of all Studebaker cars is our standard rear-wheel system," a 1925 sales brochure declared. "This system is simple, safe, economical and has our endorsement. After one year's exploitation in the United States of four-wheel brake systems, our experience and investigations justify us in saying that the public attitude toward such systems is one of indifference. We believe that those who object to them, at the present time, greatly out-number those who look upon them with favor. Members of the corporation and its dealer organization generally favor rear wheel brakes only."

Brave talk, that, but it evidently didn't play in Peoria.

However reluctantly, Studebaker bowed to public pressure. Sort of. The same sales brochure continues, "Studebaker desires to give the public what they want, however, and therefore we have designed and are producing the Studebaker 4-Wheel Hydraulic Brake System, which is simpler, more powerful and easier of operation than any system

Above: Cab has been restored with correct period graphics. *Right:* Heavy steel disc wheels enjoyed a brief vogue in mid-twenties. *Facing page, top:* Traditional MotoMeter monitors coolant temperature. *Center left:* Passengers enjoyed posh mohair seating. *Center right:* Stop/tail-lamp carries Studebaker i.d. etched in glass. *Bottom:* Styling is functional rather than beautiful.

1925-26 Studebaker
Table of Prices and Weights

	Price*	Weight
Standard Six, Model ER, 113-inch w/b, 50 hp		
Duplex Phaeton, 5-passenger	$1,145	2,870
Duplex Roadster, 3-passenger	$1,125	2,760
Coach, 5-passenger	$1,195	2,980
Country Club Coupe, 3-passenger	$1,295	2,945
Sport Roadster, 3-passenger	$1,235	2,820
Sport Phaeton, 5-passenger	$1,255	2,930
Sedan, 5-passenger (mohair trim)	$1,495	3,260
Sedan, 5-passenger (wool trim)	$1,395	3,260
Berline, 5-passenger	$1,650	3,280
TOTAL "ER" PRODUCTION, AUGUST 1924-AUGUST 1926:		147,099
Special Six, Model EQ, 120-inch w/b, 65 hp		
Duplex Phaeton, 5-passenger	$1,445	3,475
Duplex Roadster, 3-passenger	$1,395	3,360
Victoria, 4-passenger	$1,750	3,665
Sedan, 5-passenger	$1,895	3,855
Berline, 5-passenger	$2,125	3,890
Brougham, 5-passenger	$2,120	3,785
Sport Roadster, 3-passenger	$1,395	3,480
Coach, 5-passenger	$1,445	3,520
TOTAL "EQ" PRODUCTION, AUGUST 1924-AUGUST 1926:		53,780
Big Six, Model EP, 127-inch w/b, 75 hp		
Duplex Phaeton, 7-passenger	$1,795	3,785
Coupe, 5-passenger	$1,645	4,030
Brougham, 5-passenger	$2,325	4,095
Sedan, 7-passenger	$2,245	4,150
Berline, 7-passenger	$2,045	4,200
Big Six, Model EP, 120" w/b, 75 hp		
Sport Phaeton, 5-passenger	$1,795	3,505
Club Coupe, 5-passenger	$2,045	3,570
Sedan, 5-passenger	$2,245	3,785
TOTAL "EP" PRODUCTION, AUGUST, 1924-AUGUST, 1926:		40,216

*Price as of September 1925

now furnished on any American cars. We unhesitatingly recommend this system to Studebaker customers who want 4-wheel brakes, and stand ready to furnish them as optional equipment at a small extra charge."

Sixty dollars extra, to be exact, and the hydraulics were supplied in combination with steel disc wheels, replacing the usual artillery type. Cars so-equipped weighed an extra 170 pounds.

It was, in all honesty, a weird braking system. Studebaker authority Fred Fox explains: "Instead of running hydraulic brake lines to each wheel, mechanical linkages were connected to a master cylinder. Oil pressure to the master cylinder was developed by a gear type oil pump that was driven off the main shaft of the transmission. Oil from the transmission was used in the system. Depressing the brake pedal closed a bypass valve and forced the master cylinder to actuate the four wheel mechanical brake system. The problem was that the pump — because of its connection to the transmission main shaft — only worked when the car was moving. To overcome this problem, the final three inches of brake pedal travel actuated mechanical brake linkages to the rear wheels."

If this sounds like a mechanism that could only have been conceived by Rube Goldberg, so be it. In any case it evidently held little appeal for Studebaker customers, and very few cars were fitted with the system, which was reportedly hard to get used to. By 1927 it was withdrawn from sale, and conventional four-wheel mechanical brakes — internal front, external rear, after the practice of

specifications

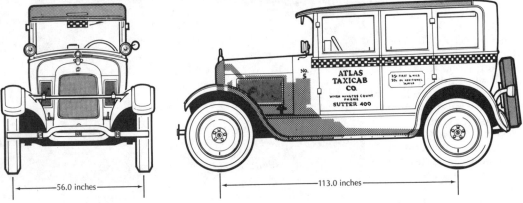

← 56.0 inches →   ← 113.0 inches →

1926 Studebaker ER Standard Six

Original price	$1,395 f.o.b. factory (sedan)
Options on dR car	Taxicab equipment, Biflex front bumper, disc wheels, MotoMeter

ENGINE

Type	6-cylinder, L-head
Bore x stroke	3.375 inches x 4.5 inches
Displacement	241.6 cubic inches
Compression ratio	4.5:1
Horsepower @ rpm	50 @ 2,200
Taxable horsepower	27.34
Main bearings	4
Fuel system	Stromberg OE-1 1-inch updraft carburetor, vacuum feed
Lubrication system	Pressure to main, connecting rod and camshaft bearings
Cooling system	Centrifugal pump
Electrical system	6-volt battery/coil

TRANSMISSION

Type	3-speed selective, floor-mounted lever
Ratios: 1st	3.24:1
2nd	1.96:1
3rd	1.00:1
Reverse	4.17:1

CLUTCH

Type	Dry disc
Diameter	10 inches
Actuation	Mechanical, foot pedal

REAR AXLE

Type	Spiral bevel
Ratio	4.6:1
Drive axles	Semi-floating
Torque medium	Springs

STEERING

Type	Worm and wheel
Turns lock-to-lock	2
Ratio	11.0:1
Turning diameter	40 feet

BRAKES

Type	External mechanical, on rear wheels
Drum diameter	15 inches
Effective area	202 square inches

CHASSIS & BODY

Construction	Body-on-frame
Frame	Heavy channel iron, 4 cross-members
Body	Composite wood and steel construction
Body type	4-door sedan with taxicab equipment

SUSPENSION

Front	I-beam axle, 36.5-inch x 2-inch semi-elliptic springs
Rear	Rigid axle, 50.125-inch x 2-inch semi-elliptic springs
Tires	31 x 5.25 (5.25/21)
Wheels	Steel disc

WEIGHTS AND MEASURES

Wheelbase	113 inches
Overall length	169 inches
Overall width	69 inches
Overall height	75 inches
Front track	56 inches
Rear track	56 inches
Min. road clearance	9.5 inches
Shipping weight	3,260 pounds

CAPACITIES

Crankcase	8 quarts
Cooling system	16.5 quarts
Fuel tank	14 gallons

CALCULATED DATA

Horsepower per c.i.d.	.207
Weight per hp	65.2 pounds
Weight per c.i.d.	13.5 pounds
P.S.I. (brakes)	16.1 pounds

Right: Owner Lawrence Siegel has proper period headgear from the original taxi firm. *Facing page, top:* Little flag on meter indicates cab's availability. *Center:* Ventilated shades allow privacy and fresh air for passengers. *Bottom:* Illuminated meter displays the bad news.

STUDEBAKER

the day — were adopted as standard issue for all models.

Whether or not the brakes had anything to do with the matter is impossible to determine, but between the record-breaking 1923 season and 1926, when our driveReport car was built, Studebaker slid from seventh to eleventh place in industry sales, as production declined by 29 percent, from 146,238 to 103,189 units. In contrast, Buick's output increased by 32 percent and Nash's by 139 percent over the same three-year period.

The Model ER Standard Six was introduced, along with the Model EQ Special Six and the Model EP Big Six, on September 14, 1924. Studebaker did not make annual model changes in those days, and production continued without major modification until August 1926. Five Standard Six body styles were offered, initially, including a five-passenger coupe, three-passenger coupe-roadster and five-passenger sedan. But the most interesting types were a pair of unique Duplex models, a three-passenger roadster and a five-passenger phaeton.

Throughout the industry, the most popular body styles in those days were the open types, the roadsters and — especially — the touring cars. Manufacturers had not yet learned to let the body sides hang down over the frame rails, with the result that closed cars were almost universally tall, ungainly and top-heavy. They outweighed the open types — in the case of the Studebaker ER, by some 400 pounds, and they cost several hundred dollars more than their fresh-air counterparts.

In some parts of the country the "California Top" was a popular aftermarket item. Designed to convert the touring car inexpensively to a semi-enclosed body style, it was a permanent, though light-weight top, equipped with windows that slid along rails mounted on the tops of the doors.

The Duplex models, designed by J. H. Bourgon, Studebaker's chief body engineer, represented an improvement on the California Top concept, combining the latter's steel-reinforced, fixed-position top with the convenience of pull-down isinglass curtains. At introduction time Studebaker was able to sell the Standard Six Duplex Phaeton for $450 less than the four-door sedan in the same series. For a brief time, the Duplex types were highly popular. But as the price of the sedan fell, from $1,595 in January 1925 to $1,495 that September, then to $1,395 a year later and $1,195 when the 1927 models appeared, demand fell off sharply, and the

STUDEBAKER

Above: Checkerboard sign hanging from visor indicates a cab coming at you. *Right:* Glass and metal divider gives passengers the feeling of riding in their own limo. *Facing page:* Taxi's steering is very quick, making it highly maneuverable in city traffic.

Duplex types were discontinued.

Meanwhile, minor styling changes were made from time to time, and other Standard Six body types were introduced. Perhaps the most significant of these was the Coach, or two-door sedan, which appeared during the spring of 1925. By that Fall, the Coach could be purchased for $1,195, just $50 more than the Duplex Phaeton. Other new types included a Sport Roadster, Sport Phaeton, Berline (offered for 1925 only), and — for a brief time — a five-passenger Brougham whose rear quarter featured oval "opera" windows and decorative landau irons.

The 75-horsepower Big Six was, of course, Studebaker's most powerful car, as well as its most luxurious. But it was the Standard Six that stood out in competitive events. Fred Fox tells us that "Early in 1925, a Standard Six Duplex Phaeton set a speed record for the 362-mile run from El Paso, Texas, to Santa Fe, New Mexico." Traveling over unim-

1926

It was, as they say, a Very Good Year. Folks were singing Rodgers and Hart's "The Girl Friend," whose lyric ("Isn't she cute/Isn't she sweet/She's gentle and mentally nearly complete") would raise the hackles of today's feminists. Other ditties of the day included "Rio Rita," "Charmaine," "I Know That You Know" (which would find new life a decade or so later in a swing rendition by Benny Goodman), and — perhaps the best of the lot — an enduring Gershwin ballad called "Someone to Watch Over Me."

Science was on the march. Transatlantic radiotelephone was established on March 7, the fiftieth anniversary of Alexander Graham Bell's telephone patent. The element illinium was discovered by B.S. Hopkins, of the University of Illinois.

Aeronautic exploits included Lieutenant Commander (later Rear Admiral) Richard E. Byrd's flight over the North Pole. On the athletic front, Gene Tunney won — by a decision, in the tenth round — the heavyweight boxing title that had been Jack Dempsey's. And Gertrude Ederle became the first woman to swim the English Channel.

Of course, life had its downside. Prohibition was the law of the land, and bootleg scotch brought $48 a case, when you could find it. Rye, of very bad quality, sold for $85, while decent champagne fetched $95. The prices were bad enough, but the real tragedy was that nearly 2,000 Americans died from consuming poison liquor that year.

Brigadier General "Billy" Mitchell, one of America's top air heroes of World War I, was court-martialed for his insistence, among other criticisms, that the tragic loss of the airship *Shenandoah* had been the result of "incompetence, criminal negligence and almost treasonable administration of the national defense by the War and Navy Departments." Mitchell was reduced to the rank of colonel and suspended from the service for five years. But Billy Mitchell was right, and in 1942, six years following his death, he was posthumously restored to the rank of major general.

Deaths during 1926 included 31-year-old Rudolpho Alfonzo Raffaelo Pierre Filibert Gugliemi di Valentina d'Antonguolla, better known as the suave matinee idol, Rudolph Valentino. Also on the casualty list was crack shot Annie Oakley, whose exploits, real and fictional, were immortalized 20 years later in the musical comedy *Annie Get Your Gun.*

On the other hand, Marilyn Monroe was born that year. So, for that matter, were Queen Elizabeth II, Andy Griffith and Jerry Lewis.

Showboat, a popular new novel by Edna Ferber, would soon provide the libretto for an immortal Jerome Kern/Oscar Hammerstein musical of the same name. Other books included Carl Sandburg's two-volume *Abraham Lincoln: The Prairie Years*, Ernest Hemingway's *The Sun Also Rises*, William Faulkner's *Soldier's Pay* and Thorne Smith's hilarious *Topper.*

The first talking motion picture was exhibited that August at the Warner Theatre, in New York City. It was *Don Juan,* featuring John Barrymore together with a synchronized orchestral accompaniment. It was a crude beginning, but sound films quickly made silent pictures obsolete. Still, among the "silents" that year were some good ones: *Ben Hur*, with Ramon Navarro and Francis X. Bushman; *Stella Dallas*, starring Belle Bennett and Ronald Coleman; *Black Pirate*, with Douglas Fairbanks; and *Volga Boatman*, featuring William Boyd, who would ultimately come to fame as Hopalong Cassidy.

San Francisco was a bustling town then, with by far the busiest seaport on the West Coast. Both the Dollar Steamship Company and Matson Navigation were headquartered there. Optimism was the order of the day. In the words of historian Felix Riesenberg, Jr., "A new generation had forgotten the great fire of '06, and in times that had never been so good the town became sheathed in gleaming tile and chromium. The enthusiasm and energy of the fifties (that's the 1850s, of course), the expansion of the seventies, and the enterprise of the nineties seemed to have combined. It was a city with space to move about in, a city that would grow. Every week more firms were opening and the red ink in Montgomery and California street offices was drying. Again San Francisco was a metropolis of millionaires, free spenders and fun."

The city's population stood at about 600,000, and another 100,000 people commuted by ferry from Oakland and Berkeley, or by train from some of the peninsula communities, to work there. Cable cars climbed the steepest hills, just as they do today; while two streetcar lines — the Municipal and the Market Street Railways — supplied transportation elsewhere. The fare was five cents.

Or, you could pick up the telephone and call Sutter 400, and the Atlas Taxicab and Auto Service, located at 118 Powell Street, would dispatch a handsome Studebaker taxi like our driveReport car.

That is, if you could afford to pay 25 cents for the first quarter-mile and ten cents for each quarter-mile thereafter.

proved roads, the Studebaker made the run in ten hours, 35 minutes, cutting one hour and 21 minutes from the previous record. But what was really remarkable was the fact that throughout the contest the car's transmission was locked in top gear.

Another interesting contest took place on New Year's Day, 1926. The object was to see which car could be the first to travel from the Pacific Coast to the entrance of Yosemite National Park. As Fred Fox tells the story, "L. G. Goodwin, an employee of Modesto, California's Wm. J. Silva Studebaker dealership, took a new Standard Six Duplex Phaeton off his boss's showroom floor and entered it in the event. Traveling over icy mountain roads covered by fresh snow, Goodwin beat all comers to Yosemite's entrance gate. Goodwin's win was all the more remarkable when you realize that it was the fifth consecutive year that a Studebaker vehicle had won the race."

Driving Impressions

Among the Model ER Studebakers produced during 1926 was our driveReport car. It evidently left the factory as a sedan, to be equipped afterward as a taxicab. The conversion was a thoroughly professional job, featuring a sliding-glass divider window, fixed-position front seat upholstered in leather, mohair passenger seat in the rear, and of course the inevitable meter — which,

by the way, is still in working order. Riding atop the right rear fender is a small, two-sided lamp which shines green to the front, clear at the rear. The taxicab's headlamps, unlike those of the stock passenger cars, are hand-adjustable and are mounted at the cowl, just forward of the windshield. The windshield itself opens out, providing ample ventilation; and the wiper is vacuum-operated. Curtains for the rear and rear quarter windows are supplied, in the interest of privacy for the passengers; and at the top of each quarter window there is a ventilating device. Assist handles are also provided, for the passengers' convenience.

Dashboard instrumentation, quite complete by 1926 standards, includes an ammeter, hydrostatic fuel gauge, oil pressure indicator and clock. A Boyce MotoMeter rides atop the radiator cap. Instruments are indirectly lighted, a progressive feature for 1926, and the dome light is controlled from the driver's seat. The odometer reads 79,353 miles, but of course it's anybody's guess how many times those numbers may have appeared. Pedal wear indicates that the cab has seen plenty of use.

During its active years the cab was owned by the Atlas Taxicab and Auto Service Company of San Francisco, whose logo, "When Moments Count," it still displays. The "Vacancy" lamp, inconspicuously located beneath the exterior visor, signals the cab's readi-

ness to return to the streets of the city.

Optional equipment, in addition to the taxicab conversion, includes a Biflex front bumper (but no rear bumper; cabbies must have driven more carefully in 1926), steel disc wheels, an after-market accelerator pedal, and the ubiquitous MotoMeter.

In most respects, the Studebaker Standard Six strikes us as an ideal vehicle for use as a San Francisco taxi. It's stoutly built and reliable, and it has torque enough to climb a wall, if only it could get the necessary traction. Admittedly, one might wish for four-wheel brakes when coming down the city's legendary hills. Even so, we found the two-wheel service brakes to be a good deal more effective than we expected, though they squeak dreadfully. The parking brake is strong enough to hold the car, even on the steepest incline.

Speed, however, is not the cab's forte. Studebaker offered a variety of axle ratios, ranging from 4.18:1 to a 5.11:1 stump-puller. This car came with 4.60:1 gearing, which is ideal for hill climbing, though it limits the car's top end to about 48 miles an hour. But then, on the streets of San Francisco the driver would have done well to travel even half that fast.

The Studebaker is not a particularly easy car to drive. With a ratio of 11.0:1, steering is very quick, requiring only two turns to go from lock to lock — which in

STUDEBAKER

continued from page 59

itself could be an advantage in city traffic. But the downside, inevitably, is that it takes a lot of muscle to turn that wheel.

The clutch is smooth, though it requires more than average pedal pressure, but the transmission, with its straight-cut gears, is a bit of a brute. Even to a driver who has had years of experience with non-synchro gear boxes, it's a challenge to change gears in the Studebaker without clashing.

The ride is firm, yet comfortable, and there is less choppiness than we anticipated. Corners are taken without excessive leaning. From the perspective of a tall driver, however, the front seat is miserable. There is no adjustment; hardly anyone offered adjustable seats in 1926. Leg room is limited, and the backrest is much too erect for comfort.

Owner Lawrence Siegel purchased the taxi in 1992 from a San Francisco public relations firm. Cosmetically, it was in good condition, though the restoration is evidently an old one. New cams had to be machined in order for the door locks to be restored to good working order. The lights were weak, because they were not properly grounded; and some detailing was required. Mechanically the car continued on page 85

Above: There's even a floor-mounted heat outlet for passenger comfort in colder climates. *Below:* Meaty wheel offers good leverage for heavy steering.

STUDEBAKER

Above: Understressed flathead six develops a whisker more than 1/5 bhp per cubic inch.
Below: Checker theme extends from front visor right around the back of the car.

could still use some help. The transmission, clutch and rear end are in excellent shape, and so are the brakes, but the front end needs new king pins and a general going over. The engine needed only a carburetor overhaul to make the cab driveable, but when the block was disassembled by Studebaker expert Jerry Washburn, it became evident that the crankshaft should be replaced. A parts car will shortly contribute its engine to the cause, and a new set of tires is also planned for the near future.

Meanwhile, however, Lawrence and Sarah Siegel displayed the taxi at the 1993 Silverado Concours d'Elegance, where we first saw it. It drew about as much attention as any vehicle on the field and, despite its imperfections, the Studebaker took Third Place in the Commercial class.

San Francisco was really in its heyday when the Siegels' taxicab was new (see sidebar, page 10). Now, if only it could talk, what stories it could tell. 🐎

Acknowledgments and Bibliography
Automotive Industries, February 18, 1926; Erskine, Albert Russel, History of the Studebaker Corporation; Fox, Fred K., "1925-26 Standard Six: An Early Success Story." Turning Wheels, December, 1986; Kimes, Beverly Rae and Henry Austin Clark, Jr. (eds.), Standard Catalog of American Cars, 1805-1942; Motor Age, November 5, 1925; Naul, G. Marshall, The Specification Book for U.S. Cars, 1920-29; Raucher, Alan R., "Albert Russel Erskine." Encyclopedia of American Business History and Biography; Studebaker factory literature.
Our thanks to Dave Brown, Durham, California; Fred Fox, Delhi, California; Ken Kiefer, Heathrow, Florida. Special thanks to Lawrence Siegel, Orinda, California.

BARGAIN CLASSIC:

1930 STUDEBAKER PRESIDENT EIGHT

T HERE really wasn't anything the matter with the Studebaker Big Six engine. Nothing at all, except that the big, bulky lump of iron had become hopelessly obsolete!

Twenty-nine percent larger than the biggest Buick powerplant and 12.5 percent bigger than the Cadillac V-8, the 353.8 cubic inch Studebaker flathead generated enough torque to pull a train. Although it was rated at a comparatively modest 75 horsepower, same as the Buick, during 1927 this engine had powered Studebaker Commanders to an impressive string of competition victories, breaking old records and setting new ones along the way. For instance:

• April, 1927, at Culver City, Califor-

By Arch Brown
photos by Dave Brown

nia: A 5,000-mile endurance run. Elapsed time 81 hours, 48 minutes, 22 seconds. Average speed of the Commander Victoria (pit stops included): 61.12 miles an hour.

• Labor Day, 1927, at Atlantic City: A pair of Commander roadsters placed first and second in a 75-mile stock car race for six-cylinder cars, in competition with two Chryslers, a Buick, a Nash, a Hudson and a Star. Winning speed: 86 mph.

• August/September, 1927, from

New York to San Francisco: Ab Jenkins, driving a Commander sedan, made the trip in 77 hours, 40 minutes, skinning more than two hours off the previous record.

• October 18, 1927, again at Atlantic City: Under American Automobile Association auspices, two roadsters and a sedan circled the track night and day for 25,000 miles. Average speed for the roadsters: 65.31 mph. The sedan, laid up for two hours after rolling over on a rain-slick turn, averaged 61.98 miles an hour.

Cannon and Fox, in their fine Studebaker history, note that "At this point Studebaker held every endurance and speed record for fully equipped stock

Originally published in Special Interest Autos #119, Sept.-Oct. 1990

Driving Impressions

Not until September 13, 1983, was any factory-bodied Studebaker recognized by the Classic Car Club of America. But on that date, the club's board of directors approved the application of Dr. C. David Hemp, a Millville, California dentist. His 1930 President Eight roadster was officially given the coveted Classic designation. Three weeks later the same recognition was extended to all 1929-32 Studebaker Presidents. So we are especially pleased to be able to feature Dr. Hemp's precedent-setting President as our drive-Report car.

Little is known about the history of this automobile prior to its acquisition by Dave Hemp in 1975. Its serial number however, reveals that it was built either in late April or early May, 1930. And at some point along the way, a previous owner substituted a Pierce-Arrow Series 132 engine for the original Studebaker unit. The Pierce engine drops into the Studebaker chassis with no modification of any kind. Its 115 horsepower rating is identical to that of the President Eight, and its displacement is nearly the same, but there are a couple of important design differences: The Pierce-Arrow uses a greater stroke-bore ratio, and it features nine main bearings in contrast to the Studebaker's five. Performance characteristics of the two powerplants would not differ markedly however.

Devotees of the Great American Race may recognize this car, for Dave Hemp — assisted by navigator Terry Rust and mechanic Darrell Dye — piloted it in the 1984 contest. The Studebaker performed flawlessly, Dave reports, and en route he stopped off at the Indianapolis Speedway, where he was clocked at 95 miles an hour! It must be confessed however, that the engine needed a ring job by the time the car returned home!

Like so many roadsters of its era, the Studebaker has a fixed-position seat. Legroom is somewhat tight for the tall driver, but this too is nothing unusual. The clutch is a bit juddery — nothing that a proper adjustment wouldn't correct. Clash-free shifts are a breeze, provided the driver remembers to use the double-clutching technique.

Steering is somewhat heavy, which is hardly unexpected, and relatively quick. Brake pedal pressure is heavy too, but the mechanical binders do their job well. Acceleration is surprisingly brisk for a big, heavy car, and the torque is fantastic. The Stude will pull a surprisingly stiff grade without downshifting, and it will crawl along smoothly at idle in top gear.

Down the road, the President Eight purrs like a kitten. Helped by a tall 3.47:1 final drive ratio, the engine seems almost to be loafing. The steering is a little loose, no doubt showing the effects of wear, and frequent corrections of the wheel are required. Engine noise is minimal, the body is tight and rattle-free. This is a well-balanced automobile, easy to control in hard cornering. Altogether, we found driving the President to be both pleasant and exciting.

It's a nicely equipped car. In addition to the twin sidemounted spares — a rare accessory for a Studebaker roadster — it is equipped with an intriguing pair of port-and-starboard running lamps, a popular aftermarket item in the 1930s. It is not a "show" car, although it took the People's Choice trophy at the 1988 Woodson Bridge Meet of the Contemporary Historical Vehicle Association (CHVA). It was there, incidentally, that son Dave, our collaborator on this report, first saw the roadster.

We found Dr. Hemp's Classic Studebaker to be an impressive automobile in every respect. Its $1,795 price represented enough money in 1930 to buy a Pontiac and two Chevrolets, but it still can be considered a bargain. For although the President Eight was 27 percent more powerful than the LaSalle or the Packard Standard Eight of its day, it was more than $600 cheaper than either of them.

We call it the Bargain Classic!

1930 STUDEBAKER

cars, regardless of price." So perhaps Guy Henry and Max Wollering, the company's chief engineer and production manager, respectively, can be forgiven for their stubborn insistence that Studebaker didn't need a new engine!

The Big Six had served Studebaker well, and long. First introduced in 1916 in a model known simply as the Studebaker Six (as differentiated from the much smaller Studebaker Four, also in production at that time), the engine was rated initially at 54 horsepower. Periodic modifications advanced that figure to 60 in 1918, to 60-65 in 1924, and finally to 75 commencing in 1925. Meanwhile, a 1918 touring car covered half a million miles as a test unit, over a five and a half year period — a remarkable record of durability!

The "Big Six" title was bestowed in 1918, at the time the 288.6-c.i.d. "Light Six" was introduced. (Parenthetically, the latter designation was a misnomer. With a shipping weight of a ton and a half — 150 pounds more than the big Buick — the Light Six was anything but light! And at $1,395 it wasn't cheap, either. The Buick Six cost $130 less.)

In the early days, as one might expect, most of the big Studebakers were open cars. In 1907 there was a towering, $2,750 limousine, but the seven-passenger touring car accounted for the

bulk of production. Over the years this changed as the closed body styles became more affordable, and by 1927 the bulk of Studebaker's production apparently consisted of closed cars.

It was during that year, 1927, that the President title was first employed by Studebaker. When the season ended, in January, there were nine body styles in the Big Six line, eight of them using a wheelbase of 120 inches. By April, these cars would be called Commanders, a title that would be a Studebaker standby throughout most of the company's remaining years.

But it was the ninth model, the biggest of the 1927 Big Sixes, that became the first Studebaker President. Built on a wheelbase of 127 inches, it initially came only as a four-door, seven-passenger sedan. Distinguishing this top-of-the-line car from lesser Studebakers was a lower body and softer, more rounded lines, as well as large, acorn-type headlamps. Double bead moldings with scallops at either end added a further stylish touch, and the interior trim was exceptionally luxurious for a car that sold for $2,245. In time the sedan was joined by two more seven-passenger President models, a duplex phaeton at $1,810 and a $2,495 limousine.

The Big Sixes — Commander and President — sold well, with production amounting to something like 40,000 for 1927. But that huge six-cylinder engine, nearly a dozen years old now, had about reached the limit of its potential. The

straight-eight configuration, first brought to the public's attention by the spectacular Model A Duesenberg, was becoming increasingly popular. Packard's excellent 1924 "Single Eight" had evidently spawned a host of medium-priced imitators. By 1925 there were eights-in-line from Auburn, Elcar, Gardner, Hupmobile, Jordan and Rickenbacker, among others. It was clear that some of the larger manufacturers would soon follow suit.

Albert Russel Erskine, Studebaker's president, has been described as a "somewhat ruthless, overbearing and ill-mannered man," who in retrospect appears to have borne more than a passing resemblance to W. C. Fields. But he was alert to trends in the industry. Perhaps he was surprised, then, at the intransigence of his engineering department when he suggested that Studebaker should have a straight-eight. For both Max Wollering and Guy Henry dug in their heels. The Big Six was a good engine, a proven engine, and look at all the records it had set!

To thwart the will of the boss is not, as a rule, the wisest course of action. Certainly not when the boss is as opinionated a man as Studebaker's stubborn president. And Erskine, an ardent fan of Notre Dame football, knew something about end runs. He quickly brought in Delmar G. "Barney" Roos as chief engineer, and both Wollering and Henry soon found themselves out of a job.

In later years, Barney Roos would come to fame as the man who took the

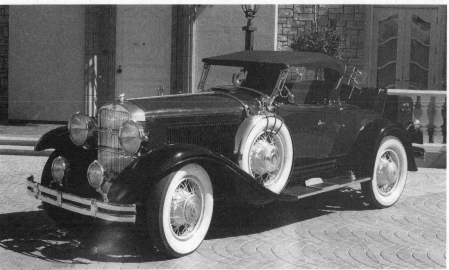

Below: More dazzle is found on the chromed sidemount tire covers and mirrors. Right: President surely has the size and style for a full Classic.

anemic old Whippet engine and transformed it into the stout little four-banger that powered the World War II Jeep (see *SIA #66*). But in his younger days he had been a racing devotee, and the nickname by which he was known throughout his adult life was taken from his hero, the legendary Barney Oldfield.

A native of the Bronx, Roos held an engineering degree from Cornell University. After a brief stint at General Electric, he moved on to Locomobile, and then to Pierce-Arrow, where for a time he served as chief engineer. He returned to Locomobile at about the time Billy Durant acquired a controlling interest in that fast-fading firm, and became an important part of the effort to revitalize it. Specifically, Roos was responsible for designing the Junior Eight (see *SIA #88*), a car which took Locomobile into a more reasonable price range than its enormous Model 48.

Moving on, Roos designed the 1927 Little Marmon. Like the smaller Locomobile, this smart little car was powered by an overhead-valve straight-eight. It must be confessed that neither of these

cars was really outstanding, in part because in both cases the engine was too small in relation to the weight of the automobile. But these two assignments, both of which started with the proverbial "clean sheet of paper" that is every engineer's dream, gave Roos invaluable experience.

Barney was not one to rest on his laurels. Just as he had done at Locomobile, he moved on before his Little Marmon made its debut, arriving at Studebaker early in 1926. By that time, he had been in the automobile business for the better part of fourteen years. If there is one thing he had learned from the experience at Locomobile and Marmon, it was that the engine must be large enough to provide plenty of power — with something in reserve.

So when the Series FA, the first Presi-

1930 Comparison Table
Representative Upper-Medium-Priced Roadsters

	Studebaker President	Buick "60"	Chrysler "77"	Gardner "150"	Windsor "8-85"
Price, f.o.b. factory	$1,795	$1,585	$1,665	$1,995	$1,695
Wheelbase	125"	132"	124½"	130"	125½"
Shipping weight (lbs.)	3,770	4,015	3,435	3,560	3,265
Engine	8	6	6	8	8
Displacement (cu. in)	336.7	331.5	268.4	298.6	268.8
Horsepower @ RPM	115/3,200	98/2,800	87/3,200	126/3,300	85/3,100
Compression ratio	5.00:1	4.30:1	5.00:1	5.25:1	5.28:1
Valve configuration	L-head	OHV	L-head	L-head	L-head
Transmission	3-speed	3-speed	4-speed	3-speed	3-speed
Final drive ratio	3.47:1	4.27:1	3.58:1	3.90:1	4.63:1
Steering	Cam & lever	Worm & roller	Cam & lever	Cam & lever	Cam & lever
Brakes	Mechanical	Mechanical	Hydraulic	Hydraulic	Hydraulic
Tires	6.00/20	6.50/19	6.00/18	6.50/18	6.00/19
Horsepower per c.i.d.	.342	.296	.324	.422	.316
Weight per horsepower	32.8	41.0	39.5	28.3	38.4

(The reader will note that a number of important manufacturers are missing from this list. Reflecting the diminishing popularity of this body style, such prominent companies as Auburn, Hudson and Nash were no longer building roadsters in 1930.)

specifications

Illustrations by Russell von Sauers, The Graphic Automobile Studio

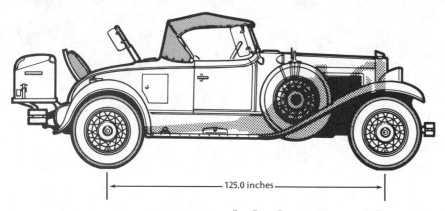
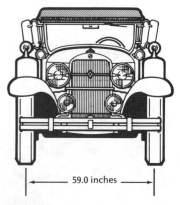

125.0 inches

59.0 inches

1930 Studebaker President Eight "FH"

Price, fob factory	$1,795 with standard equipment
Options on dR car	Bumpers, large hubcap wheels, six wire wheels with side-mounted spares

ENGINE

Type	8-cylinder, in-line
Bore x stroke	3½ inches x 4⅜ inches
Displacement	336.7 cubic inches
Compression ratio	5.1:1
Bhp @ rpm	115 @ 3,200
Taxable hp	39.2
Valves	L-head
Valve lifters	Mechanical
Main bearings	5
Lubrication system	Pressure
Induction system	Stromberg 1¼ inches 2V, Model UU2 carburetor; mechanical pump
Exhaust system	Single
Electrical system	6-volt

CLUTCH

Type	Double plate
Diameter	8¾ inches
Actuation	Mechanical, foot pedal

TRANSMISSION

Type	3-speed selective
Ratios: 1st	2.97
2nd	1.80
3rd	Direct
Reverse	3.82

DIFFERENTIAL

Type	Spiral bevel
Drive axles	Semi-floating
Torque medium	Springs

STEERING

Type	Ross cam and lever
Turns, lock to lock	2½
Ratio	15:1
Turning circle	43 feet

BRAKES

Type	Internal four-wheel mechanical
Drum diameter	15 inches
Effective area	360 square inches

CONSTRUCTION

Type	Body-on-frame
Frame	Double-drop; 8 inch siderails with 2½ inch flanges; 8 cross-members
Body construction	Steel over wood framing
Body style	Roadster, 2-4 passenger

SUSPENSION

Front	I-beam axle, 38 inch semi-elliptic springs
Rear	Conventional axle, 60 inch semi-elliptic springs
Wheels	Welded steel wire
Tires	6.00/20
Shock absorbers	Houdaille double-acting hydraulic

WEIGHTS AND MEASURES

Wheelbase	125 inches
Overall length	191 inches
Overall width	69 inches
Overall height	68 inches
Front track	59 inches
Rear track	59 inches
Ground clearance	8¼ inches
Shipping weight	3,770 pounds

CAPACITIES

Crankcase	8 quarts
Cooling system	21 quarts
Fuel tank	20 gallons

CALCULATED DATA

Hp per c.i.d.	.342
Weight per hp	32.8 pounds
Weight per c.i.d.	11.2 pounds

Winged radiator cap theme is carried through with delicate little wings on top of headlamp doors.

18

1930 STUDEBAKER

Rumble seat passengers are kept comfortable with flip-up windshield.

dent Eight, made its debut at the New York Auto Show in January, 1928, it was powered by a 100 horsepower, 312.5-cubic-inch engine — a flathead this time. Note, by the way, that although this engine was almost 12 percent smaller than the Big Six, its horsepower rating was one-third higher! The husky (2⅝-inch) crankshaft was carried in five large, bronze-backed main bearings, the connecting rods being offset to permit greater main bearing length. Six babbitt-lined, bronze-backed bearings cradled the camshaft, and valves were slightly angled in order to make possible a more compact combustion chamber. Lubrication was by pressure to the main, connecting rod and camshaft bearings, while oil was sprayed to the piston pins and cylinder walls.

Chassis components represented pretty much the state of the art in 1928, most of them supplied by specialists.

The transmission, for instance, was by Warner, a straightforward three-speed job. The double-plate clutch came from Long, four-wheel mechanical brakes from Bendix, cam-and-lever steering from Ross. One of the more interesting features was the Fafnir ball bearing spring shackles, designed to help provide a comfortable ride. Unfortunately, these proved to be prone to premature wear, one of the very few mechanical deficiencies in this fine new automobile.

The Pierce-Arrow Connection
By Dave Brown

In the United States, it seems that every automobile manufacturer has had to become a giant to survive. From several thousand producers during the industry's early years, we have now been reduced to only three.

The economic conditions which brought this about, and their effect upon the Pierce-Arrow Motor Car Company, were evidently perceived by Pierce's president, Myron Forbes, in 1928. The Buffalo, New York, firm had been producing some of the finest and most respected automobiles in the United States for over a quarter-century. But at a volume of less than 6,000 units per year, Pierce was having difficulty turning a profit. A possible solution was a merger with a larger firm.

Studebaker at that time was among the largest of the independent automobile manufacturers. Production of its mainly medium-priced line came to about 100,000 units annually. Albert Erskine, long-time Studebaker president, could see an advantage in having a prestigious, luxury marque added to his firm's lineup. Thus the merger between Studebaker and Pierce-Arrow, which took place on August 7, 1928, seemed a natural move, well-suited to the needs of both firms. Events which followed proved otherwise however, and a divorce followed five years later, coming at a time when the combined company was on the verge of collapse.

Readers who recall the merger of Studebaker with Packard a generation later, will remember that within three years of its consummation, all Packard production was consolidated into the Studebaker facilities. In fact, though the name was used a short while longer, those 1957-'58 Packards were obviously facelifted Studebaker Presidents and Hawks.

Such was never the case with the Studebaker/Pierce-Arrow arrangement. Pierce production remained at Buffalo, and the product remained distinct, still built to the old company's exacting standards. True styling of Studebakers and Pierce-Arrows moved along a converging line, and engine blocks for both were cast at the South Bend foundry. But the cars were completely different. And though for 1930 the displacement of the smallest Pierce mill was nearly identical to that of the Studebaker President Eight, its stroke/bore ratio was greater and it featured nine main bearings to the Studebaker's five.

Much has been written and said about what happened during those five sad years. A depression of unprecedented magnitude gripped the country. Studebaker sales, while suffering less for a time than those of many competitors, were by 1933 at only about a third of their 1938 level. Pierce-Arrow's new car registrations rose by 46 percent in 1929, to 8,386, apparently in response to the introduction of a new straight-eight engine — then sank by 1933 to just over 2,000 units.

Studebaker was now in the hands of receivers. An ailing subsidiary headquartered hundreds of miles away from the Studebaker home base at South Bend was more of a liability apparently, than the bankers involved could justify, so Pierce-Arrow was sold to a consortium of Buffalo businessmen. Studebaker itself was destined to be revived, and would survive as an auto manufacturer for another generation. But Pierce-Arrow was gone from the American automobile scene in another four years. A few months after the companies were separated Erskine was dead by his own hand, blamed then and since for having needlessly bankrupted his firm with an overly generous dividend policy. (See sidebar, page 21.)

In retrospect, perhaps we should not focus blame upon Erskine and Studebaker management for what happened to Pierce-Arrow or for all the woes of Studebaker itself. Economics of scale, in combination with the Depression, were gradually killing the small manufacturers, moving up through the smallest and progressively taking those larger and larger. Among the independent luxury makes, only Packard survived the 1930s, and it appears to have done so largely on sales of its medium-priced One-Twenty and One-Ten models. Jordan expired after 1930, Peerless in 1931, Marmon in 1933 and Franklin in 1934. Each of these companies had a production volume in a range comparable to Pierce-Arrow during the 1920s, and all preceded its demise.

The advent of a world war and the demand for automobiles which followed kept the largest of the independent firms in business for a number of additional years, but in time these same market factors seem to have killed them as well. Studebaker was, of course, second to the last among those to succumb.

1930 STUDEBAKER

At mid-year, there was a new President Eight — or rather, two of them, for the second-edition FA used a wheelbase of 131 inches while the FB was ten inches shorter. There were five FB models, with prices as low as $1,685 — a bargain, compared to the $2,085 to $2,485 price tags on the larger FA cars.

Both of these 1928½ cars, the FB and FA series, used a revised version of Barney Roos's straight eight. Bored to 336.7 cubic inches and with the compression ratio raised from 4.7 to 4.9:1, it developed 109 horsepower. In a further modification, the water pump was moved from the front of the block to the left side, resulting in better distribution of the coolant.

Incidentally, no end of confusion has resulted among Studebaker afficionados as the result of offering two distinct

cars during the 1928 model year, both bearing the FA designation. Not only did their engines differ, but the 1928½ cars were heavily (and very attractively) restyled. Why this confusion was perpetrated upon an unsuspecting public remains a mystery!

Obviously, with this 109 horsepower engine available in the 3,535-pound, short-chassis roadster, it was time for Studebaker to go out and set some more records. Under the direct supervision of

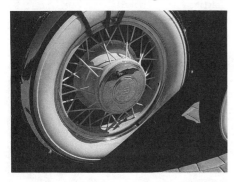

Sidemounts, large hubcaps and wire wheels were all extra-cost options on dR car.

The President Eight
Versus The Traditional Luxury Cars

To the 1930 buyer of a luxury roadster, Studebaker's President Eight presented an appealing alternative to the LaSalle of the Packard 733, at a savings of several hundred dollars. Here's how they compared:

	Studebaker	LaSalle	Packard
Price, f.o.b. factory	$1,795	$2,450	$2,425
Wheelbase	125"	134"	134½"
Shipping weight (lb.)	3,770	4,340	3,945
Engine	Straight-eight	V-8	Straight-eight
Bore x stroke	3½ x 4⅜	3 5/16 x 4 15/16	3 3/16 x 5
Bore/stroke ratio	1.25:1	1.49:1	1.57:1
Displacement (cu. in.)	336.7	340.4	319.2
Compression ratio	5.00:1	5.18:1	N/a
Horsepower @ RPM	115/3,200	90/3,000	90/3,200
Valve configuration	L-head	L-head	L-head
Main bearings	5	3	9
Clutch	Double plate	Double plate	Single plate
Transmission	3-speed	3-speed	4-speed
Final drive ratio	3.47:1	4.54:1	4.37:1
Steering	Cam and lever	Worm and sector	Worm and sector
Ratio	15:1	14:1	N/a
Brakes	Mechanical	Mechanical	Mechanical
Effective area (sq. in)	360	180	316½
Tires	6.00/20	6.50/19	6.50/20
Horsepower per c.i.d.	.342	.265	.281
Weight (lbs.) per horsepower	32.8	48.2	43.8
Pounds per sq. in. (brakes)	10.5	24.1	12.5

the American Automobile Association, two roadsters and two sedans were randomly selected. Driven to the Atlantic City Speedway, the cars were torn down to make sure they were strictly stock in every respect. Then the engines were sealed, and on July 21, 1928, the test began. With fourteen drivers spelling one another, the four cars hotfooted around the board track until each had rolled up 30,000 miles. It was a grueling test of endurance, of both man and machine!

The first roadster covered the distance in just 26,326 minutes, averaging 68.37 miles an hour and the second roadster was just three minutes behind. The two sedans, 225 pounds heavier and much more wind-resistant, averaged 64.15 and 63.99 mph, respectively, which seem equally remarkable. No mechanical difficulties were encountered, apart from the failure of one fan belt.

Then the following November it was back to Atlantic City to set a dozen more stock car records with a pair of President Eight roadsters, this time in a 24-hour run. On the three-man team, members took turns driving one of these cars, while the other car was piloted by a single driver for the entire dusk-to-dusk contest. Ab Jenkins, the iron man from Utah, was making his

Left: Windwings add comfortable, sporty touch. Below: Stude is accented by distinctive segmented taillamp design.

first twice-around-the-clock solo run in a stock car. Hall and Langworth tell us that "The Presidents ran so well that Jenkins became almost bored. The Tunney-Heeney fight was going on in New York, and on one blast by the pits,

Ab tossed a note into the slipstream: 'How's that fight coming? Give us a board.' He'd written it as the President grooved in on the banking, needing no

Albert Erskine's Dividend Policy: Formula For Disaster

In any big corporation, a certain tension is bound to exist between management and the stockholders. Stockholders, naturally, are interested in the size of their dividend checks. But sound management requires that a substantial portion of the profits be held in reserve, and re-invested in improving and updating production facilities, distribution practices, and the product itself.

Studebaker, in the early 1920s, had been a soundly managed organization, paying dividends that were substantial but not excessive. Plenty of money remained in the corporate coffers, permitting the company to maintain a highly competitive position.

All that began to change after 1923 however. Studebaker stock became one of the darlings of Wall Street because of its increasingly generous dividends. And with the coming of the Depression, Erskine and the directors actually authorized the payment of dividends out of the corporation's already too-thin reserves. During 1930, the year in which our driveReport car was built, for every dollar of earnings, Studebaker paid out five dollars to the stockholders. Consider the numbers:

Year	Income (after taxes)*	Dividends paid*	Dividends as % of income
1920	$ 9,822,000	$ 4,688,000	48%
1921	10,410,000	4,886,000	47%
1922	18,086,000	6,674,000	37%
1923	18,342,000	8,139,000	44%
1924	13,774,000	8,095,000	59%
1925	16,620,000	10,423,000	63%
1926	13,042,000	9,917,000	76%
1927	11,938,000	9,897,000	83%
1928	12,654,000	9,890,000	78%
1929	11,928,000	10,846,000	91%
1930	1,540,000	7,828,000	508%
1931	825,000	2,814,000	341%
1932	(8,687,000)	993,000	—
1933	(4,876,000)	None	—

*Rounded off to nearest 1,000
(deficit)

That Studebaker fell into receivership on March 29, 1933, seems, in retrospect, to have been inevitable. President Albert R. Erskine blamed himself for the debacle, as no doubt he should have done. But surely the board of directors must share in the responsibility for the profligate dividend policy that did so much to bring Studebaker to its knees.

Corporate vice presidents, Paul V. Hoffman and Harold S. Vance, were appointed receivers. Erskine, still nominally the president, but relieved of his duties, went home a broken man, in health and in spirit. His personal fortune, which apparently consisted chiefly of Studebaker stock, had been virtually wiped out, and the Board of Tax Appeals had issued a judgment against him for $732,000.

There was a family party at the Erskine home on the evening of June 30, 1933. It had been some weeks since anyone present had seen Albert Erskine in such good spirits, or so it seemed at the time. But the next morning they found his body with a bullet through the heart. The note read, "I cannot go on any longer." A proud man, Erskine had been unable to face the shame that he felt, both for the sad state into which his company had fallen, and for his impending personal bankruptcy.

It was a tragic end to what had been a distinguished career. A school dropout at sixteen, Erskine had risen from a fifteen-dollar-a-week job as a railroad clerk to the presidency of one of the nation's leading independent automakers, at a salary of $100,000 a year plus stock options. He had served on the board of the Federal Reserve Bank, and as president of the Board of Lay Trustees at Notre Dame University. He had been president of the South Bend Council, Boy Scouts of America. Above all, as Beverly Rae Kimes has reminded us, "he had great plans for Studebaker."

One can imagine the humiliation and the bitter regret that must have haunted the sixty-two-year-old Erskine in his last, lonely moments. But he had faith in Harold Vance and especially Paul Hoffman, so perhaps he sensed that his company would survive.

His family too would survive. For among Albert Russel Erskine's assets was a $900,000 insurance policy. More than enough to pay his debts.

Left: Golf bag door is another sign of a high-market car. Below left: Instrument panel is pleasant and plain. Below: Accessory step plate keeps wear off runningboards.

1930 STUDEBAKER

hand on the wheel!"

Altogether, Studebaker posted 114 new stock car records during 1928, some of which were destined to stand for more than thirty years. Studebaker posted some sales records too, and Albert Erskine was fairly bubbling with optimism. In 1927, he introduced a small car which he modestly named for himself (see SIA #70). Styled by Ray Dietrich, it was a handsome little machine whose Continental-built, six-cylinder engine featured a stroke/bore ratio of 1.71:1. Clearly this was in deference to British tax laws, for Studebaker was making a determined bid for the overseas market in those days. Albert Erskine called his car "The Little Aristocrat," but the Erskine — which sold for about the price of an Oldsmobile — was both overpriced and underpowered. And the 5.125:1 axle ratio, adopted in the hope of achieving acceptable performance, did nothing for engine longevity.

The Erskine Six was never a commercial success, but Albert Erskine's atten-

tion was elsewhere. Turning to the luxury field, he acquired the prestigious but unprofitable Pierce-Arrow Motor Car Company in 1928 (see sidebar, page 19).

Two new President models headed

the Studebaker line for 1929: the Model FH on a 125-inch wheelbase and the FE on a chassis ten inches longer. Horsepower of the President engine was raised to 115 by means of improved manifolding, a duplex carburetor, and

Calcutta to Bombay: Leopards and Wolves Beware!

Among the many records posted by the Studebaker President Eights, perhaps the most unusual was made during a February, 1929, run from Calcutta to Bombay, India. Here's the story, as recounted in The Studebaker Wheel:

"Piloted by C. L. Clark of the Swiss Engineering Company, Bombay, and Dewey Smith, Studebaker representative, The President Roadster checked out of Calcutta at 10:30 p.m. on February 25th, with 1,466 miles of almost unknown road ahead.

"Forty miles out of Calcutta, through endless processions of slow-moving bullock carts, in one hour and fifteen minutes. Then clear roads, and The President leaped ahead.

"Dawn found them at the Sone River. A railway trestle offered the only means of crossing — 45 minutes gone before the car was over. A hundred miles from Benares the supply line from the reserve tank became clogged with sediment. Thirty precious minutes were lost before it was blown clear.

"The East has its own ways of dealing with Western speed. Two wire wheels and tires had been shipped ahead to provide for replacements in case of tire trouble. Punctures on the way to Jhansi made it necessary to pick up these two spare wheels. But the native station master was a cautious man. Rude haste is unbecoming to those of authority. The Sahibs must first identify themselves and then secure their tires in due time.

"Official dignity was maintained at the expense of an hour and a half of delay.

"Fuel was running low as the car reached the village of Sipri. They drove up to a place handling petrol and asked if the shop had a big supply. The storekeeper answered assuringly that he had plenty and brought out two tins containing two gallons each. When told that the drivers wanted at least fifty gallons, he threw up his hands in horror and dispatched runners to all the other stores. They came back with varying quantities totalling nearly forty gallons. But before the storekeeper loaded all this into the tank he demanded cash in hand.

"The first evidence that the car was traveling game country came on the second night when a leopard crossed the road in front of the car. He leaped for safety an instant too late. More leopards, a panther, several hyenas and Indian wolves, deer and smaller game were seen. Casualties included a hyena, two wolves, a porcupine and many rabbits.

"Twenty miles of mountainous road beyond Nasik — too rough for fast travel — then the plains again, and the speedometer needle wavered between 50 and 70 miles an hour.

"Then Bombay, and an enthusiastic crowd to welcome The President.

"In spite of wasted hours, The President had made the grueling run of 1,466 miles in 40 hours, 15 minutes, clipping 7 hours, 20 minutes from the best previous record and forging just one more link in the chain of records which have won for The President Eight, the title "World's Champion Car."

Below: "Side marker" lamps mounted on runningboards are rare period accessory. Right: Flathead straight eight is good for 115 bhp. Below right: Cast step plate is simple and elegant.

another slight increase in the compression ratio. An improved Lanchester vibration damper was fitted, and a larger-diameter ring gear resulted in a final drive assembly that was both quieter and more durable. A new double-drop frame made possible a reduction in overall height, as well as a lower center of gravity. Weight was up by a couple of hundred pounds, which may have handicapped the President's performance to some degree.

Evidently the handicap was not a fatal one, however. In May, 1929, two Presidents took top honors in their displacement class at the "Double Twelve" race staged at the Brooklands racing oval in England. Only an Alfa Romeo and a Bentley came in ahead of the Studebakers in the general sweepstakes!

That same month, a President Eight roadster was selected to pace the Indianapolis "500" Classic. And in September, a Studebaker President, driven by Glen Schultz, scrambled up Pikes Peak in a record 21 minutes, 43.4 seconds to win the coveted Penrose trophy.

By 1930, rules were revised to permit stock cars of up to 366 c.i.d. to compete at Indianapolis, and for the next several years there were modified Studebaker Presidents in contention at the Brickyard. No Studebaker ever won that race, but their record was commendable nevertheless. In 1930, Russ Snowberger's Studebaker-powered Russell Eight Special took eighth place. Two years later there were five Studebaker Specials, racing in the "85% Stock" category. One of them, driven by Cliff Bergere, finished third with an average speed of 102.66 miles an hour — the first time a "stock" Indy car had averaged better than one hundred. Three factory-sponsored and two privately entered Studebakers placed "in the

money" in 1933, and Studebaker-engined racers continued to compete at Indianapolis as late as 1937.

When the 1930 models were announced, Studebaker made it known that no radical changes could be expected in the President Eight. A stylish French visor was fitted to the closed models, large-hubcap wire wheels became available, a new muffler, packed with steel wool, was said to increase horsepower substantially by reducing back pressure, and automatic shutters were fitted to the radiator. Otherwise, Studebaker wisely stood pat on a winning hand.

Meanwhile, Barney Roos had been at work designing two more Studebaker straight-eights. The 250.4 c.i.d. Commander Eight had appeared for 1929, followed by the 221.0-cubic inch Dictator Eight, introduced in mid-1929 as a 1930 model. Curiously, both of these engines used nine-bearing crankshafts, an improvement not shared by the President until 1931.

Despite the decline in sales that resulted from the ever-tightening grip of the Depression, the big President Eights remained in production through 1933. But only 635 of these fine automobiles were built during that final

season, the year the Studebaker Corporation fell into receivership. There were Studebaker straight-eights bearing the President name as late as the 1942 model year, but the classic Presidents were gone, the victim of hard times and shifting public tastes. □

Acknowledgements and Bibliography
Automobile Topics, *February 8, 1930;* Automobile Trade Journal, *April, 1930;* Automotive Industries, *February 22, 1930;* Betts, Charles, "Studebaker as Gladiator." Automobile Quarterly, *Vol. X, No. 3;* Cannon, Wm. A. and Fred K. Fox, Studebaker: The Complete Story; Hall, Asa E. and Richard M. Langworth, The Studebaker Century; Hendry, Maurice D., "Studebaker — One Can Do a Lot of Remembering in South Bend." Automobile Quarterly, *Vol X, No. 3;* Kimes, Beverly Rae, "The Big Presidents." Automobile Quarterly, *Vol. XVIII, No. 1;* Kimes, Beverly Rae and Henry Austin Clark, Jr. (eds.), Standard Catalog of American Cars, 1805-1942; Langworth, Richard M., Studebaker: The Postwar Years; Longstreet, Stephen, A Century On Wheels; New York Times, *May 22, 1977;* South Bend Tribune, May 22, 1977; Studebaker sales literature; The Studebaker Wheel *(various issues);* Carson, Richard Burns, The Olympian Cars; Hendry, Maurice D., "Pierce: An American Aristocrat." Automobile Quarterly, *Vol. VI, No. 3;* Ralston, Marc, Pierce-Arrow; Weis, Bernard J., The Pierce-Arrow Motor Car. *Our thanks to Ray Borges, Collections Manager, Wm. F. Harrah Automobile Fdn., Reno, Nevada; Dave Brown, Durham, California; Bill Jasper, Redding, California; Gene Pickett, Redding, California; Dick Quinn, Mokena, Illinois; Joe Wong, Redding, California. Special thanks to Dr C. David Hemp, Millville, California.*

Fords, and others who welded together the automotive empires of the earlier days in the industry. He was a doer.

But he could be a martinet, too. For example, when a batch of cars he'd ordered with cream stripes came through with white trim, every stripe had to be sanded off, so no ridge would mar the repaint. Then the redecorated cars were lined up in soldierly rows outside the plant. An operator sat in each one all day, awaiting Erskine's inspection. But he never showed up. Later he approved the repaints, sight unseen.

At other times, however, his sense of justice shone through. A watchman once wouldn't let him into a plant building at night. He didn't know Mr. Erskine but he had orders to admit no one without a badge. Retreating, the corporation president contacted the guard's superior. "Give this man a riase; we need more watchmen like him. I should have had some identification."

In 1928, Studebaker Corp. took control of the Pierce-Arrow Motor Car Co. of Buffalo, N.Y. This transaction came through an intricate deal involving the exchange of a specified number of shares of stock of both companies plus a cash payment of $2 million by Studebaker to Pierce-Arrow.

The manipulation resulted in Stude-baker owning a controlling interest in P-A. Mr. Erskine was named chairman of the board. Myron Forbes stayed on as president of Pierce-Arrow, with most other P-A officials continuing in their positions. Pierce-Arrow operated as a Studebaker subsidiary, rather than as a division, throughout the 5-year period of their association.

The opportunity for a Studebaker-Pierce-Arrow merger came at a good time for both companies. The complete Stude-baker line for 1928 covered a wide range, topped by a stable of commercial vehicles and trucks. Only in the prestige-car market was Studebaker lacking.

Millions of older Americans will recall

Above: Neatly laid-out instrument cluster includes all working gauges plus a dial at far left that indicates whether freewheeling is engaged or not. Someone rigged up a pushbutton starter in car, but it normally starts with Startix. *Below:* Rear compartment accessories include ash tray, courtesy lamp, center armrest, map pocket, and pull-down shades. The President represented 1932 Stude's most luxurious offering.

Above: Huge doors allow entry to rear compartment without tipping front seats. Seat upholstery material is not correct. *Below:* Fitted luggage, now gone, once came with this trunk. Spare makes it a hard reach.

by Ken Gross, *Feature Editor*

drive report

The big President 8 with extremely rare coachwork and marvelous performance can't be far from formal classicdom.

1932 Studebaker St. Regis Brougham

PHOTOS BY DARRYL NORENBERG

THE YEAR 1932 SAW AMERICA in the midst of the greatest economic depression in history: 15 million Americans, mostly heads of families, unemployed. It was the worst of times.

Studebaker Corp. wasn't in the best short-term financial condition either as the years 1932-33 rolled slowly past in South Bend, Ind., the corporate headquarters. Studebaker still stood as one of the nation's largest corporate enterprises, but the policy of its president, Albert Russell Erskine, called for uninterrupted payment

of dividends on Studebaker common stock. This came in the face of declining sales and disappearing profits. Erskine's idea was to bolster the price of Studebaker stock on Wall Street. But in his attempt, Erskine had reduced Studebaker's cash reserves to dangerously low levels. By the dawn of 1933, working capital was down to $3.5 million.

The average corporate executive would have been appalled at facing such a seemingly insurmountable obstacle to continued operation of the corporation,

but Albert Erskine wasn't an average corporate executive. Already, as we shall soon see, he'd laid plans for a financial coup that would not only solve Studebaker's current financial woes but could conceivably lay the groundwork for even greater expansion and growth in the future.

Cursed by many a Studebaker engineer as "not knowing the front end of an automobile from the rear end," Mr. Erskine has to be recorded in automotive history along with the Durants, Sloans,

25

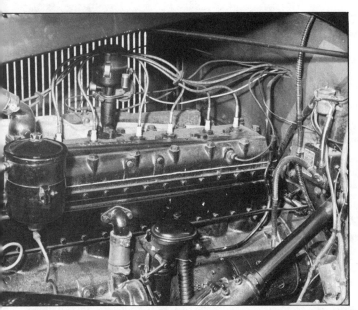

The large (336.7-cid) Studebaker 8 gives very impressive performance. Startix on the firewall came as standard equipment on the President.

Studebaker's Senior Lineup, 1932

	Six	Dictator 8	Commander 8	President 8
Model number	55	62	71	91
Bore & stroke	3.25 x 4.63	3.06 x 3.75	3.06 x 4.25	3.50 x 4.38
Displacement, cu. in.	230.2	221.0	250.4	336.7
Rated bhp @ rpm	80 @ 3200	85 @ 3200	101 @ 3200	122 @ 3200
Compression ratio	5.1:1	5.0:1	5.2:1	5.1:1
Wheelbase, in.	117.0	117.0	125.0	135.0
Weight, lb. (dry sedan)	3150	3240	3545	4260
Tire size	5.50 x 18	5.50 x 18	6.00 x 18	6.50 x 18
Axle ratio	4.27:1	4.73:1	4.73:1	4.31:1
Price range	$840-$1090	$980-$1230	$1350-$1665	$1690-$2095
Production (model yr.)*	13,647	6021	3551	2399

Studebaker's Senior Lineup, 1933

	Six	Commander 8	President 8	Speedway President 8
Model number	56	73	82	92
Bore & stroke, in.	3.25 x 4.63	3.06 x 4.00	3.06 x 4.25	3.50 x 4.38
Displacement, cu. in.	230.2	235.7	250.4	336.7
Rated bhp @ rpm	85 @ 3200	100 @ 3800	110 @ 3600	132 @ 3400
Compression ratio	5.5:1	5.5:1	5.0:1	5.5:1
Wheelbase, in.	117.0	117.0	125.0	135.0
Weight, lb. (dry sedan)	3310	3385	3725	4465
Tire size	5.50 x 17	6.00 x 17	6.50 x 17	7.00 x 17
Axle ratio	4.31:1	4.73:1	4.36:1	4.36:1
Price range	$865-$1145	$1025-$1315	$1320-$1635	$1655-$2060
Production (model yr.)*	6861	3841	1194	635

*Source: The Production Figure Book for U.S. Cars, by Jerry Heasley; Motorbooks International

1932 Studebaker driveReport

the year 1928 as the beginning of the "Great Boom of the 1920s." Sales of new cars were up sharply and would continue through 1929. This was particularly true of luxury cars.

Only Pierce-Arrow wasn't sharing in this sales bonanza—not because P-A quality had deteriorated in the least, but rather due to the fact of the ultraconservatism of Pierce-Arrow management. Pierce-Arrow was offering only 6-cylinder powerplants in 1928, while its major American competitors had been selling 8- and 12-cylinder motorcars for several years. Additionally, Pierce-Arrow had failed to keep styling pace with the competition.

With the assumption of control of Pierce-Arrow by Studebaker in 1928, Erskine pushed hard through his board position to accelerate the introduction of the smartly restyled and brilliantly engineered new 1929 Pierce-Arrow models. Announced in Jan. 1929, they became an instant success.

During this 5-year association between the two companies, there was a minimum of liaison between the various departments except for the sales offices. Sales, of necessity, had to be coordinated to a degree. Studebaker did make some forgings for Pierce-Arrow, but strictly on a job-lot basis and under the control of Pierce-Arrow personnel at all times. The same held true of a few bodies framed in the Studebaker body plant to alleviate temporary bottlenecks in Buffalo. Bodies were then shipped to Buffalo for finishing and installation there. One major deviation from the above pattern involved Stude-

baker engineering and the five exotic 1933 Pierce Silver Arrows.

STUDEBAKER REPLACED its time-honored Big 6 in its President series with the 1928 models in Jan. 1928. Powering the new Presidents was a new 313.1-cid Straight 8 designed and then constantly improved under the watchful eye of Barney Roos, Studebaker's new chief engineer (see *Barney Roos* biography, SIA #43). With a 3.375 x 4.375 bore and stroke, the 1928 engine developed 100 bhp at 2600 rpm. Its crankshaft was carried in five main bearings, and lubrication was by pressure feed to all bearing surfaces.

After the production of approximately 9000 engines, bore went to 3.5 inches, which brought displacement up to 336.7 cid and made a very noticeable difference in the engine's performance. For the 1931 model, a 9-bearing crankshaft was added to the 336.7 engine to bring it in conformity with the 250.4-cid Commander 8 and the 221.4-cid Dictator 8, which had been announced in 1929. This was the last major change to an engine that brought Studebaker so much glory on the raceways of the world.

Stylewise, Studebaker made very little change in its line of 1928-30 motorcars. They remained handsome, big, and regal during those years. The major styling change for 1931 consisted of a veed grille shell that sloped slightly to the back and oval headlamps on the top-line models. The rakish roadsters of the previous three years were replaced with a new and unique model known as the Four Seasons convertible roadster. While keeping much of the low, rakish appearance of the former roadster, the new model offered roll-up windows.

The 1932 Studebakers had a narrowing

of the radiator grille and a more pronounced vee. The line carried two completely new body styles: a stunningly beautiful new convertible sedan for five, which replaced the former tourer, and novel-for-Studebaker concept known as the St. Regis brougham. This latter body is considered by many to be one of the most innovative and beautiful styles ever produced by Studebaker and, like the convertible sedan, was available in all four senior series of Studebaker cars then being offered.

The St. Regis brougham combined the coziness of a coupe with the roominess of a sedan, seating five comfortably while at the same time providing adequate trunk space without undue rear overhang. Additionally, it provided an excellent ride as all passengers were cradled between the front and rear axles—a considerable improvement over the traditional sedans and coaches of that era.

We asked former Studebaker production chief Otto Klausmeyer about the St. Regis. "I remember the body style well," Klausmeyer said. "I have a body exactly like it on my Pierce-Arrow. The bodies have a great family resemblance—but they're not the same.

"The St. Regis brougham was designed by Jim Hughes, Studebaker's chief body engineer. Perry Sullivan was Jim's assistant. Those two, along with Paul Auman, used to build the sample bodies. I believe the St. Regis brougham was designed in 1931. Pierce picked up the design and widened it and lengthened it slightly. The general proportions were about the same in both cars, which made for a very striking 2-door.

"Unfortunately, though, the design had some defect," Klausmeyer explains. "You see, the doors were extremely wide. They

Above & below: Opening, adjustable windshield plus accessory windwings and cowl flap aid ventilation, as do roll-down rear quarter panes.

Left: Kick-panel pockets hold maps or an owner's manual. Tiny tag on far right of instrument panel is the sole emblem proclaiming this the President series. Right: Studebaker introduced oval headlamps in 1931 on its top-line series and extended them to all its senior models in 1932-33.

1932 Studebaker driveReport

continued

were hinged on the windshield pillar, which was slanted—and the windshield slant ran all the way down to the frame sill. The floor sill and the hinges were mounted on that. And it was because of this angle that, when you opened the door and got in, if you didn't get in quickly, the door would knock you in.

"The weight of the door made it close very quickly on you and the car was awkward to get into because of this feature. Aside from that, it was a very, very striking body design."

Although some people have felt that Studebaker and Pierce interchanged stampings for the doors of their broughams, this isn't true. Pierce bought some stampings from Budd and Murray—while most of Studebaker's stampings were produced right in South Bend. The convertible sedan body style was made by the Central Manufacturing Div. of Cord Corp. at Connersville, Ind. So while the St. Regis was strictly a Studebaker body, the convertible sedan body was designed and built for Studebaker by Central Mfg. "They used to ship them from Connersville to South Bend," says Mr. Klausmeyer, "by flatbed truck—three bodies on each truck.

"You see, we didn't have capacity for that type of body in South Bend. All the buildings were filled up and we were working like mad on various different designs. Furthermore, the volume on those bodies was so small that they were practically a handbuilt item. Studebaker couldn't afford to build framing jigs to turn out just a few bodies a month." As a result of this arrangement, these bodies were very similar to those used on the beautiful Auburn and L-29 Cord cars of the same period. They were unique in being the only purchased bodies ever installed on cars bearing the Studebaker nameplate, with the exception, of course, of 1938-39 convertible sedans and a few showcars fitted with bodies by the outstanding coachbuilders of the day, such as LeBaron, Derham, etc.

Built-in lube record on the President includes instructions for break-in and maintenance.

Sidemounted spares were probably originally supplied with this car, but either a dealer or an owner converted it to a trunk-mounted spare.

specifications

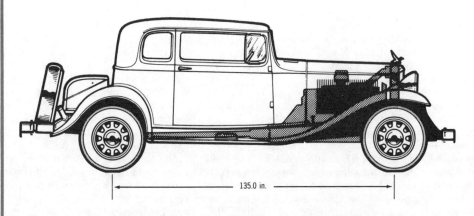

135.0 in.

59.0 in.

1932 Studebaker 91 President St. Regis brougham

Price when new .... $1750 f.o.b. South Bend (1932).

ENGINE
Type .... In-line, L-head 8, water cooled, cast-iron block, 9 mains, full pressure lubrication.
Bore & stroke .... 3.50 x 4.375 in.
Displacement .... 336.7 cid.
Max. bhp @ rpm .... 122 @ 3200.
Max. torque @ rpm .... N.a.
Compression ratio .... 5.1:1.
Induction system ....Single updraft carburetor, mechanical fuel pump.
Exhaust system .... Cast-iron manifold, single muffler.
Electrical system .... 6-volt battery/coil.

CLUTCH
Type .... Single dry plate, molded asbestos lining.
Diameter .... 11.0625 in.
Actuation .... Mechanical, foot pedal.

TRANSMISSION
Type .... 3-speed manual, floor lever, silent 2nd, freewheeling.

Ratios: 1st .... 2.86:1.
2nd .... 1.65:1.
3rd .... 1.00:1.
Reverse .... 3.44:1.

DIFFERENTIAL
Type .... Spiral bevel, Hotchkiss drive.
Ratio .... 4.31:1.
Drive axles .... Semi-floating.

STEERING
Type .... Ross cam & lever.
Turns lock to lock ....3.5.
Ratio .... 17:1.
Turn circle .... 42.0 ft.

BRAKES
Type .... 4-wheel mechanical drums, internal expanding, vacuum booster.
Drum diameter .... 15.125 in.
Total swept area .... 289.0 sq. in.

CHASSIS & BODY
Frame .... U-section steel.
Body construction .... Composite, steel sheet over hardwood framing.
Body style .... 2-door, 5-pass. close-coupled brougham.

SUSPENSION
Front ....I-beam axle, semi-elliptic longitudinal springs, hydraulic lever shock absorbers.
Rear .... One-piece axle, semi-elliptic longitudinal leaf springs, hydraulic lever shock absorbers.
Tires .... 6.50 x 18 4-ply.
Wheels .... 10-spoke steel artillery wheels, lug-bolted to brake drums.

WEIGHTS & MEASURES
Wheelbase .... 135.0 in.
Overall length .... N.a.
Overall height .... 69.125 in.
Overall width .... N.a.
Front tread .... 59.0 in.
Rear tread .... 61.5 in.
Ground clearance .... 7.8 in.
Curb weight .... 4300 lb. approx.

CAPACITIES
Crankcase .... 8 qt.
Cooling system .... 23 qt.
Fuel tank .... 20.5 gal.

T HE BIGGEST NEWS involving Studebaker in 1932, however, was the corporation's re-entry into the low-priced field. The Rockne put Studebaker in competition with Ford, Chevrolet, and Plymouth (see SIA #33). Studebaker hadn't been represented in the low-priced field since dropping the small Erskine at the end of the 1929 model run. Now Studebaker once again spanned the entire range from the lowest priced Rockne ($585) up to the top of the Pierce-Arrow prestige and luxury line.

With the shadows of a worldwide Depression deepening, you'd think that Erskine *would* retrench. But not at all. He was busily engaged in an effort to shore up Pierce-Arrow's sagging fortunes by commissioning an exotic new motorcar targeted to sell for $10,000, the Pierce Silver Arrow. The Rockne 75 evaporated, but the Rockne 65 continued into 1933 virtually unchanged except for its redesignation as the Rockne 10. Base price of the two-passenger coupe remained $585. Studebaker's line was

For 1932, 10-spoke metal artillery wheels were optional, with wires standard. In 1933, Studebaker's artillery wheels received 14 spokes.

revised considerably for 1933 (see sidebar, page 26).

A total of 22 models were offered in the 1933 Studebaker line. Included, once again, were the beautiful St. Regis brougham, the convertible sedan, and the Four Seasons convertible roadster, which were available in all four series.

S OUTH BEND, in Graham's footsteps, approached streamlining with the claim, for example, that the air resistance on the long-wheelbase President 8 was reduced eight percent with a resultant four percent increase in speed. The 1932 clamshell front fenders gave way in '33 to full valenced ones, which blended into the radiator apron and concealed the front suspension. Runningboards curved to match the new bodies and blended smoothly into the rear fenders.

The new, sharply raked radiator and windshield posts made for striking lines. The rear deck was now concave, and the

1932 Studebaker

tail panel spread out and slightly downwards to conceal the springs and shackles. Interestingly, in January 1933, Studebaker stopped including handcranks as standard equipment.

In a further effort to visually lower the cars, wheel diameters were reduced from 18 to 17 inches—with a newly designed standard metal spoked wheel (our driveReport car has the new wheels—wires were still an option). The distinctive oval headlamps, sidelights, and single-bar, center-dip bumpers were common to both 1932 and 1933 models.

Studebaker engineering was particularly proud of their power brakes. Bendix-Kliesrath booster brakes were an improved mechanical two-shoe stopper with quarter-inch molded linings. Foot pressure was assisted by vacuum.

Including Studebaker's line of commercial vehicles and light-to-medium trucks, the corporation was offering much too broad a range of products for Depression-bound 1932. The outlook for the year wasn't bright. Studebaker's working capital at the beginning of the calendar year was down to $3.5 million—only enough to cover normal day-to-day operating expenses for a very short period. Additionally, the corporation had some very sizable bank loans coming due in March 1933. The financial outlook was indeed bleak, but Albert Erskine felt he had a plan to not only solve Studebaker's immediate fiscal problem but to turn it to the corporation's long-term advantage.

Since the beginning of the Depression, the ultra-conservative White Motor Co. of Cleveland had guarded their corporation's cash position well. As a result, their balance sheet showed a sizable nest egg. Nevertheless, White management was surprisingly amenable to a discussion of a takeover by Studebaker. The arrangement was to be somewhat similar to the acquisition of Pierce-Arrow, with an exchange of stock and a cash payment by Studebaker.

Erskine pledged Studebaker's working capital as a show of good faith while the White stockholders voted on the proposition. Following this formality and according to plan, the adequate cash resources of the White Motor Co. would immediately become available to Studebaker—plus its expanded truck coverage through the addition of the heavy White line to the already existing range of lighter Studebaker trucks.

The plan seemed almost foolproof and just what the doctor ordered for ailing Studebaker. Then a hitch developed. A minor White Motor Co. stockholder sued to prevent the sale of the company's assets. When the case went to court, it tied up the working capital Erskine had pledged. Almost concurrently, the Studebaker loan from the Chase Manhattan Bank came due.

Mr. Erskine made a hurried trip to New York to arrange an extension of the loan, but the bank's officers balked. The end of the road seemed near.

Back in South Bend, a local creditor, the Edwards Iron Works, filed a friendly suit to place the Studebaker Corp. into receivership. The petition was heard before Judge Thomas J. Slick, and granted. Judge Slick named Paul Hoffman, Harold Vance, and Ashton Bean as receivers in charge of the corporation, granting them permission to operate the plant, in an effort to put the ailing giant back on its feet. Both Hoffman and Vance were Studebaker vice presidents, while Bean was White's board chairman.

Erskine retired to his estate, Twychenham Hills, in the south part of South Bend, a sick and broken man. Three months later, in July, he tragically took his own life.

ONE OF THE FIRST ACTIONS taken by the new receivers was to temporarily close the Studebaker plant until the firm's entangled financial affairs could be unraveled and arrangements made with creditors. The proposed takeover of White was abrogated and arrangements made for the sale of Pierce-Arrow.

The "friendly" receivers, as they were called in the press, were about to make automotive history. Never before had a car company in receivership been rescued by its own management. Studebaker's "friendly factory policy" toward its dealers had its origins back in 1924. Under its mandate, any Studebaker dealer had a right to walk in on any Studebaker executive, put his feet on the desk, and gripe. The prime receiver of the complaints was vice president of sales, Paul G. Hoffman. His cool handling of dealers won the confidence of the entire organization. And when the receivership crisis came, Hoffman, FORTUNE said, "...was the company's No. 1 hope of survival."

Hoffman felt he could save Studebaker if he could just hold his dealers together. Sympathetic, Judge Slick listened to Hoffman's plans, which revolved around the theory that the best defense is attack. Hoffman felt the best way to protect the stockholders' $4.8 million inventory equity was to tune up his whole organization to actually *increase* Studebaker's sales. He presented his bold plan to Judge Slick for nearly an hour—and the Judge okayed a $100,000 advertising campaign.

Harold S. Vance and Hoffman put the finishing touches on a massive sales drive. They'd already wired or telephoned 300 of their top dealers, explaining the grave situation and insisting that, if the dealers could just remain loyal, Studebaker would survive.

They introduced an elaborate sales incentive program with special prizes and temporary additional discounts of $45-$75 per car. By the following Monday, Stude sales were skyrocketing; by the following week, dealers had sent in 2,200 orders. As FORTUNE noted, "...the shock had been weathered and the entire organization was on the offensive."

But there was more to come. With the support of receiver Ashton Bean, Judge Slick bought a proposal for $700,000 retooling in May 1933 for new models. To pay the bills, Studebaker's Pierce-Arrow stock was unloaded for $1 million, to a group of Buffalo, New York, financiers. By December 31, 1933, Studebaker had produced a $55,000 new operating profit for its first nine months of receivership—with a loss of only about 15 percent of its dealer force!

Public confidence was restored and further buoyed by a study which proved Barney Roos' engineers were as good as any in the industry and Studebaker could manufacture at a competitive cost in any price field except the lowest (they were later to prove even this wrong with the successful Champion launch in 1939).

Careful management at this point cemented Studebaker's survival. By the end of 1934, Vance and Hoffman still had most of their working capital and sold off all their receivership leftover cars. They retooled twice for new models, consistently employed 5,000-6,000 South Bend workers, and sold 89,000 vehicles in the most difficult sales environment imaginable.

Studebaker's phoenix-like success in surviving receivership set a precedent which

helped the passage of the Summers Bill—a law designed to rescue Depression-hit companies *in extremis*.

Through the faith and efforts of Hoffman and Vance, South Bend had weathered its darkest hour.

THE 1932 STUDEBAKER President St. Regis brougham you see depicted here has had several well-known owners, among them Phil Hill, TV producer Jim Packer, and Don Williams, co-owner of Davis-Williams, in Beverly Hills, California.

SIA talked to all three of these gentlemen and asked for their driving impressions. States Jim Packer: "I've owned over 200 full classics, and I'd rank this car—in driving performance—among the top five. It's as smooth as a Packard. Marvelous ride. It's not bouncy.

"With the single exception of the Packard V-12 of the mid-1930s, this Studebaker handles better than any classic, in my opinion. It always gave me the feeling that it would do what I wanted it to. Very responsive, and yet very solid. It had the maneuverability of a lighter car, plus the road-holding characteristics of a luxury car."

Don Williams concurs. "This car, mechanically, is on a par with a Packard as far as steering and acceleration go. It's far better than a Cadillac of the same period. My personal feeling is that the best driving cars of the classic era were the Packard and the Pierce, and this Studebaker is on a par with any of them." Phil Hill, former race driver and long-time collector, doesn't agree—at least not so unreservedly. In his opinion, the Studebaker can't possibly match the quality of a classic Pierce, Packard, or even a Cadillac. It had to be built to a lower standard. Yet, dollar for dollar, Hill agrees that the President was an awfully good deal.

"I think you were getting, really, quite a bargain. But then that's often the case with smaller cars sold in larger numbers. The more expensive the car gets, the greater the tendency for getting less for the money.

"The question is," he continues, "how do you take a car that's a pretty high-order design concept—in this case the Pierce equivalent of a St. Regis brougham—and lop a thousand dollars off its price, and then end up with something that isn't a compromise?"

The St. Regis incorporates several interesting nuances. The doors are so long, for example, that you hardly need to tip the front seatbacks to get into the rear compartment. In fact, thin people can walk right through. Of course, as Mr. Klausmeyer observes, the size of these doors makes them heavy and awkward to manage, especially if the car is parked on an incline.

But there's plenty of leg room front and rear in this 135-inch-wheelbase brougham. Interestingly, the same brougham body was mounted on Studebaker's 117- and 125-inch chassis. On those, the doors came all the way back to the rear fenders—actually had a slight C-curve in the bottom rear edges to clear the fenders.

Starting the engine of this elegant machine is strikingly modern. Since the President was equipped with Startix (see SIA #14), you merely turn the key. The engine starts immediately, and it restarts itself automatically should it stall.

One reason might be freewheeling, which few owners ever used. But freewheeling, when engaged, sometimes resulted in a dead engine when slowing abruptly or turning corners.

The President's instrument panel is handsome and complete, with a bold clock and speedometer centermost, flanked by gauges for all normal functions. Without meaning this as a serious criticism, some drivers prefer the speedometer nearer themselves and, likewise, the key.

The St. Regis steers with amazing ease, yet it's precise and relatively quick. Vacuum-boosted brakes take gentle pressure to bring the car to a confident halt. A "pass-around" cigarette lighter (as opposed to the variety on the end of a wire) comes as standard President equipment, as do twin ashtrays in the rear compartment.

Shifting feels silky smooth; likewise clutch action. Altogether, this car is a dream to drive. Even visibility is good except to the 3/4 rear, where it's about average for the era.

With Studebaker producing such a good deal for the money, it's a shame not more customers had the cash to enjoy it. Only 2,399 Presidents were sold in 1932, and although we have no precise figures, it's unlikely that more than 10 percent of them were broughams. ☎

Our thanks to E.T. Reynolds, Ponchatoula, Louisiana; Otto Klausmeyer, South Bend, Indiana; Phil Hill, Santa Monica, California; Don Williams, Beverly Hills, California; Jim Packer, Los Angeles, California; Fred Fox and members of the Studebaker Drivers Club, Box 3044, South Bend, IN 46619; and Bill Cannon and members of the Antique Studebaker Club, Inc., Box 142, Monrovia, CA 91016.

1940 STUDEBAKER COMMANDER

Middle Class Value

by Arch Brown
photos by Bud Juneau

THE Studebaker Corporation had its origins in a humble South Bend, Indiana, blacksmith shop, 'way back in the early 1850s. The firm achieved some prominence during the Civil War as a builder of freight wagons for the Union Army, but the real foundation of the Studebaker brothers' rather considerable fortune was laid during the Boer War (1899–1902), once again through the building of horse-drawn vehicles for military use.

Then in 1902, at the instigation of Fred Fish, John Mohler Studebaker's son-in-law, the company undertook to build automobiles—as a sideline, at first. This, over the initial opposition of J. M. Studebaker, who declared, "To me the gasoline automobile is a clumsy, dangerous, noisy brute of a vehicle. They're going to catch fire, they're not safe, they blow up, accidents will happen, a lot of people are going to be killed, the damned things stink to high heaven, they shake your liver to pieces,

they always break down at the worst moment, and in short they are a public nuisance and even worse, a public menace."

Having thus expressed his sentiments, 67-year-old John Mohler, last survivor of the five Studebaker brothers, gave his blessing to Fred Fish's bold, forward-looking plan. And within a year John Studebaker himself was using a new Studebaker-Garford automobile.

By 1911 Studebaker was second only to Ford as a builder of motorcars—a distant second, to be sure—with production totalling 26,827 automobiles. The company was unable to sustain that ranking; yet by 1915, two years before J. M. Studebaker's death, the company was in sixth place, just behind Buick. Profits that year came to more than $9 million, and Studebaker was firmly established as a leading builder of medium-priced cars.

The company's pre-war peak came in 1923, when production reached 146,238 cars, and profits exceeded $18 million. The directors, under the leadership of Albert Russel Erskine, who had become president of the firm in 1915, declared dividends totalling just over $8 million amounting to about 44 per-

Originally published in Special Interest Autos #157, Jan.-Feb. 1997

Above left: *Loewy-designed hood accents add character to Commander.* **Top:** *Taillamps are of very sleek, modern design.* **Above right:** *Headlamps and parking lamps are in clean combo unit.* **Below:** *Stylized "S" in runningboards gives custom touch to prosaic part of car.*

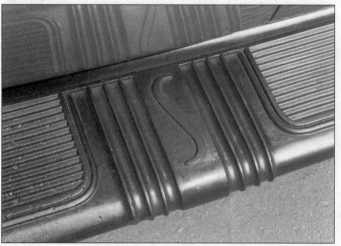

cent of profits. This was good business practice, leaving a healthy balance for product development, plant improvement and reserves.

But then A. R. Erskine—himself a major stockholder in the company—embarked upon a policy of paying out an ever-increasing share of profits in the form of dividends to the stockholders. Studebaker became one of the darlings of Wall Street on the strength of this largess, which by 1929 totalled 91 percent of profits. The frugal John M. Studebaker would have been horrified.

And then came the Depression. By 1930 the nation's economy was in bad shape, and getting worse. Studebaker posted a slim profit of $1.5 million that year. Even that much was a major achievement in view of the fact that sales were considerably less than half their pre-Depression level. But Erskine, a perennial optimist, insisted on paying out five times as much in dividends as the company had received in profits, thus seriously depleting Studebaker's reserves.

At the very pit of the Depression, 1932, Studebaker lost $8,687,000; yet that year the directors, urged on by A. R. Erskine, paid out nearly a million dollars in dividends. It was a policy that verged on madness; and on March 18, 1933, Studebaker, unable to meet $6 million in bank loans, went into receivership. Corporate vice presidents Paul G. Hoffman and Harold S. Vance were appointed receivers, along with Anton G. Bean, president of the White Motor Company. Erskine retained the title of president, but he was relieved of his duties. He cleaned out his desk and

went home, a man broken in both spirit and health. Three months later he was dead by his own hand.

All of which is getting somewhat ahead of the story. Back in 1927, in an effort to expand Studebaker's market by taking his company into a lower-priced field, Albert Erskine introduced a new, small car which he modestly named for himself. Built on a wheelbase of 108 inches and powered by a 146-c.i.d. Continental engine, the Erskine was a handsome little machine, styled by the great Ray Dietrich. But it was not, by most people's definition, a "low-priced" car, costing as it did, about nine percent more than either a Pontiac or a Dodge.

Evidently with European tax laws in mind, the Erskine was designed with the unusually long stroke/bore ratio of 1.71:1. But it failed to make so much as a dent in the overseas market, while here at home it was considered to be both over-priced and under-powered. Furthermore, the combination of its

high-winding engine and a 5.125:1 axle ratio led to premature engine wear, and the Erskine soon developed a dismal reputation for durability. Then in 1928 Albert Erskine moved in the opposite direction, acquiring control of Pierce-Arrow. Pierce, at that time, was losing money, but a handsome new line of straight-eights was planned for 1929, and had it not been for the coming of hard times during the 1930s, this might have been a highly profitable acquisition. But the costly Pierce was the wrong car for hard times, and it proved to be a money-loser for Studebaker. One month after Albert Erskine's death, Pierce-Arrow was sold (for $1 million cash) to a group of Buffalo businessmen. And by 1938 it was out of business, though for many more years its magnificent V-12 engine was used to power Seagrave fire engines.

By 1931 the "Low-Priced Three," Chevrolet, Ford and Plymouth, held, among them, two-thirds of the new car market in the United States. Studebaker's share, in contrast, amounted to barely 2.5 percent of the total. Albert Erskine began to think small again.

As explained in *SIA* #33, it happened that a pair of independent auto engineers, Ralph Vail and Roy Cole, had developed an excellent light six, expecting to sell it to Willys. But Willys, lacking sufficient capital to tool up for this as yet un-named car, dusted off its 1927 Whippet engine and brought out the 1933 Willys 77 instead. Vail and Cole were left with two prototypes, along with the rights to the design of their car, including that of the engine. Vail, driving west toward his farm near Michigan

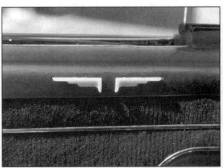

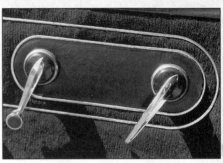

Above: Split grille is intricately cast and handsome in appearance. **Top right:** Fine detailing continues inside on window cappings and, **right,** door and window handles.

1940 STUDEBAKER

City, Indiana, in one of the prototypes, made a fortuitous stop in South Bend,

where his car was shown to Albert Erskine.

The result was the Rockne, named for Knute Rockne, just then on the verge of retirement after a distinguished career as Notre Dame University's football

coach. The plan was that Coach Rockne, who for several years had been doing public relations work for Studebaker during the off season, would be named head of a Studebaker subsidiary where the car would be produced, but on March 31, 1931, he was killed in a tragic airplane crash.

Plans went forward, and toward the close of 1931 production of the Rockne car got under way in the Detroit plant where Erskines had previously been built. Actually, there were *two* Rocknes that season. The larger of the two, the Rockne 75, was essentially a rebadged Series 54 Studebaker Six, while the smaller model was the Cole-Vail car, advertised as the Rockne 65. The latter was a beautiful little automobile of excellent quality. A trifle larger, ten percent more powerful and $100 more expensive than the Chevrolet, it was one of the best buys on the already overcrowded market.

But 1932 was not a propitious time to market a new automobile. The 75 lasted just one season, while the 65, retitled the Rockne 10, remained in production only until the summer of 1933—by which time, of course, Studebaker was in receivership.

The Cole-Vail engine, however, remained a Studebaker stalwart long after the Rockne automobile was gone. Bored to 205.3 cubic inches (up from 189.8 in the Rockne), it resurfaced in the 1934 Studebaker Dictator. Caught in the turmoil of receivership, the company's 1933 model year production had amounted to only 12,531 Studebakers plus about 13,000 Rocknes. The calendar year figure of 43,024 units looked much better, thanks to the September 1933 introduction of the 1934 models accompanied by an extraordinarily effective advertising campaign conceived by Paul Hoffman and aimed chiefly at

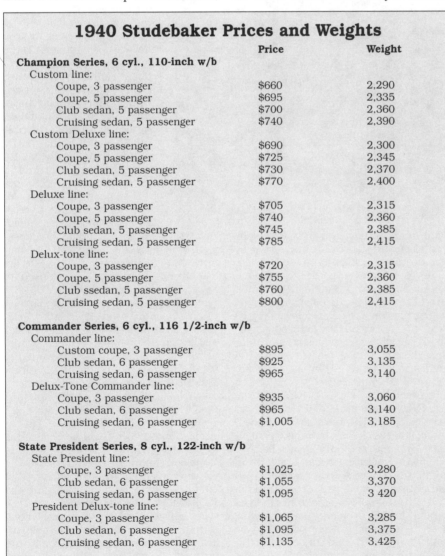

1940 Studebaker Prices and Weights

	Price	Weight
Champion Series, 6 cyl., 110-inch w/b		
Custom line:		
Coupe, 3 passenger	$660	2,290
Coupe, 5 passenger	$695	2,335
Club sedan, 5 passenger	$700	2,360
Cruising sedan, 5 passenger	$740	2,390
Custom Deluxe line:		
Coupe, 3 passenger	$690	2,300
Coupe, 5 passenger	$725	2,345
Club sedan, 5 passenger	$730	2,370
Cruising sedan, 5 passenger	$770	2,400
Deluxe line:		
Coupe, 3 passenger	$705	2,315
Coupe, 5 passenger	$740	2,360
Club sedan, 5 passenger	$745	2,385
Cruising sedan, 5 passenger	$785	2,415
Delux-tone line:		
Coupe, 3 passenger	$720	2,315
Coupe, 5 passenger	$755	2,360
Club ssedan, 5 passenger	$760	2,385
Cruising sedan, 5 passenger	$800	2,415
Commander Series, 6 cyl., 116 1/2-inch w/b		
Commander line:		
Custom coupe, 3 passenger	$895	3,055
Club sedan, 6 passenger	$925	3,135
Cruising sedan, 6 passenger	$965	3,140
Delux-Tone Commander line:		
Coupe, 3 passenger	$935	3,060
Club sedan, 6 passenger	$965	3,140
Cruising sedan, 6 passenger	$1,005	3,185
State President Series, 8 cyl., 122-inch w/b		
State President line:		
Coupe, 3 passenger	$1,025	3,280
Club sedan, 6 passenger	$1,055	3,370
Cruising sedan, 6 passenger	$1,095	3 420
President Delux-tone line:		
Coupe, 3 passenger	$1,065	3,285
Club sedan, 6 passenger	$1,095	3,375
Cruising sedan, 6 passenger	$1,135	3,425

bolstering the morale of the company's dealer body.

The big, 337-cubic-inch Speedway President was gone before the 1934 season opened, leaving two smaller Studebaker Eights: the 250.4-c.i.d. President, priced (in sedan form) at $1,285, and the 221.0-c.i.d. Commander, with sedan prices starting at $1,025. But nearly 77 percent of Studebaker's 1934 model year output was comprised of a newcomer, the $845 Dictator Six, powered by an 88 horsepower version of the Rockne engine

By 1936 Studebaker was out of receivership. The Cole/Vail engine had been stroked to 217.8 cubes, yielding 90 horsepower. That car, with only minor styling changes, was continued into 1937. But at that point somebody at Studebaker was astute enough to see that with Hitler's Nazis running roughshod over Europe, the Dictator name might carry some negative connotations. Accordingly, the following year the six-cylinder Studebaker—its engine bored an additional 1/16-inch to 226.2 cubes—was given the more acceptable Commander title. And it is that engine, rated at 90 horsepower, that was fitted to the handsome 1940 Commander coupe that serves as our driveReport car.

With the March 1939 introduction of the Champion, Studebaker attempted once again—with conspicuous success, this time—to field a low-priced car. Custom and Deluxe trim levels were offered in three body types, at prices ranging from $660 to $800, figures com-

Above: Sturdy flathead six began with Rockne. It's understressed at 90 bhp from 226 cubes. *Below:* Full set of gauges surrounded by woodgrain greets the driver.

Studebaker's Durable Cole-Vail Engine
1932-1960

The competent and durable six-cylinder engine developed by Ralph Vail and Roy Cole for Studebaker's 1932 Rockne was fated to far outlast the car for which it was designed, though bore, stroke and compression ratio were increased from time to time. Note that our drive/Report car is among the many models listed here.

Year	Model	Bore/Stroke	C.i.d.	C/R	Hp/rpm
1932	Rockne 65	3 1/8 x 4 1/8	189.8	5.25:1	65/3200
1933	Rockne 10	3 1/8 x 4 1/8	189.8	5.50:1	70/3200
1934	Dictator	3 1/4 x 4 1/8	205.3	6.3:1	88/3600
1935	Dictator	3 1/4 x 4 1/8	205.3	6.3:1	88/3600
1936	Dictator	3 1/4 x 4 3/8	217.8	6.3:1	90/3400
1937	Dictator*	3 1/4 x 4 3/8	217.8	6.0:1	90/3400
1938	Commander*	3 5/16 x 4 3/8	226.2	6.0:1	90/3400
1939	Commander*	3 5/16 x 4 3/8	226.2	6.0:1	90/3400
1940	Commander	3 5/16 x 4 3/8	226.2	6.0:1	90/3400
1941	Commander	3 5/16 x 4 3/8	226.2	6.5:1	94/3600
1942	Commander	3 5/16 x 4 3/8	226.2	6.5:1	94/3600
1947	Commander	3 5/16 x 4 3/8	226.2	6.5:1	94/3600
1948	Commander	3 5/16 x 4 3/8	226.2	6.5:1	94/3600
1949	Commander	3 5/16 x 4 3/4	245.6	6.5:1	100/3400
1950	Commander**	3 5/16 x 4 3/4	245.6	7.0:1	102/3200
1951	Light trucks	3 5/16 x 4 3/4	245.6	7.0:1	102/3200
1952	Light trucks	3 5/16 x 4 3/4	245.6	7.0:1	102/3200
1953	Light trucks	3 5/16 x 4 3/4	245.6	7.0:1	102/3200
1954	Light trucks	3 5/16 x 4 3/4	245.6	7.0:1	102/3200
1957	Light trucks	3 5/16 x 4 3/4	245.6	7.5:1	106/3400
1958	Light trucks	3 5/16 x 4 3/4	245.6	7.5:1	106/3400
1959	Light trucks	3 5/16 x 4 3/4	245.6	7.5:1	118/3400
1960	Light trucks	3 5/16 x 4 3/4	245.6	7.5:1	118/3400

*Also used for Coupe-Express
**Also used for light trucks

specifications

illustrations by Russell von Sauers, The Graphic Automobile Studio

© copyright 1996, Special Interest Autos

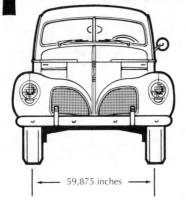

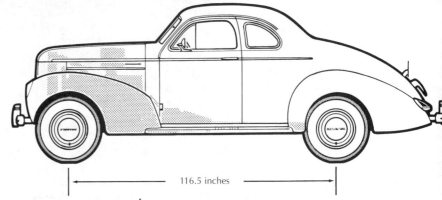

|←——— 59,875 inches ———→|

|←——— 116.5 inches ———→|

1940 Studebaker Commander

Base price $895 f.o.b. factory
Price as equipped N/A
Std. equip., this model Hill-holder, dual windshield wipers, hood latch on steering column, concealed gas filler cap
Options on dR car Overdrive, white sidewall tires, Studebaker heater, aftermarket left outside mirror

ENGINE
Type 6-cylinder, in-line, L-head
Bore x stroke 3.3125 inches x 4.375 inches
Displacement 226.2 cubic inches
Compression ratio 6.00:1
Horsepower @ rpm 90 @ 3,400
Torque @ rpm 174 @ 1,200
Taxable horsepower 26.3
Valve lifters Mechanical
Main bearings 4
Carburetor Stromberg 1.25-inch single downdraft
Fuel feed Camshaft pump
Lubrication system Pressure
Cooling system Centrifugal pump
Exhaust system Single
Electrical system 6-volt battery/coil

TRANSMISSION
Type 3-speed selective, synchronized 2nd and 3rd speeds, column-mounted lever; overdrive, hill-holder
Ratios: 1st 2.57:1
2nd 1.55:1
3rd 1.00:1
Overdrive 0.70:1
Reverse 3.48:1

CLUTCH
Type Single dry disc
Diameter 9.25 inches
Actuation Mechanical, foot pedal

DIFFERENTIAL
Type Hypoid
Ratio 4.55:1
Drive axles Semi-floating
Torque medium Rear springs

STEERING
Type Ross cam-and-lever
Turns lock-to-lock 5.25
Turning diameter 41 feet 3 inches

BRAKES
Type 4-wheel internal hydraulic
Drum diameter 11 inches
Effective area 150 square inches

CHASSIS & BODY
Construction Body-on-frame
Frame Double-drop; partial box section side rails; X-member
Body construction All steel
Body type 3-passenger coupe

SUSPENSION
Front Studebaker Planar independent; 49.5-inch x 2.5-inch 15-leaf transverse spring
Rear Rigid axle, 54-inch x 1.75-inch, 10-leaf longitudinal springs
Shock absorbers Houdaille double-acting

Tires 6.25/16 4-ply originally; now 6.00/16
Wheels 16-inch x 4.5-inch steel disc

WEIGHTS AND MEASURES
Wheelbase 116.5 inches
Overall length 197.5 inches
Overall width 72 inches
Overall height 66 inches
Front track 59.875 inches
Rear track 61 inches
Min. road clearance 7.875 inches
Weight 3,055 pounds

CAPACITIES
Crankcase 6 quarts
Cooling system 14.5 quarts
Fuel tank 18 gallons
Transmission 2 pints (plus 3/4-pint overdrive)
Differential 3 pints

CALCULATED DATA
Horsepower per c.i.d. .398
Weight per hp 33.9 pounds
Weight per c.i.d. 13.5 pounds
Weight/sq. in. (brakes) 20.4
Rev. per mile 3,349
Stroke/bore ratio 1.31:1

Right: Studebaker wheel motif harks back to the early days of the firm's automaking. **Facing page, top:** Ride is smooth and highly controllable. **Below:** driveReport car was originally ordered with minimal accessories, not even a radio.

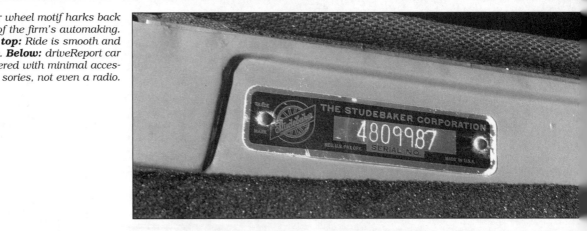

1940 STUDEBAKER

petitive with the familiar "Low-Priced Three." Advertisements stressed the Champion's outstanding economy, and the smaller Studebaker was a success from the start. By 1940 it accounted for 62 percent of the factory's total passenger car production.

Still, Studebaker's reputation rested to a considerable extent on its full-sized Commander Six and President Eight models. In fact, there are those among the army of Studebaker aficionados who will tell you that the best cars the company ever built were the 1940 Commanders and Presidents. Their engineering was excellent, craftsmanship was superb, economy was literally unbeatable, and styling, developed under the leadership of the internationally acclaimed Raymond Loewy, was (and remains) nothing short of stunning.

Commanders (and the State Presidents as well) came in two trim levels for 1940, each available in three body types: coupe, club sedan (two-door) and cruising sedan (four-door). Priced only $40.00 higher than the corresponding "regular" models was the Delux-Tone line, introduced during April 1940, As befitted their upscale status, the Delux-Tone cars offered two-tone upholstery, dual horns, deluxe steering wheel, standard white-sidewall tires, and five different two-tone color combinations.

One of Studebaker's most popular

standard features for many years was the Hill-Holder, which prevented the car from rolling backward on an incline. Many years ago we owned a Studebaker equipped with that very handy device;

and when we traded it in on a Plymouth, the lady of the house insisted that it, too, be equipped with a Hill-Holder. It's possible, I suppose, that ours was the only new Plymouth ever to be delivered with this particular piece of equipment.

Other standard features on the 1940 Studebakers included "Planar" independent front suspension. Developed by Delmar G. "Barney" Roos when he was chief engineer for the company, it employed a transverse front leaf spring in lieu of the coils used by most of the competition. First introduced in 1935, the Planar system remained a Studebaker characteristic through 1949.

Options abounded. The "Climatizer," apparently patterned after Nash's "Weather Eye," was a complete fresh air

filtering and ventilating system, mounted under the front seat. A conventional heater was also available at lower cost; and it is one of these units with which our driveReport car came equipped.

Other "extras" included fender skirts, bumper wing guards, master grille guard, wheel trim rings and a dashboard clock.

But perhaps the automatic overdrive was the option for which Studebakers were most noted. It was this device, which cut engine revolutions by 30 percent at speeds above 35 miles per hour, that helped make possible Studebaker's long string of awards in the Gilmore (later Mobilgas) Economy Runs. In the 1940 contest, for example, Studebaker scored a clean sweep, with the Champion, Commander and President models all taking top honors in their respective classes. Winners were determined on the basis of ton miles per gallon, computed by multiplying the weight of the car in tons times the average miles per gallon. Here's how the Studebakers scored:

Model	Miles per gallon	Ton m.p.g.
Champion	29.19	53.448
Commander	24.72	54.750
President	23.40	54.573

By way of comparison, as Fred Fox has noted, the Chevrolet achieved just 48.022 ton mpg and 22.87 mpg in the 1940 contest.

Driving Impressions

Lou and Debbie Raimondi's Commander coupe was delivered to its origi-

Above: Well-designed interior light illuminates coupe's interior adequately. Below: Hood support is like that of many new cars.

1940 STUDEBAKER

nal owner, Mona M. Huntzinger, of Reedley, California, on February 12, 1940. Obviously, the lady gave the car meticulous care, for it was still in exceptionally good original condition when Lou acquired it, 41 years later.

This is not to say that restoration work wasn't needed. A friend reupholstered the car and new paint was professionally applied during 1982, but although its oil pressure was a little low, the Studebaker ran so well that no major mechanical work was undertaken until 1994. At that point, Lou pulled the head and found to his delight that the cylinder walls were flawless, showing virtually no taper. Lou installed a new set of standard pistons and rings, replaced the main, connecting rod and camshaft bearings, and fitted new exhaust valves and guides, A new clutch was next, followed by a complete overhaul of the brakes.

At some point, the odometer numbers had dropped from view. One of the minor tasks still facing Lou is that of pulling the speedometer and correcting that situation. Meanwhile, of course, he has no idea how many miles the Studebaker may have traveled. Obviously, though, the mileage is far from excessive.

Ms Huntzinger was obviously not one for loading her car with options. The Hill-Holder was standard equipment, of

The Commander Versus The Competition

	Studebaker Commander	Buick Special	Chrysler Royal	Nash Ambassador
Price, 3-pass. coupe	$895	$895	$895	$925
Shipping weight (lb.)	3,055	3,505	3,075	3,290
Wheelbase	116.5"	121"	122.5"	121"
Overall length	197.5"	203.9375"	202.5"	203.1875"
Front tread	59.875"	58.03125"	57"	56.875"
Rear tread	61"	58.15625"	60.28125"	60.25"
Engine	6 cylinder	Straight 8	6 cyl.	6 cyl.
Displacement (cu. in.)	226.2	248.0	241.5	234.8
Compression ratio	6.00:1	6.10:1	6.50:1	6.00:1
Horsepower/rpm	90/3,400	107/3,400	108/3,600	105/3,400
Torque/rpm	174/1,200	203/2,000	188/1,200	190/1,050
Carburetor (dwnddrft)	Single	Dual	Single	Single
Main bearings	4	5	4	7
Valve configuration	L-head	Ohv	L-head	Ohv
Clutch diameter	9.25"	10"	10"	10"
Front springs	Transverse	Coil	Coil	Coil
Rear springs	Semi-elliptic	Coil	Semi-elliptic	Semi-elliptic
Final drive ratio	4.55:1	4.40:1	4.10:1	4.10:1
Overdrive available?	Optional	No	No	Optional
Steering	Cam/lever	Worm/sector	Worm/sector	Worm/sector
Turning diameter	41' 3"	41' 0"	45' 3"	39' 0"
Braking area (sq. in.)	150.0	158.7	155.5	169.0
Drum diameter	11"	12"	11"	10"
Tires (factory)	6.25/16	6.50/16	6.25/16	6.25/16
Stroke/bore ratio	1.31:1	1.33:1	1.33:1	1.30:1
Horsepower per cid	.398	.431	.447	.447
Crankshaft revs per mile	3,349	3,190	2,870	3,018
Weight per hp	33.9	32.8	28.5	31.3
Weight per c.i.d.	13.5	14.1	12.7	14.0
Weight/sq. in. (brakes)	20.4	23.3	19.8	19.5

course. Beyond that, this car has an overdrive and a recirculating heater (rather than the more expensive Climatizer). Period! No radio, no fancy stuff. Lou added a set of white sidewall tires and a left outside mirror, but that's the crop when it comes to "extras."

I was privileged to drive this fine old car for several miles, over rural roads near Lou and Debbie Raimondi's home in Clovis, California. This is not a hot-shot performer; wasn't meant to be. Figure it this way: The Commander engine's displacement is only five cubic inches greater than that of the 1940 Ford V-8, yet the Studebaker outweighs the Ford by more than 250 pounds. Still, acceleration is entirely adequate. The clutch is smoother than most, and gear-changes are quick and fairly precise. The car corners flat, the ride is smooth, and the driver has the feeling of being totally in control. (A 61-inch rear tread is helpful in this respect. Who says Pontiac invented the Wide Track?) Steering is rather slow: five and a quarter turns, lock-to-lock, and a little heavier than I expected until the car gathers speed. The brakes pulled a bit to one side during my test drive, but that's easily corrected. Lining surface is more than adequate.

But of course, the Studebaker is at its best when it can stretch its legs, out on the open road. With the overdrive engaged, one is scarcely aware of engine noise, and when the loud pedal is pressed to the floor the car automatically downshifts to direct drive, providing that extra punch for passing or climbing hills.

Raymond Loewy was famous for supplying attractive little touches that provided the cars he designed with that indefinable something called "class." Certainly that is true in the case of the Raimondi car. Consider, for instance, Bud Juneau's photograph of the Studebaker's very attractive dash panel.

There were several minor features that I found attractive. The hood release, for example, is inside the car, on the steering column—an idea many years ahead of its time. The gas filler cap is hidden behind a small door in the right rear fender. Door hinges, except for the lower ones, are concealed so as not to be visible when the doors are closed. Door handles are smoothly faired into the stainless steel side moldings.

Altogether, I found the Commander to be a particularly attractive automobile. So did the judges at the 1996 Concours of Champions, where it brought home a First Place trophy. ๛

Acknowledgments and Bibliography

Cannon, William A. and Fred K. Fox, Studebaker: The Complete Story; Fox, Fred K., "1940 Commanders and Presidents: Studebaker's Best?" Turning Wheels (bulletin of the Studebaker Drivers Club), August 1987; Fox, Fred K., "1941 Studebaker Land Cruiser: Loewy's Prewar Masterpiece," Special Interest Autos, December 1985; Hall, Asa E., and Richard M. Langworth, The Studebaker Century; Hendry, Maurice D., "Studebaker: One Can Do a Lot of Remembering in South Bend," Automobile Quarterly, Vol. X, No. 3; Kimes, Beverly Rae and Henry Austin Clark, Jr., Standard Catalog of American Cars, 1705-1942; Langworth, Richard M., Encyclopedia of American Cars, 1940-1970; Lamm, Michael, "1933 Rockne," Special Interest Autos, March 1976; Maloney, James H., Studebaker Cars.

Our thanks to Dave Brown, Durham, California; Bill and Laura Gillum, Clovis, California; Don Phillips, Kerman, California. Special thanks to Fred K. Fox, Delhi, California, of the Studebaker Drivers Club, who provided invaluable help, and Lou and Debbie Raimondi, Clovis, California, owners of our driveReport car.

Above left: Original jack and tools hide in their own compartment. **Right:** More than enough room for luggage for two. **Below left:** Spare stores behind seats, keeping it clean and leaving more trunk room. **Right:** Heater was one of the few options ordered for this car. **Bottom:** Rear styling is far less distinctive than other aspects of car.

1947 CHAMP
Coming or Going?

Designed on the sly in a basement and initially engineered to a scheme nearly as radical as the Tucker's, the clean, unpretentious 1947 Studebaker became this country's postwar trendsetter.

PEOPLE COULDN'T believe it. Here came a car out of Buck Rogers —something from another world and time. It leapt more than the 3½-year chasm caused by the war. We can't imagine today what emotions the 1947 Studebaker brought forth when it first appeared in dealer showrooms in June 1946.

People poured in to see it. No one made a head count, but it's safe to say that crowds numbered in the hundreds of thousands. And for months afterward, pedestrians would stop and stare at a new Studebaker rolling by. When they got over the initial shock, kids would yell, "Hey, mister, are you coming or going?", which everyone considered very funny and appropriate.

But despite the jokes, people judged the back-to-front Studebaker as something of a miracle, particularly the Champion and Commander Starlight coupes, with their huge wraparound backlight. The Champion Starlight was a standard, 5-passenger production car priced among the Big Three, but instead of being another tall, rehashed prewar model, it hugged the ground. The average *woman* could see over the roof. The car's lowness alone made it impressive, not to mention the pleasingly angular, simple lines. The Starlight coupe stood out as "ultimately futuristic" and "daringly postwar."

Radical as they were, the 1947 Studebakers might well have been more so. Earlier in their planning stages, postwar Studes had been almost as radical as the 1948 Tucker. That's because Studebaker engineers had done considerable wartime testing of an opposed, water-cooled 6. This engine was meant for rear placement in a postwar passenger car. Too, Studebaker had planned to use torsion-bar front suspension under all its 1947 models. That continued as the plan right up to a few weeks before production actually began.

The 1946 Frazer had had its New York unveiling that January, so Frazer led the industry as the first all-new postwar production car.

Alongside it stood a prototypal front-drive Kaiser. It wasn't until June 1946, though, that rear-drive production Kaisers reached dealer showrooms, and those came at the same time as 1947 Studebakers, not ahead of them. Studebaker had staged public showings of its 1947 models as early as Apr. 1946, but supplier strikes, steel shortages, and OPA price dalliances delayed Stude's debut until June.

As it was, creation of the 1947 Studebaker involved a tremendous race with time—a crash program in the best wartime tradition. Studebaker had honed crash programs to an almost routine finesse. The Army, for instance, had given Studebaker exactly 180 days during the war to design, develop, and build 600 Champion-engined Weasels (all-terrain amphibians). Those 180 days meant from blank paper to 600 Weasels ready for a projected invasion. Studebaker body engineering went to work on a full-sized draft of the Weasel hull on a Friday and sent finished drawings to the sheetmetal shops that Sunday. At the end of 180 days, there stood 600 invasion-ready Weasels.

That same sort of compressed timing happened with the 1947 Studebaker. Preliminary work started in 1942-43. Virgil M. Exner, who claims credit as the postwar Studebaker's designer despite protests from Raymond Loewy, remembers, "Gene Hardig [chief chassis engineer] and I went to Roy Cole [engineering vice president] about this time, 1942-43, because neither of us was too busy with war projects. We sold him on the idea of letting us do an advanced design. This would be engineered to some degree toward production. We sold Cole on this, and I built a ¼-scale model. Soon after that we built a full-sized wooden mockup in the Studebaker die-model shop.

"This was a flush-sided job, and that's what convinced me that the first postwar car *shouldn't* be completely flush-sided. It should have a pontoon rear fender because of the beltline at that time. It seemed to have an awfully heavy look. But the upper structure, the curved one-

Originally published in Special Interest Autos #19, Nov.-Dec. 1973

The 1947 Studebaker's styling remains controversial even today, with Loewy and Exner both claiming credit. This ¼-scale plaster model was made around May 1944 from Exner's original "basement" clay designs.

Production styling created a sensation when introduced in Apr. 1946. Champion's owner Floyd Swan used to work for Stude in South Bend.

Going back to mid-1943, Exner, in Loewy's employ, came up with this full-scale wooden mockup. It could have accepted rear engine. Exner felt that straight-through fender gave design a too-heavy look.

Studebaker gave serious thought to bringing out postwar woody, publicized it in several magazines, but decided not to at last minute.

Starlight coupe's huge backlight became a conversation piece from the beginning. Same basic 1947 body shell served Studebaker until 1953.

Electric screw jacks operate top. Designers first tried to make convertible by cutting down Starlight coupe. This proved too narrow, so final version used 2-door sedan sheetmetal with 4-door decklid.

piece windshield and wraparound back window and rear deck—those turned out quite a bit like the postwar production car."

Exner and Gordon Buehrig headed Raymond Loewy's Studebaker studios on an equal footing toward war's end. But Exner never really got along with Loewy. Loewy's office was in New York, Exner's in South Bend, so during the war they saw relatively little of each other. With Exner worked a small team of highly talented designers: Gordon Buehrig (Cord 810 and Auburn speedsters), Bob Bourke and Holden Koto (1953 Studebaker Starliner: Koto also did the 1949 Ford), John Reinhart (1956 Continental Mark II), Vince Gardner, Jack Aldrich, and Frank Alhroth, an excellent surface modeller.

Exner had long nursed a growing dislike for Loewy, feeling that he (Loewy) was taking full credit for designs he had very little to do with—designs created by Exner. Bob Bourke comments, "In essence it was a lack of respect. Ex was a designer, and Loewy was a promoter—a promoter/designer, you might say. Whereas Loewy would principally get all the credit for everything, this to Exner was wrong in principle."

All Studebaker advertising, all its press releases, plus all articles about the 1947 models credit only Loewy for the postwar design. Loewy's prestige and name meant a good deal to Studebaker at that time, particularly on so radical a body configuration. Harold Vance, Studebaker's board chairman, wasn't overly enthusiastic about Loewy either, according to Exner, but he went along with the other board members who'd originally hired Loewy and who still acted as his patrons.

The postwar car actually started in the early spring of 1944, according to Exner, when engineering v.p. Roy Cole came into Exner's office along with Harold Vance. They asked Exner if he'd be willing to do a complete postwar car *off* the Studebaker premises, in secret, unbeknownst to Loewy or the board or to anyone else except a few department chiefs in body drafting and chassis engineering.

Cole liked Loewy perhaps less than Exner did, because Cole wanted his own design team under the engineering banner. He didn't care for styling dictated or sold to him by an outside consultant from New York and Paris. Vance went along in this case because he valued speed. He wanted Studebaker to be first out with a new postwar car. The fewer people involved, he reasoned, the faster the work. Vance had full confidence in both Cole and Exner and saw no reason to involve Loewy.

Exner continues: "I agreed to start immediately. I first cleared out

1947 Champ driveReport

one of my bedrooms at home—this was in the spring of 1944—and they sent me out an 8-foot drafting board. Then we went into my basement and installed an overhead fluorescent light, and they built me a ¼-scale clay modeling table down there. This was my job, then, to be worked on nights and weekends. That's the way it started, and Gene Hardig, who was then chief of chassis drafting, came out every day.

"To begin with, we worked on seating and chassis layouts under his supervision. In the meantime they built me an armature [base] for a clay model, and I started that. This period in my home lasted about 3-4 months. On completion, it was still a pretty good secret even at Studebaker. Some rumors leaked out because some of the chassis had to be done right there.

"As was the custom, we next built a full-sized wooden mockup. Unlike a clay, on a wooden mockup the doors open and shut; also the interior can be trimmed just like the real thing. This gave us a chance to sit in and evaluate the car as to dimensions, vision, seating, wheel angle, and all that.

"While I was still working in my home, there were several meetings with the Budd people from Philadelphia, who came out to follow progress. Budd had to know about this project, because they were going to build the tools and supply stampings for our postwar cars. Studebaker also sent to my home, regularly, one of their top body draftsmen, Tom Dingman, who worked with me on engineering problems. We then sent the ¼-scale model and all drawings to Philadelphia [Budd], where the full-scale mockup was built and completed.

"The original mockup turned out to be too small. It was all painted and trimmed and everything, standing on the old Champion's 110-inch wheelbase, with a 67-inch overall width. Roy Cole had a thing at that time—his philosophy was that a car cost so much a pound. He stuck to that rigidly, and these were the dimensions he laid down. They were a little tough to work to, but it turned out that the chassis had too much tread—or I had a body with only so much width. In other words, what happened when the front wheels jounced? The only way to get front-wheel jounce was to open the wheel wells way up and then add a fender lip. This lip treatment started a sort of trend, which is still in use today.

"We decided the car was too small, so we increased wheelbase to 111.5 inches and gave the width another two inches. We then built an all-new wooden mockup right there in the model shop at Studebaker, because most everybody knew about the car by that time. The body drawings were simply opened up and a 2-inch strip put down the center without changing the profile, and the rear wheels were moved back 1.5 inches. [Eventually wheelbase went to an even 112 inches.] Then the front end looked too short to me; this was quite a departure as far as the hood and rear deck went. I convinced Roy Cole we should add three inches to the front end, principally the fenders, and two inches in the hood. The new wooden model was then finished up like that." Vince Gardner designed the grille textures, and John Reinhart finished up the "racetrack" gauge cluster.

"So toward the fall of 1944, they called in the board of directors and all the people from New York and Chicago to a one-day showing," continues Mr. Exner. "This was a tremendous surprise to a great many of them. Because Loewy hadn't seen this car or even heard about it, we went from there—finished up the details, designed the interior, and that was about it."

Actually that wasn't it by a long shot. When Loewy first heard about the car in 1944, too late to do anything about it, he was furious. Who could blame him—he's been bypassed, and his own studio chief had conspired against him. Loewy fired Exner on the spot, but Cole immediately hired Exner as a full-time Studebaker engineering employee. Loewy then tried to hire Exner back, but Exner wouldn't go back.

To compound the misery, Cole and Exner had let Loewy's group work on another set of postwar designs, knowing full well they'd never come to anything. For this, they fed or at least let Loewy labor with wrong dimensions and specifications. Bob Bourke, who worked under Exner during the war but who'd been busy more with military projects, recalls, "Frank Alhroth and Ex and I worked on the initial advanced styling mockups at the beginning and end of the war. We got into the thing later than Ex. I don't know how Loewy found out what was going on, but we [the Loewy team] showed cars that, for instance, were given wrong dimensions. We worked on a car that was narrower and with worse proportions than Ex had to work with. It was sort of an under-handed deal on the part of Roy Cole, because he was trying to get Loewy out of there. We [Loewy] did two full-sized plaster automobiles, and when management viewed them, they said they were just too narrow. Well, those were the dimensions that we had to work with. Then we took those, and in a matter of a week's time, we cut them right down the middle and expanded them out to where the other [Exner] jobs were."

Bourke considered the Loewy designs at least as good as Exner's, but Exner admits that by the time the board of directors viewed the wooden mockups, die models for his designs had been 40% finished, and Budd was rapidly tooling for production.

• •

Champions were called G-Models, and the immediate prewar (1942) Champ was the 4-G. Right after the war, Studebaker built about 20,000 1942-like 5-G Champions before introducing the flush-sided postwar 6-G in June 1946.

Except for the engine and transmission, nearly everything about the 6-G was different from the 5-G. It had two inches more wheelbase and a flanged, box-section frame, double dropped for a low body profile. This frame was largely the work of Harold Churchill, who later took Cole's place as engineering v.p. after Cole's death. The frame proved very rigid.

According to E.T. (Ed) Reynolds, who worked at the South Bend proving grounds, "The box-section frame—and even the body—was initially designed to handle the engine either up front or at the rear. The people in engineering felt that there was a very good chance that the industry trend might be toward rear-engine design, so the car was balanced out so the engine would fit in back. Then, too, the first postwar car in development had torsion-bar front suspension. The postwar double A-frame planar setup was a modification of the torsion-bar suspension. It wasn't until just weeks before we went into production that the car went back to the modified planar. These torsion bars were very similar to Chrysler's. You could control carrying height, same as Chrysler's. The main difference was that Chrysler's torsion bars mount to the lower A-arm, while Studebaker's mounted to the upper one."

Ed reports that prototypes running the torsion-bar suspension rode and handled beautifully. The only reason Studebaker went to a revamped planar setup was because they were afraid they couldn't get a good supply of the sort of steel needed for torsion bars. As it was, Studebaker did have problems getting steel after the war, same as everybody else, so they bought the Empire Steel Co. in Ohio. Since Empire made industrial, not automotive steel, Studebaker used it as trading stock and sold Empire again after the shortage eased.

"We had a little Flat 6 under development right after the war," adds Reynolds. "It was water-cooled, and displacement was around 200 cubic inches. We never installed one in the rear of a car, but they installed

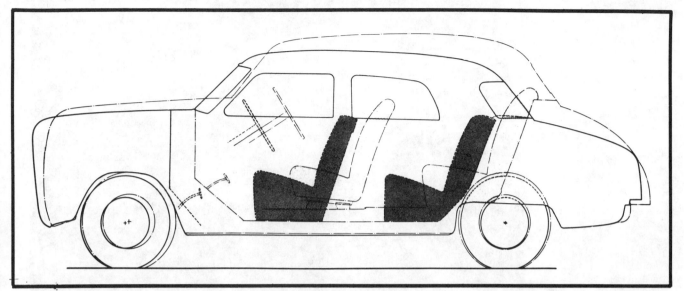

Restyled Champ placed passengers and engine nearly a foot ahead of previous design. Rear seat was five inches lower and 10 inches wider than before.

Budd in Philadelphia supplied Stude's stampings during postwar era. We've often wondered what ever became of these ¼-scale models.

Champion 6 had oil pan turned around to compensate for engine's move forward. Otherwise it remained virtually unchanged from 1939 til 1961.

Nothing fancy about Champion convertible's upholstery pattern. Lack of pleats in leatherette material makes interior easier to keep clean.

Designer Vince Gardner built sport roadster from '47 business coupe in late 1940s, drove it for years. Car was recently saved from crusher.

John Reinhart detailed the "racetrack" dash panel. Champion used 100% gauges, and this car has optional clock. Knobs are well marked, easy to reach.

Though originally slated for torsion-bar front suspension, postwar Stude stuck with planar.

John Reinhart also did the postwar emblems. Commander had a large one with spread wings.

Shallow trunk suffers from top encroachment & spare. Rear compartment almost got a Flat 6.

1947 Champ driveReport

three of them up front in cars for testing and development. By that time the trend was back to conventional, so they dropped it."

Studebaker ran olive-drab, handbuilt mechanical prototypes around the South Bend test track as early as Apr. 1945. These used versions of the Exner body plus the torsion suspension.

When Roy Cole, Gene Hardig, and Virgil Exner drew up the initial postwar Champion package, one of their primary objectives was to get as much interior space into the car as possible without unduly expanding its exterior. Today we'd class the Champion as a true compact. (Interestingly, the first Falcon and Valiant of 1960 both used 170-cid 6s, same as the Champion, although with shorter strokes.) With the Champ's flush sides, maximum seat width became 60 inches. This beat the 5-G Champion by a full 10 inches.

The double-dropped frame let the car's planners move the rear seat 11 inches ahead of its previous location, plus five inches down. The front seat got a similar shove forward and down. To accomplish this, though, the engine had to be moved ahead nine inches, bringing its centerline astraddle the front axle. To give enough jounce clearance, the engine oil pan had to be turned around backward so the sump stood toward the front. Other Champion engine mods for 1947 included adding bearing inserts (learned from the Weasel program), which greatly increased

reliability, and changing the locations of the starter and oil filler tube.

Along with its full line of 3- and 5-passenger coupes, 2- and 4-door sedans, and a convertible, Studebaker also hoped to bring out a station wagon. A wagon was listed up to the last minute before introduction, and references to it appeared in LIFE, POPULAR MECHANICS, CONSUMER RESEARCH BULLETIN, AUTOMOTIVE INDUSTRIES, and other publications. The wagon never made it, of course, although SIA showed some of the prototypes considered (*SIA #6, pp. 10-17*), one with a plastic roof and another, more conventional wood-bodied wagon. The woody would probably have been the one for production.

• •

Uncle Tom McCahill tested the 1947 Champion in MECHANIX ILLUSTRATED for Sept. 1946. We like his comments better than our own, so the following are his impressions, reprinted with permission. Tom's test of the Champ took place at Studebaker's 800-acre proving grounds in South Bend.

"...visibility has been made superb by increasing the windshield area 144 square inches and the rear window [of the 4-door sedan] 239 square inches. [The Starlight coupe's total glass area ran to 2430 square inches, an industry record.] This rear window is the outstanding feature of the design, for it is nearly as large as the windshield and curves clear across the back. At a glance, it's hard to tell which end of the car is which, because the rear luggage compartment tapers back in lines like those of the hood.

specifications

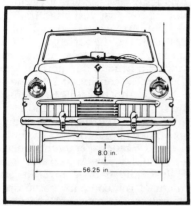

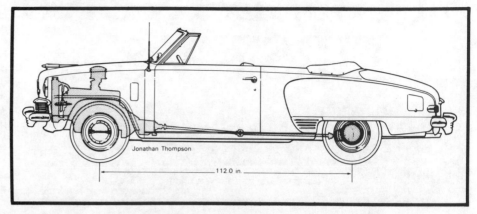

Jonathan Thompson

8.0 in.
56.25 in.
112.0 in.

1947 Studebaker Champion convertible coupe

Price when new.... $1902 f.o.b. South Bend (1947).

Current valuation*.. Xlnt $2730; gd $1365; av $435.

Options.......... Radio, overdrive, spotlight, turn signals.

ENGINE

Type........... In-line L-head 6, water cooled, cast-iron block, 4 mains, full pressure lubrication.
Bore & stroke...... 3.0 x 4.0 in.
Displacement....... 170.0 cid.
Max. bhp @ rpm.. 80 @ 4000.
Max. torque @ rpm.. 134 @ 2000.
Compression ratio.. 6.5:1 (7.0:1 opt).
Induction system.... 1-bbl. carburetor, mechanical fuel pump.
Exhaust system.... Cast-iron manifold, single muffler.
Electrical system.... 6-volt battery/coil.

CLUTCH

Type........... Single dry plate, molded asbestos lining.
Diameter......... 8.0 in.
Actuation........ Mechanical, foot pedal.

TRANSMISSION

Type........... 3-speed manual with overdrive, column lever.
Ratios: 1st........ 2.61:1.
2nd....... 1.63:1.
3rd....... 1.00:1.
Overdrive.. 0.70:1.
Reverse.... 3.54:1.

DIFFERENTIAL

Type........... Hypoid, Hotchkiss drive.
Ratio:......... 4.56:1.
Drive axles........ Semi-floating.

STEERING

Type........... Cam & twin lever, variable ratio.
Turns lock to lock... 3.9.
Ratio............ 24:1 to 30:1.
Turn circle........ 39.0 ft.

BRAKES

Type........... 4-wheel hydraulic drums, internal expanding, self-adjusting.
Drum diameter...... 9.0 in.
Total lining area..... 148.0 sq. in.

CHASSIS & BODY

Frame........... Box-section steel, ladder type, 5 cross-members, double dropped.
Body construction... All steel.
Body style........ 2-dr., 5-pass. conv. coupe.

SUSPENSION

Front........... Independent, planar, transverse leaf spring, upper and lower A-arms, lever hydraulic shock absorbers.
Rear............ Solid axle, semi-elliptic leaf springs, lever hydraulic shock absorbers.
Tires........... 5.50 x 15 tube-type.
Wheels.......... Pressed steel discs, drop-center rims, lug-bolted to brake drums.

WEIGHTS & MEASURES

Wheelbase........ 112.0 in.
Overall length...... 192.75 in.
Overall height...... 60.75 in.
Overall width...... 69.75 in.
Front tread....... 56.25 in.
Rear tread....... 54.00 in.
Ground clearance.... 8.00 in.
Curb weight....... 2875 lb.

CAPACITIES

Crankcase........ 5 qt.
Cooling system..... 11 qt.
Fuel tank......... 18 gal.

FUEL CONSUMPTION

Best........... 28-30 mpg.
Average.......... 19-23 mpg.

*Courtesy **Antique Automobile Appraisal,** Prof. Barry Hertz.

"For speed tests on the track, I selected a car with only a few hundred miles on it. In trying out the pick-up, I went through all gears a number of times. The car had considerable snap, considering the engine size, but the performance could not be considered outstanding. In high gear I allowed the speed to drop to 10 mph a number of times before opening the throttle wide and holding it there, and again the performance was excellent but not flashy. Perhaps I should point out that this engine is the smallest from the standpoint of developed horsepower of any American car I have tested this year with the exception of the 1946 Studebaker.

"For ride testing, I drove the Champion over the standardized rough road of the proving grounds, which presents just about every road hazard.... It consists of long and sharp dips and deep man-made ruts, single and double, so that at times both the right and left wheels are hitting the ruts and at other times only the right or left wheels. I drove over this course at several different speeds, from low to high, and if any faulty roadability existed, it was bound to show up; but it didn't. The little Champion is a remarkably good road car. On the hill test, which meant starting from a dead standstill and going up a terrific grade, the low horsepower was noticeable, but a climb as extreme as that will seldom...be encountered."

SIA should add that among the Champion's hidden charms were fantastic gas mileage (up to 30 mpg with overdrive and careful feather-footing), variable ratio steering (30:1 near the locks for easier parking and 24:1 dead ahead for better response). Then, too, all 1947 Stude-

bakers had self-adjusting brakes, a postwar first and a great trend-setter.

The entire car started a trend, or several trends, particularly in the way it looked and the economy and lightness of its engineering. Harley Earl, GM's styling boss, was one of Studebaker's first customers for a 1947 model. He brought it back to his studios for his designers to study. The '47's applied rear fenders probably influenced similar treatments in GM's 1949 models—and in Chrysler's, too. Ford Motor Co. likewise bought an early 1947 Stude—a Champion—and disassembled it completely. Ford engineers weighed and tagged each part, using the figures to compare their own 1949 components. Roy Cole's weight consciousness apparently worried Harold Youngren and other planners of the 1949 Ford. So in its day, the Champ became the car to shoot for. 🔗

Our thanks to Floyd F. Swan, Anaheim, Calif.; Virgil M. Exner, Birmingham, Mich.; Raymond Loewy, New York; Eugene Hardig, South Bend, Ind.; Bob Bourke, Westport, Ct.; Gordon Buehrig, Grosse Pointe, Mich.; John M. Reinhart, Dearborn, Mich.; Vince Gardner, Detroit; E.T. Reynolds, Ponchatoula, La.; Holden Koto, Boynton Beach, Fla.; Fred Fox, Marv Silverstein, and the Studebaker Drivers Club, Box 791, Oswego, Ill. 60543; Otto Klausmeyer, South Bend; Strother MacMinn, Los Angeles; Burt Weaver, Oakland, Calif.; Jonathan Thompson, South Laguna, Calif.; and Mechanix Illustrated, copyright 1946 by Fawcett Publications.

STUDEBAKER'S FIRST V-8

Arrow at the top, and a wide range of Studebaker and Pierce-Arrow commercial vehicles, Erskine was very close to achieving his goal. Although they produced more vehicles, neither Ford nor Chrysler offered the variety that Studebaker did. Even the stock market crash of 1929 did little to dampen Erskine's optimism. He continued to issue big dividends, and in 1932 Studebaker gained control of the White Motor Company, producer of White and Indiana trucks. Then in March 1933 the bubble broke and Studebaker found itself in receivership. Pierce-Arrow and White were lost, and court-controlled management of the company came under the auspices of co-receivers Paul G. Hoffman, Harold S. Vance and Ashton G. Bean. Both Hoffman and Vance were long-time Studebaker employees, and Bean was president of White. Under the able guidance of these men, especially Hoffman, Studebaker recovered.

Paul G. Hoffman, who had been a very successful Studebaker dealer in southern California and later Studebaker's vice president in charge of sales, took over as president of the reorganized Studebaker Corporation. Harold Vance became chairman of the board. Hoffman had a good understanding of exactly what it took for an independent American automobile manufacturer to survive. Progressive ideas, good design, engineering excellence, aggressive sales

1951 COMMANDER STARLIGHT

by Fred K. Fox
photos by John & Connie Stanton

AMERICA'S independent automobile manufacturers are now history, and the world is a poorer place for it. Great makes, such as Packard, Hudson, Nash, Auburn, Reo and dozens more challenged the big boys, and in doing so greatly accelerated the engineering and styling advancement of the automobile. Today, Detroit's challengers come from Europe and the Land of the Rising Sun. If some of the independents had survived, we might very well be looking at a Packard Infiniti on the cover of *Motor Trend* or *Car and Driver*.

One of the best remembered independents was Studebaker, a proud old company that in 1928 proclaimed itself "The Great Independent." Actually, in 1928 Studebaker's president, Albert Russel Erskine, had optimistic plans for the Studebaker Corporation to become another General Motors. The previous year he had introduced the Erskine line of small cars (see *SIA* #70), and in 1928 he purchased Pierce-Arrow, the luxury car company from Buffalo, New York. With the Erskine at the low end, Studebaker's Dictator, Commander and President models in the middle, the Pierce-

and responsible management were all on Hoffman's "must" list.

Mechanical innovations quickly adopted by the new Studebaker company included overdrive, which was offered first as an option on 1935 Presidents, and the Hill Holder, a 1936 anti-roll device that became one of Studebaker's most famous options. Ride and handling were greatly improved in 1935 with the adoption of Studebaker's unique transverse spring "Planar" independent front suspension.

In 1936 Hoffman hired the well-known industrial designer Raymond Loewy and his associates to direct the styling of the new 1938 Studebakers, a series that the *Magazine of Art* picked as "The Car of the Year." In 1939 Studebaker unveiled its low-priced Champion (see *SIA* #35), a smartly styled pre-compact car that could haul as many people as a Chevrolet, but weighed less and got considerably better gas mileage (a 1940 Champion obtained 29.19 mpg in the 1940 Gilmore Economy Run).

Hoffman's tactics had worked very well, and by the time the United States entered World War II, Studebaker was again making consistent profits for its

Driving Impressions
by Lynn Eyerly

Our feature car, a 1951 State Commander Starlight coupe, is an excellent representative of Woron's "strong originality" of design. It is owned by John and Connie Stanton of Salem, Oregon, and was purchased new by John's grandparents, Frank and Juanita Kellogg.

When John, a neighbor, invited me to test-drive his Starlight Coupe I leapt at the chance for several reasons.

First, he has been a great source of technical and sometimes physical help in things mechanical. We both share an enjoyment in older cars, and even though he prefers Detroit iron and I stick to those automobiles of foreign origin, we have enjoyed an undeniable camaraderie for several years. When the coupe, which had been in his family since new, came into his possession, I wasted no time in inspecting the new arrival. Even though it had only seen a little over 50,000 miles and showed only moderate wear and tear, John spent the next three years improving the car until it reached its current outstanding condition. During this time, I've been restoring a once-speedy British six-cylinder car of similar vintage, and the chance to drive a medium-priced American V-8 for comparison was not to be passed up.

The design of the car creates few neutral first impressions. One either likes or dislikes the controversial styling, and as one approaches the car, the bullet-nose and panoramic rear window stand out as two features that must have been quite avantgarde in their time. John tells me that Studebaker was sensitive about the nose styling; it's actually a less prominent "bullet" and a more conservative front end than that of the previous year.

Once settled in the driver's seat, you find yourself in the classic fifties driving position: loads of leg and elbow room, a cloth-upholstered bench seat on which to rest your posterior, and a big steering wheel close to your chest, complete with a chrome horn ring that glares in your eyes on sunny days. The instruments, though a million miles away on the distant dashboard, are housed in three large, round, very legible dials directly in front of the driver.

Starting procedure is rather unusual: You turn the key and push the clutch pedal down until its backside presses on what looks like a spare headlight dimmer switch. This engages the starter. A simultaneous stab at the gas pedal, and the ohv V-8 purrs into life. It's a quiet idle — you can hear the clock ticking. One can feel that it is a V-8 rather than a six; however, the steering wheel shakes just enough to let you know that it is not an in-line cooking under the hood. This engine, by the way, was very much state-of-the-art in an era when flatheads still held sway. With only 232 cubic inches, however, one cannot say that its potential had been fully tapped in 1951.

Transmitting the power from that engine is achieved by that favorite American setup, the three-speed column shift (with non-synchro first). But the linkage is mercifully precise enough to prevent this from becoming an onerous chore. I like the four-on-the-floor of my car better. John tells me that the manual shift and V-8 combo was relatively rare. All those owners who chose automatics must have had rather leisurely acceleration and a shorter range, but then we weren't in such a hurry then.

As I eased out of John's driveway, the clutch pedal displayed its next trick: Part way up, it releases its "hill holder" brake, and only nearer to the top of its travel does it do what most clutches do. Not much later, having accidently killed the engine on an incline and trying to restart, I realized just how handy that brake could be!

Driving is very much typical of the era. One takes corners slowly, and you had better leave a little extra room ahead to allow for the standard "stomp and pray" brakes. The low-stressed V-8 does not develop much low-speed torque on hills. There are several items in which this car excels, however. Once into overdrive on the highway, you can almost forget that you are in a 38-year-old auto; only the bias-ply tires remind you to mind the helm occasionally. Also, for its size, the coupe's sharp-turning abilities make it surprisingly tractable in tight places and U-turns. In contrast, my old Brit can't do tight corners. Finally, for a car of its age, the outward visibility is something in a class of its own. In contrast, looking out of the windows of my old car reminds me of a view through a series of bunker slits. Two adult rear-seat passengers will find their side and rear view especially panoramic. They also get leg room enough to suit a six-footer, and huge cubbyholes which are hidden under the hinged armrest lids. Not bad for a coupe.

All told, I found the car to be just as entertaining and friendly to drive as my old British sedan, and in several ways its equal or superior in performance.

STUDEBAKER

stockholders. During the war, Studebaker produced military trucks, aircraft engines and the in-house designed Weasel, a sort of go-anywhere Jeep. All during the war Hoffman was making plans for what Studebaker would do when peace was achieved. He realized that initially there would be an overwhelming seller's market, but after that he knew Studebaker would have to be on its toes or it would be overrun by the Big Three.

What resulted from Hoffman's 1942-45 planning brought Studebaker its greatest fame. Hints of the forthcoming triumph came in March 1944 when Hoffman and Vance included the following in their 1943 Annual Report:

"Although the end of the war is not in sight, the Corporation's management is

Above: Fender vents were a familiar Studebaker feature. Above right: Headlamp/sidelamp design was a refinement from 1950 shape. Right: Coupe has a trunk nearly as long as its nose. Below: Wheel covers are also close to 1950 design. Facing page: "Bullet nose" design appeared only in 1950 and '51, yet was one of Studebaker's most memorable styling benchmarks.

increasingly aware of its responsibilities to stockholders and to employees with respect to the prompt and orderly transition of this business from a wartime to a peacetime basis. Generally speaking, the planning and development stages of our war production responsibilities are behind us, and so, a few men in our organization can be assigned to postwar planning without any detrimental effect whatever to our current war production.

"We believe that with the resumption of civilian production of passenger cars and commercial cars, Studebaker will have an unusual opportunity. We are planning boldly, but carefully and thoroughly to take full advantage of it.... We are studying the merits and availability of new materials and of new methods arising out of war experience. We are working out a detailed program for distribution of our products after the war. We are doing all of this with the hope that the time is not far distant when we can see the end of the war and the beginning of a new era in the affairs of this 92-year-old enterprise."

The results of all this wartime planning were the newly styled 1947 Studebakers (see *SIA #19*), the first postwar designs from a prewar company. Introduced in mid-1936 after a short run of prewar-styled Champions, the new Studebaker hit the industry like a storm. Not since the Model A Ford was introduced in late 1927, had there been so much interest in a new automobile. The company proclaimed that they were "First by Far With a Postwar Car," and jokesters had a field day kidding about how one couldn't tell which way the new Studebakers were going. *Life* magazine was so impressed by Studebaker that they gave the company and its products a big ten-page color spread in their September 16, 1946, issue.

The new styling was mainly the work of Virgil Exner. Much of the design was accomplished in Exner's home, without Raymond Loewy's knowledge, but Loewy's company ended up receiving all the credit. The most dramatic body style of the new line was the five-passenger coupe, later identified as the Starlight coupe. The five-passenger coupe featured four large wraparound rear windows that went from B-pillar to B-pillar. All the new bodies, except the long-wheelbase Commander Land Cruiser, were offered as either Champions or Commanders.

The new 1947 models put Studebaker on a roll, but Hoffman was keenly aware that the momentum had to be maintained. By 1947, Studebaker was undoubtedly aware of General Motors' development of new, modern, overhead-valve V-8s for its Cadillac and Oldsmobile lines. Studebaker's new models may have attracted a lot of attention, but their power plants offered little excitement. Both the Champion and Commander were powered by L-head sixes that produced, respectively, 80 and 94 horsepower. The more powerful L-head straight-eight President engine was not returned after the war. Realizing that GM's new engines would be trend setters, Hoffman and Vance gave Studebaker's engineering department the green light to start the development of their own ohv V-8.

Hoffman also wanted to maintain the styling lead that the '47s had established. New designs were considered for 1949, but in the end, a dramatic facelift was introduced for the 1950 model year. Called the "Next Look," it featured an airplane-inspired "bullet-nose," revised rear fenders and vertical taillamps. The front-end styling had some Tucker similarities, but it was not a Tucker rip-off. Actually, Loewy's stylists had been considering an airplane spinner nose since 1941. It could be that the Tucker did give Studebaker's management nerve enough to go ahead with the radical styling. And radical it was! It caused as much or more comment than the original 1947s. Everyone and his brother had a nickname for the new Studebaker. Needle-nose, two-row corn picker and torpedo-nose were just a few of the many monikers applied. Initial reaction from Studebaker personnel, dealers and the buying public was mixed. Some hated it, while others thought it was exactly the kind of dramatic new design that Studebaker needed to maintain its bold image. Tom McCahill called it the "best looking car in its class," but one big West Coast dealer shoved the front ends into potted plants so they would not shock his customers!

The 1950 facelift of the 1947 models was handled by Robert Bourke, Loewy's South Bend styling chief. Bourke still remembers Loewy's directive, which said that the new front should "look like ze aeroplane." Today, Bourke is better remembered for his design work on the 1953 Studebaker Starliner hardtop and Starlight coupe, models that have long been recognized for their beautifully clean aerodynamic lines.

Initial sales of the 1950 Studebaker models were a little sluggish, but several mid-year maneuvers, including price reductions, introduction of a low-price Custom Champion, more chrome on other models and a new Automatic Drive transmission all helped improve sales. A gradual acceptance of the styling and a fear of Korean War shortages also helped increase sales. By the end of the 1950 model year, Studebaker had produced 343,164 automobiles, the all-

specifications

©copyright 1990, Special Interest Autos

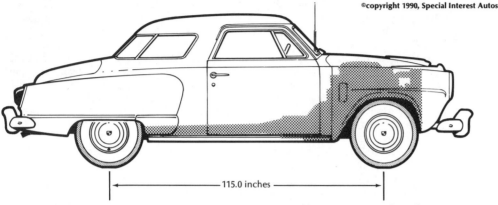
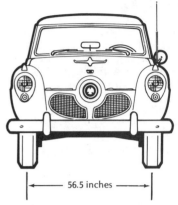

115.0 inches

56.5 inches

1951 Studebaker Starlight Coupe

Base price	$2,137
Options and Accessories	Overdrive, Hill Holder, Climatizer heater defroster, white sidewall tires, full wheelcovers, Strat-O-Vu exterior rear view mirror, Fram oil filter

ENGINE
Type	Overhead 90-degree V-8, cast iron block and heads, five main bearings, solid valve lifters
Bore and stroke	3⅜ inches x 3¼ inches
Displacement	232.6 cubic inches
Max bhp @ rpm	120 @ 4,000
Max torque @ rpm	190 @ 2,000
Compression ratio	7.0:1 (7.5:1 optional)
Carburetor	Stromberg model AAUVB-26, two-barrel
Exhaust system	Cast iron exhaust manifolds with crossover pipe and single muffler and tail pipe
Electrical system	6-volt, positive ground with Delco-Remy starter, generator, regulator and distributor

TRANSMISSION
Type	Standard 3-speed with overdrive
Actuation	Shift lever on steering column, H pattern
Ratios: 1st	2.57:1
2nd	1.55:1
3rd	1.00:1
Overdrive	0.70:1
Reverse	3.48:1

DIFFERENTIAL
Type	Spicer Hypoid
Ratio	4.56:1
Drive axle	Semi-floating

STEERING
Type	Cam and twin lever with variable ratio
Ratios	24:1 straight ahead; 33.8:1 full turn
Turns lock to lock	5.5
Turning circle	39 feet

BRAKES
Type	Self-adjusting, self-centering hydraulic drum brakes
Front	11-inch cast-iron drums
Rear	9-inch cast-iron drums
Total lining area	163 square inches

CHASSIS & BODY
Frame	Ladder-type with double-flanged box section side rails and five cross members
Body construction	Steel
Body style	5-passenger, 2-door coupe
Configuration	Front engine, rear wheel drive

SUSPENSION
Front	Independent coil springs with upper and lower unequal length A-arms, direct acting tubular hydraulic shock absorbers and anti-roll bar
Rear	Solid axle, 4-leaf semi-elliptic springs, "sea-leg" mounted direct-acting tubular hydraulic shock absorbers
Wheels	Five lug, 15-inch x 5-inch steel disc
Tires	Tube-type bias ply 7.10 x 15

WEIGHTS AND MEASURES
Wheelbase	115 inches
Overall length	197.5 inches
Overall height	61.75 inches
Overall width	70.69 inches
Front track	56.5 inches
Rear track	54.0 inches
Ground clearance	8.0 inches
Shipping weight	3,025 pounds
Curb weight	3,168 pounds

CAPACITIES
Crankcase	6 quarts (7 w/filter change)
Cooling system	18.75 quarts (w/Climatizer)
Fuel tank	18 gallons

PERFORMANCE
Top 0-60 time	12.5 seconds (*Mechanix Illustrated*, January 1951)
Top fuel economy	28 mpg (1951 Mobilgas Economy Run)

This page: Starter is activated by pushing all the way down on clutch pedal. Facing page, top: Combination armrest/storage bin is a neat feature for back seat passengers in coupe.

STUDEBAKER

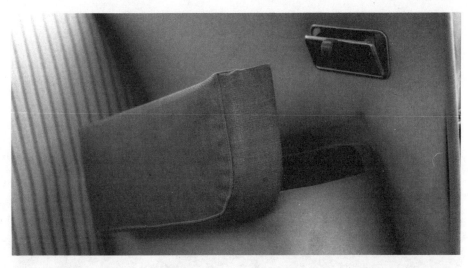

time record for the company. For the calendar year, sales were $477 million and profits were $22.5 million. All this looked good for Studebaker, but there were many underlying factors that soon caused major problems for Studebaker and later for Studebaker-Packard. Among these were an antiquated assembly plant that was still using many buildings constructed before the turn of the century; a spoiled work force whose productivity was way below the Big Three, and the lack of dynamic leadership. Part of the leadership problem occurred in April 1948 when Harry Truman talked Paul Hoffman into stepping down from his Studebaker presidency and becoming the head of the Economic Cooperation Administration, an agency that spent $5 billion a year of US taxpayers' money to rebuild the economy of war-torn western Europe. Of course, Truman had made a good choice — a point made clear in a Hoffman cover story in the April 4, 1949,

issue of *Life* magazine — but ECA's gain was Studebaker's loss.

Before Hoffman left, Studebaker's new engine program was well in gear. Directed by engineering chief Stanwood W. Sparrow, the ohv V-8 was ready for the 1951 model year. The new engine, which was made standard on Commander models, was quite a coup for Studebaker. Only Cadillac and Oldsmobile introduced — in 1949 — a modern ohv V-8 before Studebaker. Concurrent

with Studebaker's introduction was Chrysler's famous Hemi V-8. Studebaker's new V-8 featured a wedge-type combustion chamber and displaced 232.6 cubic inches. With a bore of 3⅜ inches and a stroke of 3¼ inches, it narrowly qualified as an over-square engine. The new power plant produced 120 horsepower at 4,000 rpm.

At the time the Studebaker V-8 was introduced, many people surmised that it was just a baby Cadillac V-8. Whether

Living With A Bullet-Nose

One of the enjoyments of doing articles on special interest autos is that it gives the writer a chance to learn — through research — about various models, and many times drive the featured vehicles. For this article, Lynn Eyerly stood in for the driving assignment, so I missed the opportunity to take the 1951 Commander Starlight through its paces.

Although I did not have a chance to drive John Stanton's Studebaker, I don't feel completely in the dark, for during the past 39 years, I have been able to ride in and — when I became old enough — drive a bullet-nose Studebaker. The story starts back in February 1950. My parents, who had babied a 1935 Packard One Twenty through the war, were seriously looking for a new car. Being quite satisfied with a 1949 Studebaker truck they had purchased in December 1948, they were easily talked into buying a slightly used 1949

Bermuda Green Commander four-door sedan. After taking delivery of the Commander on February 28, my mother and father quickly became disenchanted with the car. Its design was pleasing and it ran perfectly, but it lacked the expansive rear leg room of the old Packard. With one son over six feet and another one — me — heading that way, they decided the Commander had to go. After just five days of ownership, they traded it in on a brand new 1950 Studebaker Land Cruiser, a stretched wheelbase model that had considerably more leg room than the regular Studebaker four-door sedan. I went with my father when he picked up the car, a Fiesta Tan model with black, gold and gray striped nylon upholstery. To me, the color was not as impressive as the green Commander, but the new front-end styling with its protruding rocket nose put the Fox family right into the 21st century,

or so it seemed.

Of course, the 21st century image only lasted about two years. The fast-paced styling evolution of the 1950s quickly dated the Land Cruiser and, by the mid-fifties, I was anxious for my folks to buy a more modern car. This was not to be. They were farmers, so the Land Cruiser was only used for weekly shopping and occasional pleasure trips. The rest of the time it sat in the garage growing older and more out of date. By 1960, when my parents finally acquiesced and bought a new 1960 Studebaker Hawk, the dealer would only offer them $100 trade-in for the old Land Cruiser. The Land Cruiser was still in very good condition, so my father decided, as he had done several times in the past, just to keep it. Well, that was 29 years ago, and although my parents are now gone, we still have the Land Cruiser. Its original paint still holds a good shine, and the tough nylon upholstery proved long ago that Studebaker was not fooling about durability. It passed the 100,000-mile mark several years ago, but the pan has never been off the engine.

The Land Cruiser's dated styling, which made it almost worthless in the late fifties and early sixties, has taken a major turnabout. Because of its unique and easily identifiable design, the 1950-51 Studebaker bullet-nose is now — especially in convertible form — one of the most sought-after postwar Studebaker models. Current price guides show a 1951 Commander convertible on a par with Studebaker's famous Avanti sports coupe. Midwest farmers would call it the revenge of the two-row corn picker.

STUDEBAKER

Right: Mathews, Bourke and Loewy work on postwar Studebaker designs. Below: Studes always did very well in Mobilgas Economy Runs. Bottom: 1951 V-8 on dynamometer test. Facing page, top: P-38 Lightning was inspiration for "bullet nose" front. Center: '43 Studebaker Champion styling study featured tri-star nose treatment. Bottom: Wartime "bullet nose" styling study.

this assumption hurt or helped Studebaker is impossible to ascertain, but it was certainly untrue. The following chart lists the major differences.

	1949 Cadillac V-8	1951 Studebaker V-8
Camshaft	chain driven	gear driven
Valve lifters	hydraulic	solid
Pistons	"slipper"	standard
Piston pins	floating	locked-in rod
Water pump	integrated w/manifold	separate from manifold

Studebaker's V-8 water pump was an ingenious invention that could be changed easily without disconnecting any hoses. Both Studebaker and Cadillac had their spark plugs placed above the exhaust manifold, a much more desirable position than that used on the first Ford and Chevrolet ohv V-8s.

Like any new product, the modern high-revving ohv V-8s introduced in the late forties and early fifties had their share of teething problems. One that got a lot of publicity, especially for Studebaker, was the so-called "soft camshaft." The problem was much more complex than just soft cams, and it was one that plagued all the companies, not just Studebaker. A thorough review of this problem was given by H.R. Johnson, Jr.,

in a major article in *Turning Wheels*, the journal of the Studebaker Drivers Club. Explaining the basis for the problem, Johnson made the following comments:

"Why were these new breed V-8 engines more susceptible to this type of failure? The reasons were many and there were as many theories. One inescapable fact, and perhaps one of the primary reasons, was the increased contact load between the cam lobe and valve lifter surfaces. In the "L"-head engines the lifter acted directly on the end of the valve stem. Valves were smaller due to limited space in the combustion chamber and were, consequently, lighter. Valve spring loads were less because of less valve weight. In the V-8 engines, cylinder bores were larger, permitting the use of larger and heavier valves. Also introduced into the valve train was a push rod and rocker arm. All this mass had to be accelerated when the valve was opened, creating high unit stress on the contact surface. Valve springs had to have a higher load to keep the valve train components from separating at the higher engine speeds. Every major engine part from bearings to valve train in these new engines was higher stressed — some, like the cam and lifters, to a point that the materials and some oils of the day could not withstand. In other words, the critical point had been passed."

When the "critical point" was passed, spalling of the lifter surface occurred,

Above: From inside the car, Studebaker's rear glass has a definite aircraft, or possibly even a spaceship appearance. *Below:* Stude's first V-8 appeared in 1951. It was the first "independent" to offer this kind of engine.

STUDEBAKER

and this in turn wore down the lobes on the camshaft. The solution involved new metallurgical methods, better oils, and design changes that reduced valve load without limiting engine speed. Studebaker's engineers and technicians put thousands of hours into the problem. Other companies also worked on the problem, but Studebaker's efforts were probably the most intensive. Harold Vance was very concerned about Studebaker's image. People who bought new 1951 Studebaker Commanders and had camshaft problems were given special attention. Emory Bonander, a former Northern California Studebaker dealer who now sells GM products, commented that "Studebaker's handling of the camshaft failures in the early fifties represented the best factory dealer support I ever encountered."

As mentioned, the new V-8 was installed in all 1951 Commanders, including the long-wheelbase Land Cruiser. The Champion continued with the small L-head six, but since the V-8 was actually shorter than the six, both lines were able to use the same 115-inch-wheelbase chassis (the Land Cruiser had a 119-inch wheelbase).

Styling changes for 1951 were made to de-emphasize the bullet nose. The center of the nose was made of silver-gray plastic and the outer ring was painted. The grille was enlarged and made flush with the body instead of being recessed as it was in 1950. For the first time, exterior sheet metal was exactly the same on Commanders and Champions. Except for different emblems and instruments, the only major visual difference between the two series was under the hood.

Body styles included a three-passenger business coupe (available only as a Champion), the Starlight five-passenger coupe, a two-door sedan, a four-door sedan, a convertible, and the Land Cruiser (only available as a Commander). The Champion was available with Custom, DeLuxe, or Regal trim. The Commander came with Regal or State trim.

Although the styling was now five years old, the five-passenger Starlight coupe with its large four-section wraparound rear windows was still Studebaker's most dramatic body style.

Easily identifiable as a Studebaker, the Starlight gave rear-seat passengers unprecedented visibility. Other makes later copied the concept (e.g., certain late fifties and early sixties GM products), but nobody ever equaled Studebaker's boldness.

One of the 1951 Studebaker Commander's greatest achievements was excellent fuel economy. Since the early days of the prewar Gilmore Economy Runs, Studebaker had been the country's leading fuel economy champion. (During the entire history of the prewar Gilmore and postwar Mobilgas runs, Studebaker won more class firsts than any other company.) At the 1951 Mobilgas Economy Run, Studebakers, especially the new Commander V-8, made excellent showings. Winning Class B, the Commander with overdrive obtained 28.0 mpg (58.2 ton-mpg) on the 840-mile run from Los Angeles to the Grand Canyon via Death Valley. Although awards were based on ton-mpg (the weight of the car in tons times its average miles per gallon), it is interesting to note that of all the full-sized cars entered, the Commander obtained the second best mpg figure. It was edged out by just 0.62 mpg by a 1951 Studebaker Champion. Compared to the previous year, the '51 Commander got 4.2 mpg better than the 102 horsepower, 1950 L-head six-cylinder Commander.

Besides being economical, the '51 Commander was a good performer for its day. Tom McCahill wrote in the January 1951 *Mechanix Illustrated* that the new V-8 "transforms the maidenly Studie of recent years into a rip-roaring hell-for-leather performer that can belt the starch out of practically every other American car on the road." Tom was able to make the '51 Commander go from zero to 60 mph in 12.5 seconds, an excep-

Above: Instrument panel is understated and easy to read. Below: Trunk offers hefty amount of storage space.

tional figure for an American car in 1951.

Because of Korean War production restrictions, and a shorter model year, 1951 Studebaker automobile production dropped to 268,565, but Commander sales, because of the popular new V-8, were way up. In 1950, Commander production represented 21 percent of Studebaker's car sales; in 1951, it was up to 46 percent. Because of war materiel production for the government—mainly 6x6 military trucks—

Studebaker's sales set a new record of $503 million, but profits were down to $12.6 million. Outwardly, Studebaker's situation looked good as it prepared to celebrate its 100th anniversary in 1952.

In an overview, the 1950-51 Studebakers, especially the Starlight coupes, were cars that could not be confused with any other make. Walter Woron, in the June 1951 *Motor Trend*, noted the following: "The appearance of the Studebaker causes an immediate reaction in the minds of most persons: They either like it or have a positive distaste for it. It is not for us to state whether or not the lines are good or bad from an esthetic point of view; however, they do possess strong originality." A current Motor Trend journalist would be hard pressed to say that about any 1990 car! ∂

Acknowledgments and Bibliography

William Cannon and Fred Fox, Studebaker: The complete Story; *Fred Fox, "1951 Studebaker Cars,"* Turning Wheels, *December 1985; H.R. Johnson, "Studebaker's Camshaft Story,"* Turning Wheels, *August 1986 and October 1987; contemporary Studebaker Service Bulletins, Service Letters, and sales literature; and contemporary automobile related magazines.*

Our thanks to John and Connie Stanton, of Salem, Oregon, for providing the featured car and the photographs. Special thanks to Lynn Eyerly for driving the featured car and for writing the "Driving Impressions" report.

STUNNING STUDEBAKER

1953 CHAMPION STARLINER

MICHAEL Lamm has called it "the most beautiful car ever mass-produced in America." And Richard M. Langworth, in his post-war Studebaker history, wrote: "Ask any industrial designer for the best automotive shape of the fifties, and he'll almost certainly pick the 1953-54 Studebaker coupes — the pillarless Starliner, the five-window Starlight.... They were, and are, magnificent-looking machines. Before their first year was up they'd won *Motor Trend*'s award for 'the most aesthetically styled cars.' They've been cited since as the outstanding industrial design of the decade by authorities who never before considered an automobile for that title." Langworth might have added that these stunning Studebakers were recognized early-on as certified Milestone cars.

They're popularly known as the "Loewy Coupes," after Raymond Loewy, for many years Studebaker's chief design consultant. But they actually represented the work of "Bob" Bourke, the Loewy Studios' chief designer, assisted by Holden "Bob" Koto.

The original intent had been to build a "show" car, a one-off intended for public relations purposes. But as the design developed, Bob Rourke began to nourish the hope that somehow, it might be put into production. "Normally," Bourke has written, "you'd just

by Arch Brown
photos by the author

run a thing like this off clean-slate, with no thought of production. But something prompted me to keep it practical, on the slim chance that it just might appeal to management."

Time was short, for it was the spring of 1951 before work on the project got under way, and Bourke found himself working, literally, day and night. It could easily have become, in Shakespeare's phrase, "Love's Labours Lost." But fortunately, Studebaker president Harold Vance liked the clay model. So did Paul Hoffman, former president and future chairman of the company. And Raymond Loewy, who wielded considerable influence with the directors, enthusiastically recommended that this sensational new design be adopted.

In the end the directors consented: The slinky, low-slung Starlight and the Starliner were to be put into production for the 1953 model year. In addition a line of sedans was to be developed, with styling derived from the coupes but more conventional in concept. This agreement represented a tremendous gamble on Studebaker's part: It required the factory to tool up for two dif-

ferent types of automobile, since no body panels could interchange between the coupes and the sedans. The investment was therefore a major one — and a risky one in a sense, for a company as small as Studebaker.

In order to give the Starlight and the Starliner their long, sweeping lines, Bob Bourke used the 120.5-inch wheelbase of the premium-priced Land Cruiser, rather than the 116.5-inch chassis employed by the rest of the line. The coupes' height was held to 58.3 inches — lowest in the industry, and five and a half inches lower than the Studebaker sedans. This meant that the driveshaft tunnel was somewhat intrusive, especially in the rear compartment. Bourke solved that problem by employing a permanent center armrest, separating the two rear-seat passengers.

Mechanical changes were few. Perhaps they were considered unnecessary; probably they were simply impossible, given Studebaker's limited financial resources. As before, two series were offered, the V-8-powered Commander and the six-cylinder Champion. Each was available in either Deluxe or Regal trim, while the Champion sedans also came (at rock-bottom prices) in bare-bones Custom form.

Engines were essentially the same as the 1952 Studebakers. The Commander's powerplant was a thoroughly mod-

Driving Impressions

Those of our readers who have visited Reno's National Automobile Museum will recall that in addition to the four "galleries," each devoted to a different era in the development of the automobile, there are a number of charming "street scenes" in which several of the museum's fine cars are displayed. Parked by a fireplug in the 1950s section (and displaying a parking ticket on its windshield) is a gorgeous 1953 Studebaker Champion Starliner, finished in Coral Red with an Ivory Mist top.

(Incidentally, although we find the color scheme very attractive, Bob Bourke detested it. Writing years later in *Automobile Quarterly*, he noted, "although new exterior colors were constantly being developed by us, many of the colors that reached production were incredibly gauche. As I recall, there was a sort of deep salmon that was particularly excruciating.")

For $25 a year, Reno residents are permitted to "adopt" any car in the museum. Their names are displayed on the descriptive card that accompanies the car, and they are expected to participate by periodically cleaning and waxing the car. Out-of-towners, unable to take part in the wax-and-shine parties, may become non-participating "adoptive parents" for an annual contribution of $75. It happens that the author and his wife were among the first to enroll in this program as absentee "parents," with the "adoption" of the Starliner. So we were particularly pleased when Chuck Hilton, the museum's executive director, agreed to break the Studebaker out of the museum in order for it to serve as our driveReport subject.

This car was purchased at auction on November 28, 1977, by the Harrah Museum, predecessor to the present National Automobile Museum. Nothing is known about its prior history, although it was obviously a well-cared-for example. It's not a lavishly equipped unit. The only options are the overdrive, hill-holder, heater and white-sidewall tires. A smartly styled metal plate covers the hole where the radio would go.

The hardtop's condition suggests that the 85,382 miles registered on the odometer is probably the accurate figure. At some point it has evidently been repainted, and the vinyl upholstery on the seats has been replaced. Otherwise, the interior appears to be original.

We'll also hazard a guess that at some point the engine has had some attention, for it starts readily, runs very quietly, and emits no visible exhaust smoke. The clutch displays a very slight chatter, not at all unusual for a Champion. There's some play in the steering, and the brakes tend to pull a bit to one side — easy problems to remedy, and hardly surprising in a car that spends its life in a museum.

Front leg room is ample, and head room is better than one might expect, given the Starliner's low silhouette. Driver and passenger sit low and rather erect, perhaps more so than some people might prefer, though we did not find the position uncomfortable. Rear seat accommodations are somewhat cramped, however, at least for six-footers. The seat is very low, and getting in and out of the rear compartment is something of a struggle. The trunk is spacious, though shallow, and the spare tire is somewhat intrusive.

Steering is just a bit on the heavy side; the power assist would be helpful, though we don't consider it a necessity. Pedal pressures, both clutch and brake, are moderate. Shifts are easy, and the synchronizers do their job well.

The Studebaker's ride is very comfortable — just a little on the firm side, a characteristic that suits our personal preference. The '47 Starlight Coupe that we owned, years ago, tended to heel over rather heavily in hard cornering, thanks presumably to its "Planar" front suspension. In contrast, this car, with its conventional front end, takes the turns with aplomb.

If the Champion has an Achilles' heel, it is the torque output of the engine: 138 pounds-feet at 2,400 rpm, compared to the Chevrolet's 200 at 2,000. Given a decent start, these cars will climb hills rather readily, but if the momentum is lost, it's very difficult to regain. The low-end torque simply isn't there. In order to compensate, we found second gear/overdrive to be a useful combination.

The Champion's final drive ratio, with either the standard transmission or the automatic, was 4.10:1, but cars equipped with the overdrive came with 4.56:1 cogs. With the 0.70:1 overdrive engaged, this gives our driveReport car an overall ratio of 3.19:1, ideal for open road driving. It cruises smoothly and quietly at modern freeway speeds.

Motor Trend, road-testing a 1953 Champion sedan, recorded 24.9 miles per gallon at a steady 60 miles an hour. Overall, at speeds of 30, 45, 60 and 75 mph as well as in city traffic, their car averaged a commendable 26.5 mpg. Studebaker's reputation for economy was well-deserved.

Studebaker had already sown the seeds of its own destruction by the time our driveReport car was built. Its factory was outmoded and hopelessly inefficient; its labor contract was the most costly in the industry. Bob Bourke recalled that "after the Starliner was put into production, every component was laid out by Engineering and price tagged to compare with the contemporary Chevrolet. The result of this cost analysis showed that if General Motors had produced this car it could have been built for $385 less than the Chevy. Yet Studebaker sold it at Buick prices. They had to, as their unit costs were much higher than GM's."

But General Motors didn't build the Starliner and the Starlight. It would have been out of character for the giant corporation to produce anything so daringly different. Studebaker built them, and Bob Bourke's stunning coupes stand as monuments not only to his talents, but also to the courage of the men of South Bend.

1953 STUDEBAKER

ern, short-stroke, overhead-valve job, developing a respectable 120 horsepower from 232.6 cubic inches. First introduced in 1951, the V-8 had quickly developed an outstanding reputation for durability, economy and performance.

The six-cylinder engine, on the other hand, was the familiar flathead, developed by Barney Roos during his tenure as Studebaker's chief engineer and first introduced in the 1939 Champion (see *SIA* #35). It was a tough, reliable little powerplant, though its L-head configuration together with its long-stroke design meant that it was essentially obsolete by 1953. Displacing 169.6 cubic inches, it was rated at a modest 85 horsepower, which was no more than barely adequate for a 2,760-pound automobile. We'll have more to say about that in our Driving Impressions.

Above: Bob Bourke's front-end treatment is low-slung, simple and elegant. **Facing page, top left:** *Wheel covers are also attractively simple in design.* **Top right:** *Subtle Stude i.d. on trunk lid.* **Below left:** *Modern Studebaker symbol complements styling of car.* **Below right:** *Fender air vents are an old-time touch.*

SIA Interview:

Shortly before the close of 1990 a new executive director was appointed for the National Automobile Museum. Charles C. "Chuck" Hilton is no stranger to the operation, having started with the Museum as an accountant back in 1984, when it was still owned by Harrah's. Appointed comptroller when the non-profit William F. Harrah Foundation was formed, he served in that capacity while the present museum was under construction. Then in the period just preceding his present appointment he served as the museum's assistant director.

In recent months there have been many rumors concerning the status and probable fate of this fine museum; so while we were in Reno *Special Interest Autos* called on Chuck Hilton to ask for clarification — and to inquire about his plans for the future.

SIA: It has been said that the National Automobile Museum has been granted a "reprieve" by the city of Reno. Would you clarify for our readers just what its status is?

Chuck: What transpired between the Foundation and the City of Reno was that the city agreed to issue short-term (five year) bonds in the amount of $9.1 million, to pay off the construction debt owed by the Foundation to the Interstate Bank.

SIA: In order to reduce the interest rate?

Chuck: Right. It brought the rate down from 11 percent to somewhere around 5¼ percent, reducing our $87,000 a month interest payments to about $49,000.

The misconception is that the city has effectively paid off that debt. That's not accurate. What they've actually allowed us to do is to re-finance it. The Foundation and the museum still owe the $9.1 million, due and payable at the end of five years. The whole reason behind the re-

financing plan is, we thought that if we had the opportunity to operate the museum for a couple of years, we could get ourselves in a better position, looking well financially.

SIA: In other words, get your traffic up.

Chuck: Right. Exactly. Get our attendance numbers to where we're at least at the break-even point — or close to it. And I think we can do that, given the opportunity to operate a little while longer.

SIA: So this is a five-year "reprieve"?

Chuck: Well, it could effectively be less than that. What we're looking at is that in addition to us being able to re-finance, we also have a one-percent room tax that's in effect in Washoe County. For a 12-month period, receipts will go toward the operation and debt service of the museum. So that will give us a year in which we will be creatively reducing the debt service.

What the city — and most everyone — is worried about is that if the museum continues to operate at less than a break-even point, we will be in serious financial trouble about two and a half years from now. We will have exhausted all our current funds, we will have eaten up the room tax money, and we will be operating at a loss position.

SIA: So you have, in effect, a 2½-year "window." How will you take advantage of it?

Chuck: Well, we launched an aggressive marketing campaign. We hired a great director of marketing, who came to us from the Henry Ford Museum in Dearborn. We launched a number of local campaigns. We introduced an annual pass program. That's an inexpensive yearly ticket; you buy it one time and you can visit the museum any time you wish. We introduced a number of weekend activities that we hope will draw both the local

public and the tourists. We introduced a number of campaigns for kids. We're working now with the Washoe County schools to make the museum part of their curriculum, so that every school-age child in the county will come through the museum at some time during their educational period. We're going to be training teachers here at the museum, on the different types of assets that the museum offers — not only the technological aspects, but for use in history classes as well. So these are some of the programs that we've started.

SIA: You lost that marketing director, did you not?

Chuck: Yes. He returned to Detroit just recently. What we have is the groundwork laid down. We have a three-year marketing plan outlined. Jackie [Assistant Director Jackie Frady, a ten-year veteran with the museum] and I feel like we can keep that active until such time as we can replace the marketing director.

SIA: So you expect to get somebody with professional experience as a campaign director?

Chuck: Yes. One of my criteria is that

For an extra $231, the Champion could be purchased with an automatic transmission. Developed jointly by Studebaker and Borg-Warner engineers, this was an excellent unit combining a three-speed planetary gearset with a torque converter. (As a matter of fact, Ford had attempted to purchase the rights to the Studebaker automatic, but officials at South Bend wanted it to be exclusively Studebaker's. Their refusal would cost the company dearly in badly needed revenue in the years that followed.)

Champions equipped with the automatic were fitted with 7.5:1 aluminum cylinder heads, in lieu of the standard 7.1:1 cast iron jobs. Even so, their already marginal performance was handicapped somewhat. The new transmission was much better suited to the more powerful Commanders. A far better bet for buyers of the six-cylinder cars was the Borg-Warner overdrive, optional at $105.

A new Studebaker option for 1953

Chuck Hilton

the person must have a proven track record in fund-raising, and that's where we're going to go with it.

SIA: Will the library continue to offer research services to car owners? [The position of librarian is now vacant, following the recent resignation of Linda Huntsman.]

Chuck: Yes. We've advertised for a professional librarian.

SIA: A trained librarian who knows something about automobiles? Not the most common combination in the world!

Chuck: Right. But we're hoping to find that perfect mix. We'll just have to try. And Linda [Huntsman] has offered to be a resource for us, and [former museum staffers] Bob Jackson and Pete Grosso. All these people are volunteers, and we'll have them as resource people.

SIA: Will you continue to show cars at the various Concours d'Elegance?

Chuck: We will. The only aspect that is changed is that we used to fund those trips. The new criteria is that our expenses must be paid or we don't go to these events. Pebble Beach may be the exception. We can cover that because we have a friend whose grandmother has a house down there. So by staying there, it's not quite as expensive as staying at the Lodge.

SIA: In your view, what sets the National Automobile Museum apart from other museums?

Chuck: In my mind, several things. The span of our collection is significant. The fact that we begin in 1890 and run through brand new Porsches in our "modern street" is important. We really do run the gamut of the automobile, as best one can in a 200-car collection.

I think the way the cars are displayed is unique and interesting. And I think we're very fortunate in the quality of the cars in

the collection. We have a number of "celebrity cars." We have several one-of-a-kind prototypes that add interest. But we also have the cars that were owned by the common every-day Joe, from 1900 up to modern times. You don't see row after row of classic cars. You see the cars that you probably would have seen most frequently on the street during that period of time. And I think that's important.

If you look at the collection as a whole, it really is a nice cross-section of the development of the automobile. And of course there are the "period" street scenes and the little extra trappings that are built into the museum that I think are significant. But not as significant as the collection itself.

SIA: You're presenting the automobile as history.

Chuck: Right.

SIA: Is there one car that you consider to be the "crown jewel" of the collection?

Chuck: It would have to be the Phantom Corsair, if only because of the recognition that it has gotten over the past couple of years. I think it's significant that it won Best of Show at the International Classic and Sports Car Show in Birmingham [England] that it was the featured car at Meadow Brook [concours] this year, and the feature car at the Santa Barbara concours. It's just gotten an awful lot of attention, and it really is a spectacular car!

SIA: Apart from achieving solvency, have you any special aspirations for the museum?

Chuck: I'm really interested in taking the museum to the point where I think it could be, with regard to its educational program. I'd like to see some additional exhibits built into the museum. Jackie and I are working right now on putting together a program, ready for a grant, to build a children's center down in the

arcade area, which would be all hands-on exhibits where the kids can get into an automobile simulator. And do some other things for children, things that are a little more active than what we have now.

I think the strongest goal for the museum, after it pays for itself, must be to develop our educational program. That's Number One! Secondly, I really would like to see us branch slowly back into the restoration process. I think that's part of what we need to do as a facility that shows the automobile. I think we should always have an ongoing restoration. Not to the degree that we did at Harrah's, but maybe one car at a time.

SIA: Do you have any contact with the various marque clubs?

Chuck: Yes. We've developed a good rapport with most all the clubs. We've had the Cadillac-LaSalle Club here, and the Al Jolson Cadillac has been featured in their publication. We've just had the Oldsmobile Club here. We've had the NorCal Classic Car Club. We mail to all the clubs, and make suggestions for them when they come. We do after-hours events for them, cocktail parties, whatever they need. We work as closely as we can with them.

SIA: How do you assess your chance of success?

Chuck: I firmly believe that if we can make a dent in the overall amount that we owe, if we can show the community and the public in general that the management of the facility and the board of trustees really want to retire that debt, I think we'll get to the point where we can take care of the rest. I have great faith in this community, and people in general. The support we've received for the museum has been overwhelming. I don't believe the public wants to see the facility have to close its doors.

SIA: Nor do we.

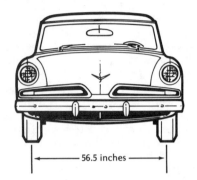

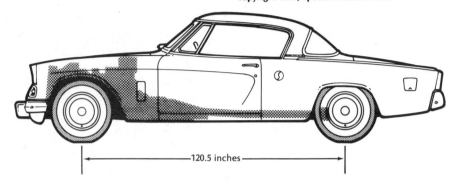

56.5 inches

120.5 inches

1953 Studebaker Champion Starliner

Price $2,116 f.o.b. factory with standard equipment
Options on dR car: Overdrive, hill-holder, heater, white sidewall tires

ENGINE
Type Six-cylinder, L-head
Bore x stroke 3"x4"
Displacement 169.6 cubic inches
Compression ratio 7.0:1
Hp @ rpm 85 @ 4,000
Torque @ rpm 138 @ 2,400
Taxable hp 21.6
Valve lifters Solid
Main bearings 4
Fuel system Carter WE-989SA 1-bbl downdraft carburetor
Lubrication system Full pressure
Cooling system Centrifugal pump
Exhaust system Single
electrical system 6-volt

CLUTCH
Type Single dry plate
Diameter 8.0"
Actuation Mechanical, foot pedal

TRANSMISSION
Type 3-speed selective with overdrive; synchronized 2nd and 3rd gears; column-mounted lever
Ratios: 1st 2.61
2nd 1.63
3rd 1.00
Reverse 3.54
Overdrive 0.70:1

DIFFERENTIAL
Type Hypoid
Ratio 4.56:1
Drive axles Semi-floating

STEERING
Type Saginaw worm & roller
Ratios 19.0 gear, 20.0 overall
Turning diameter
(curb/curb) Right 40'0", Left 41'0"
Turns of wheel,
lock-to-lock 3½

BRAKES
Type 4-wheel hydraulic drum type
Drum diameter 10" front, 9" rear
Effective area 168.0 square inches

CONSTRUCTION
Type Body-on-frame
Frame Ladder type
Body construction All steel
Body style Hardtop coupe

SUSPENSION
Front Independent A-arms, coil springs, link stabilizer bar
Rear Rigid axle, longitudinal leaf springs
Shock absorbers Tubular hydraulic
Wheels Pressed steel, drop-center rims
Tires 8.40/15 originally; now G78/15

MEASUREMENTS AND WEIGHT
Wheelbase 120.5"
Overall length 201.9"
Overall width 71.0"
Overall height 56.3"
Front tread 56.5"
Rear tread 55.5"
Minimum road
clearance: 6.8"
Shipping weight 2,760 pounds

CAPACITIES
Crankcase 5 quarts (less filter)
Transmission 1½ pints (overdrive 1¼ pints)
Differential 3 pints
Cooling system 10 quarts
Fuel tank 18 gallons

CALCULATED DATA
Stroke/bore ratio 1.33:1
Hp per c.i.d. .501
Lbs. per hp 32.5
Lbs. per c.i.d. 16.3
Lbs. per sq. in.
(brakes) 16.4

PERFORMANCE
Standing ¼ mile 22.7 seconds/60.4 m.p.h.
zero to 30 m.p.h. 6.3 seconds
zero to 60 m.p.h. 21.7 seconds
Top (average
of 4 runs) 85.59 m.p.h.
Stopping distance,
from 30 m.p.h. 46 feet
Stopping distance,
from 60 m.p.h. 192 feet
Fuel consumption
overall 26.5 m.p.g.

(From a September, 1953 *Motor Trend* road test of a Champion 4-door sedan, weighing approximately the same as the Starliner)

This page, right: Wraparound rear window fits the design perfectly. **Far right:** *Flying S nicely fills space between grille openings.* **Facing page, top:** *It still looks fresh and modern after nearly 40 years.* **Below left:** *Vinyl bench provides slippery seating.* **Below right:** *Interior treatment is also simple and sporty.*

1953 STUDEBAKER

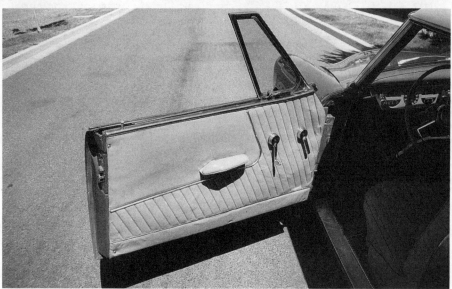

was power steering. Initially the company announced that Commander models would be available (for an extra $161) with a mechanical unit developed by Borg-Warner. This device was soon replaced, however, by the more traditional (and less costly, at $134) Saginaw hydraulic power steering, which was offered eventually to buyers of the Champions as well as the Commanders.

Also on the option list was Studebaker's familiar hill-holder, which prevented the car from rolling backwards when stopped on a hill. Priced at a reasonable $15, this was a useful device, and a highly popular one, as this writer can personally attest. (When we traded in our 1947 Studebaker Champion on another make in 1953, the lady of the house insisted that the new car be fitted with a hill-holder, supplied by the local Studebaker dealer.)

If Studebaker officials had any doubts about the public's acceptance of the Starlight and the Starliner, their anxieties were soon relieved. The coupes didn't come to market until January 1953, several weeks after the sedans

1953 Studebaker Table of Prices, Weights and Production

	Price	Weight	Production
Champion Series, 116½" wheelbase, 85 horsepower			
Custom Sedan, 2-door	$1,735	2,690	3,983
Custom Sedan, 4-door	1,767	2,710	5,496
Deluxe Sedan, 2-door	1,831	2,700	7,584
Deluxe Sedan, 4-door	1,863	2,735	17,180
Regal Sedan, 2-door	1,917	2,715	2,968
Regal Sedan, 4-door	1,949	2,745	17,897
Champion Series, 120½" wheelbase, 85 horsepower			
Deluxe Starlight Coupe	1,868	2,695	9,422
Regal Starlight Coupe	1,995	2,700	16,066
Regal Starliner Hardtop	2,116	2,760	13,058
Commander Series, 116½" wheelbase, 120 horsepower			
Deluxe Sedan, 2-door	2,089	3,055	2,371
Deluxe Sedan, 4-door	2,121	3,075	10,065
Regal Sedan, 4-door	2,208	3,095	7,454
Commander Series, 120½" wheelbase, 120 horsepower			
Land Cruiser Sedan, 4-door	2,316	3,180	15,981
Deluxe Starlight Coupe	2,127	3,040	6,106
Regal Starlight Coupe	2,213	3,040	14,752
Regal Starliner Hardtop	2,374	3,120	15,981

Note: All prices f.o.b. factory, with standard equipment.

Acknowledgements and Bibliography
Automotive Industries, *March 15, 1953;*
*Bourke, Robert E., "The Starlight and
the Starliner,"* Automobile Quarterly,
Vol. X, No. 3; Bridges, John, Bob Bourke
Designs for Studebaker; *Cushing, Harry,
"Studebaker Pioneers & New Style."* Mo-
tor Trend, *March 1953;* Gunnell, John
A. (ed.), Standard Catalog of American
Cars, 1946-1975; *Hendry, Maurice,
"Studebaker — One Can Do a Lot of
Remembering in South Bend."* Auto-
mobile Quarterly, *Vol. X, No. 3;* Lang-
worth, Richard M., *Encyclopedia of
American Cars, 1940-1970;* Langworth,
Richard M., Studebaker: The Postwar
Years; *"Studebaker Blazes & Styling
Trail."* Motor, *February, 1953; "Stude-
baker — Penny-Pinching Champion,"*
Motor Trend, *September 1953.*
*Our thanks to Dave Brown, Durham,
California; Linda Huntsman, Lemon
Valley, Nevada; the following members
of the National Automobile Museum
staff, Reno, Nevada: Jackie Frady, Assistant Manager; Bob MacMillan, Master Technician; Rod Lungstrom, Auto-
motive Technician. And special thanks
to Charles C. "Chuck" Hilton, Executive
Director, National Automobile Museum, Reno, Nevada.*

1953 STUDEBAKER

continued from page 17

made their appearance. Even so, the
Starlight and Starliner models accounted for an astonishing 46.4 percent
of Studebaker sales for the 1953 model
year. This was, of course, highly unusual, for sedans are traditionally the
mainstay of any automaker's business.
(At Chevrolet, for instance, coupes and
hardtops accounted for only 10.6 percent of the division's total 1953 volume.)
This unexpected development created
some production delays, unfortunately,

and early in the year some potential
buyers — including this writer —
turned to other makes when the Studebaker coupes were unavailable.

Whether or not Studebaker's management foresaw the accolades that Bob
Bourke's neo-classic design would re-
ceive, surely nobody could have anticipated that with periodic modifications
— "facelifts," if you will — the coupe
would remain in production for 12 seasons, evolving eventually into the famed
Hawk GT (see *SIA #25*). It was an incredible record of longevity, especially for
those times. And it stands as a tribute to
the design genius of Bob Bourke.   □

*Top: At just 85 bhp, flathead six in
driveReport car provided decidedly unsporty
performance.* ***Above:*** *Dash uses sports-car
style instrumentation.* ***Above center:*** *Trunk
room is low and long.* ***Above right:*** *Vertical
taillamps finish off the fender shape well.*
Right: *There's not a bad line on the car
coming or going.*

1953 Studebaker Champion Starliner "Hard-top" Convertible for 5

There's plenty of room in every Studebaker! Leg room, elbow room, head room and seating space have been increased. The passenger compartment is positioned ahead of the rear axle in the cradled "comfort zone."

Automatic dome light flashes on when either of the front doors of a Land Cruiser or a sedan is opened (except Custom Champion).

Studebaker Automatic engine controls assure better gas mileage, reduced engine wear. Automatic spark provides correct timing. Automatic choke means easier starting.

Easy-to-operate pedals. New positioning of the clutch and brake pedals reduces the effort of driving.

Glare-proof "perimeter" dial illumination. Studebaker dash gauges are lighted from the edges to reduce inside glare. This serves to cut down fatigue and eyestrain and helps make night driving safer.

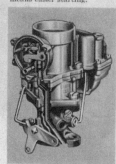

South Bend Ferrari

drive report

1956 Studebaker Golden Hawk

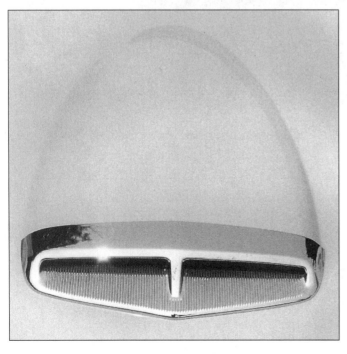

Originally published in Special Interest Autos #165, May-June 1998

Above left: Modest fins, accent area in rear cove help update original 1953 Loewy design of Stude hardtop. **Top right:** *Grille design was undoubtedly inspired by the cars from Maranello.* **Above right:** *Wheel covers are ultra-flashy.*

by John F. Katz
photos by Vince Wright

Driving Impressions

ART Hettinger bought our drive-Report Golden Hawk in 1994, from the daughter of the original owner. Her father, a dentist named Palmer, had spent his leisure hours back in the fifties playing golf with doctors and lawyers, many of whom drove Thunderbirds or Corvettes. Doc Palmer wanted something a little different, so he bought a Golden Hawk. Like his buddies, he used his special car sparingly, mostly for drives to the country club — and occasionally for a little racin' in the street. "They were always heckling him about his Studebaker," Art told us, "so it really satisfied him when he beat a Corvette."

Dr. Palmer had his Hawk inspected for the last time in 1978, then stored it in his basement garage, taking it out only occasionally for cleaning. Art found the car remarkably well preserved, with no rust but needing some cosmetic work. He replaced the tires and carpets, repaired some minor collision damage at the right rear, and repainted the body its original Mocha and Doeskin hues. The front bumper has been re-chromed, and the headlight rims replaced, but

the rest of the shiny stuff — indeed, the rest of the car — is original, with just 52,786 miles.

I have to duck low to squeeze into the Hawk, but once inside I'm sitting surprisingly high and bolt upright, in typical mid-fifties fashion. The steering wheel lays low, down in my lap, although the spokes and grips are well placed. Visibility isn't too bad all around, with the fins at the rear and high fenders up front helping to locate the corners of the car. Despite the Hawk's long wheelbase, there isn't that much car ahead of the windshield, and what little there is slopes away very neatly.

The Hawk instrument panel is so purely functional, you might wonder if the engineers locked the stylists in a closet and then gleefully ordered generic gauges out of a Stewart-Warner catalog. As plain and straightforward as the control panel on a fire pump, it's also one of the best looking dashboards of the decade. Its only functional flaw is the location of the radio, which requires a little reach.

The rear seat looks low and skimpy, but it's really no worse back there than in most mid-fifties hardtops. The lower cushion is generous, the backrest angle comfortable, and there's enough headroom to wear a cap. Admittedly, the dishpan-sized foot wells are a little weird.

The shift pattern of the two-speed

Packard Ultramatic is P-N-'D'-L-R, where the hash mark to the left of the D corresponds to High in a Packard, meaning that the transmission starts in high gear and relies on the torque converter alone for torque multiplication. The mark to the right of D corresponds to Packard's Drive, with the low gear kicking in for faster getaways.

The Packard V-8 rumbles — *no, sings* — a deep baritone song; this is how Ezio Pinza would have sounded if he were a race car. Even at low rpm, its prodigious torque rewards the smallest throttle opening with an urgent forward thrust. Get on it hard, and the rush toward Eternity will convert non-believers. Just as an experiment, Art said, he once tried flooring the gas from rest on dry pavement; the rear tires lost traction completely, spinning and smoking while generating only negligible forward progress.

The Hawk maneuvers with surprising ease, its narrow body, high seats, and good visibility suggesting a compact more than a mid-priced, full-size automobile. It glides smoothly over rough roads, with body motions well under control. The optional power steering responds accurately but offers little feedback. It does compensate for the weight of that Packard V-8; in normal driving, the Hawk feels no more nose-heavy than any big-block muscle car from a decade later.

Stude Golden Hawk

If anything, the Hawk's brakes are its weak point. The pedal is offset way over to the left, feels dead and unyielding, and delivers little in the way of results.

Nonetheless, this first child of the Studebaker-Packard marriage showed great promise, combining South Bend's flair for extroverted styling ("damnable fins" and all) with the smooth and certain power of a Packard. It handles no worse than most of its contemporaries, and better than some. The Golden Hawk was easily strong enough to take on the Big Three; it's a pity that Studebaker-Packard was not.

History and Background

The marriage was hasty, and perhaps not well considered. But for richer or poorer, for better or for worse, Studebaker and Packard took the vow on October 1, 1954. The first child of their union was the finny, flashy, Packard-powered Golden Hawk of 1956.

Former Packard president James M. Nance, now president of the Studebaker-Packard combine, championed the Golden Hawk as a conspicuous flagship and fabulous performer that would show the world what Studebaker and Packard could accomplish together. Bob Bourke, who headed Raymond Loewy's design team at Studebaker, described "Big Jim" as "a great promoter, an electric personality." A decade later *Car and Driver* (see "Who Killed Studebaker," page 70), called him a "one-man, three-ring circus."

Certainly, Nance exuded confidence — and justifiably so, if one read the right statistics. South Bend's sales had expanded from a healthy $268 million in 1947 to $594 million in 1953, with an after-tax profit of $108 million in six years. Packard, producing fewer cars for a more rarefied market, had generated $48.5 million in profit in the same period. Taken together, the two nameplates had sold 5.5 percent of all new cars in America in 1950–53. As if to display its industrial dynamism, Studebaker-Packard operated two company-owned DC-3s on a daily schedule between Detroit and South Bend.

Bold plans were laid for an all-new line of '56 Studebakers, sharing the Packard-built 320-c.i.d. Clipper V-8 and Ultramatic transmission. The new sedan

Above: *In 1956 Hawk was the most European of American cars.* **Below:** *False air-scoops provide beginning for fins.* **Facing page, top:** *Graceful roofline wasn't changed from '53 design; taillamps carried over from earlier cars.*

The Fastest of the Fast in 1956

	Studebaker Golden Hawk	Buick Century	Chevrolet Corvette	Ford Thunderbird	Dodge D500	Chrysler 300B
Base price	$3,061	$2,963	$3,295*	$3,151	$2,833**	$4,242
C.i.d.	352	322	265	312	315	354
Compression	9.5:1	9.5:1	9.25:1	9.0:1	9.25:1	10.1:1
Carburetion	1x4v	1x4v	2x4v	1x4v	1x4v	2x4v
Bhp @ rpm	275 @ 4,600	255 @ 4,400	225 @ 5,200	225 @ 4,600	260 @ 4,800	340 @ 5,200
Torque	380 @ 2,800	341 @ 3,200	270 @ 3,600	324 @ 2,600	330 @ 3,000	385 @ 3,400
Transmission	2-speed auto	2-speed auto	3-speed manual	3-speed manual	2-speed auto	2-speed auto
Axle	3.07	3.36	3.55	3.31	3.73	3.08
Wheelbase	120.5	122.0	102.0	102.0	120.0	126.0
Track, f/r	56.4/55.6	59/59	57/59	56/56	58.9/59.2	60.4/59.6
Weight, lb.	3,360	3,890	2,870	3,088	3,505	4,360
Lb./bhp	12.2	15.2	12.8	13.7	13.5	12.8
Acceleration: 0-30	3.4	3.4	3.4	3.3	3.4	N/A
0-60	9.2	9.6	7.5	9.3	9.6	N/A
50-80	8.5	11.0	N/A	N/A	na	N/A
1/4-mile	17.3 @ 80	17.1 @ 80.5	15.9 @ 91	17.0 @ 85	17.2	N/A
Max mph	117.2	109.8	118.5	112.2	115.4	N/A
Mpg	12.2	11.1	12.0	13.5	N/A	N/A
60-0 braking	171 feet	155 feet	N/A	N/A	N/A	N/A

*includes optional engine tested
** Custom Royal Lancer with D500 package

Dimensions, unless noted otherwise, are in inches; torque in foot pounds; speeds in mph; times in seconds. Test results are from the following sources: Studebaker, *Motor Trend*, February 1956; Buick, *MT*, June 1956; Corvette, *Sports Cars Illustrated*, May 1956; Dodge, *SCI*, August 1956; T-Bird, *Road & Track*, August 1956. We could find no comparable test of a '56 Chrysler 300-B but have included its specifications for comparison.

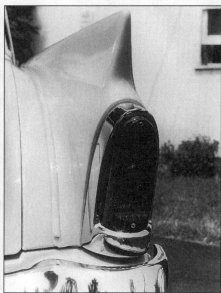

new car until early '57 (of course it wouldn't arrive then, either) and called for a rapid and economical face-lift of the current Studebaker line.

Celebrated industrial designer Loewy had run Studebaker styling as an independent consultant since 1936, dropping in three days a month to keep everything on track. His full-time crew in South Bend consisted of ten designers and about 30 clay pushers, wood carvers, and other supporting cast members, all headed by Bourke. Loewy billed South Bend around $1 million a year for the entire operation, including salaries—a not-outrageous fee by the standards of the times. Nonetheless, his contract was up in '55, and Nance decided not to renew it. Instead, the former Packard chief farmed out the '56 facelift to free-lancer Vince Gardner, who in seven weeks squared up the ends of the '53–55 sedans—and charged $7,500.

Nance still hoped to develop new two- and four-door hardtops out of the face-lifted sedan bodies, so he could phase out the separate line of Starlight and Starliner coupes that shared very little sedan tooling. And even with the older, smaller body shell, the Packard V-8 might still go into top-of-the-line President models. Alone among the independents, Packard had developed its own overhead-valve V-8 *and* automatic transmission, and Nance wanted to amortize some of that considerable investment by supplying engines and transmissions to Studebaker. Once again, however, the figures wouldn't mesh: Studebakers could be produced

would have been stunning: longer and wider than its predecessors, with a Buick/Olds-inspired greenhouse, very clean flanks, and an upright, trapezoidal grille. In December 1954, Loewy himself presented the full-size clay to Studebaker's somewhat skeptical management, who worried about the car's slightly tapering fenders.

But it didn't matter what they thought, because the real numbers wouldn't add up. Of that $108 million profit from 1947–53, almost half—$47 million—had been earned in 1948–49. By June '54, South Bend was *losing* $2.5 million per month. Packard had lost $1 million in the first quarter of the year, and the combined market share of Studebaker and Packard had fallen to 2.5 percent. Studebaker couldn't afford tooling for an all-new body. In late January 1955, Nance postponed the

Ultramatic

GM was the first automaker to introduce a modern, fully automatic transmission. Second was Packard, which launched its Ultramatic in mid-1949. None of the other independents ever built an automatic of their own. Even Ford wouldn't have its own automatic until '51, and Chrysler would debut its PowerFlite in mid-'53.

Even more remarkably, the Packard Ultramatic—at least in theory—combined the best characteristics of the HydraMatic and the Dynaflow in a way that GM wouldn't even approach until the sixties.

Packard chief research engineer Forest M. McFarland had been experimenting with torque converters for as long as anyone at GM. Wartime projects diverted his attention for awhile, but then McFarland—assisted by development project engineer Warren Bopp and staff engineer Herbert Misch—returned to his automatic transmission research in 1944.

McFarland was convinced that he could improve on GM's corporate HydraMatic and its "godawful number of shifts." With a simple fluid coupling that provided no torque multiplication, HydraMatic delivered relatively good engine braking and lit-

tle "slip" but depended on a four-speed gearset for acceleration. Buick's Dynaflow torque converter, McFarland believed, was closer to the mark, but it allowed so much slip it felt as though it "was in second gear all the time."

McFarland's solution was a twin-turbine torque converter with an even higher maximum ratio than Buick's. As in the Dynaflow, a planetary gearset provided reverse and an emergency low. Ultramatic drivers could select High range and rely exclusively on the converter for smooth, unhurried starts (like a Dynaflow), or select Drive to accelerate in low gear and then automatically shift up to high (like Chevrolet's Powerglide). Naturally, Packard also provided a Low position to lock the transmission in low gear.

But what made Ultramatic unique was an internal, 11-inch, oil-bathed cork clutch that locked the torque converter solid at cruising speed. This combination of features gave Ultramatic the smoothness of a Dynaflow, with superior torque multiplication, plus—once the clutch engaged—the engine braking and fuel efficiency of a manual gearbox.

GM used locking converters on its buses, and in 1956 Borg-Warner added a lock-up clutch to the automatic transmission it supplied to Studebaker and Jaguar (a hybrid unit that depended on both a torque converter and a three-speed gearset for torque multiplication). But it wasn't until Chrysler re-invented the idea in 1978 that any of the Big Three offered a locking converter on a passenger car.

For Packard, the Ultramatic would prove more of an engineering achievement than a business success. The company poured $15 million into Ultramatic, and by 1954 still hadn't sold enough cars to recoup its investment. It was hoped that the merger with Studebaker would create a whole new market for Ultramatic. But the two-speed transmission proved a poor match for the underpowered, six-cylinder Champion, and was judged only "moderately satisfactory" with the Studebaker V-8s. Ultimately, it couldn't compete cost-wise with off-the-shelf units available from Borg-Warner or Detroit Gear, and so it expired with the last of the traditional Packards at the end of 1956.

illustrations by Russell von Sauers, The Graphic Automobile Stud

specifications

56.4 inches

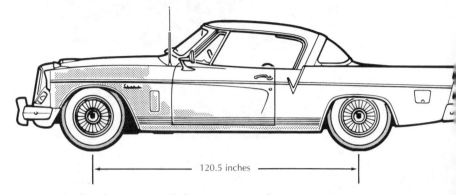

120.5 inches

1956 Studebaker Golden Hawk

Price	$3,061
Std. equip. includes	Sky Power 352 V-8, finned iron brake drums, overdrive (with manual transmission), complete instrumentation with vacuum gauge and tachometer, full wheel covers
Options on dR car	Twin-Ultramatic transmission, power steering, power front windows, radio, heater, dual outside mirrors, tinted glass, whitewall tires, deluxe wheel covers
Est. price as tested	$3,565

ENGINE

Type	V-8
Bore x stroke	4 inches x 3.5 inches
Displacement	352 cubic inches
Compression ratio	9.5:1
Horsepower @ rpm	275 @ 4,600 (gross)
Torque @ rpm	380 @ 2,800 (gross)
Taxable horsepower	51.2
Net bhp at rear wheels	104 @ 3,000 rpm (80 mph)
Valve gear	Ohv
Valve lifters	Hydraulic
Main bearings	5
Induction system	1 Carter 4-bbl downdraft
Fuel system	Mechanical pump
Lubrication system	Pressure, gear pump
Cooling system	Pressure, centrifugal pump
Exhaust system	Dual
Electrical system	12-volt

TRANSMISSION

Type	Two-speed automatic with locking torque converter
Ratios: Low	1.82:1
High	1.00:1
Reverse	1.63:1
Max. torque converter	2.90:1 @ 1,650 rpm

DIFFERENTIAL

Type	Hypoid, semi-floating
Ratio	3.07:1

STEERING

Type	Saginaw recirculating ball with hydraulic servo
Turns lock-to-lock	4.25
Ratios	18.2:1 gear; 20.0:1 overall
Turning circle	41 feet, curb-to-curb

BRAKES

Type	Wagner 4-wheel hydraulic with vacuum servo
Front	11.0 x 2.5-inch drum
Rear	10.0 x 2.0-inch drum
Effective area	195.3 square inches
Parking brake	Mechanical, on rear drums

CHASSIS & BODY

Construction	Separate box-section ladder frame with 5 crossmembers
Body	Welded steel stampings cross members
Body style	5-seat pillarless coupe

SUSPENSION

Front	Independent, upper and lower A-arms, coil springs
Rear	Live axle, semi-elliptic leaf springs

Shock absorbers	Tubular, direct acting, front an rear
Tires	Firestone Deluxe Champion 7.10 x 15
Wheels	15-inch stamped steel disc

WEIGHTS AND MEASURES

Wheelbase	120.5 inches
Overall length	203.9 inches
Overall width	70.4 inches
Overall height	58.1 inches
Front track	56.4 inches
Rear track	55.6 inches
Min. road clearance	6.5 inches
Shipping weight	3,360 pounds

CAPACITIES

Crankcase	5 quarts
Transmission	11 pints
Rear axle	3.0 pints
Cooling system	26.5 quarts (with heater)
Fuel tank	18 gallons

CALCULATED DATA

Bhp per c.i.d.	0.781
Stroke/bore	0.875
Lb./bhp	12.2 pounds
Lb./sq. in. brake area	17.2
Production	4,071, Golden Hawk; 19,165 total 1956 Hawk

*Right: Vacuum gauge and tach is in keeping with sporty image. **Facing page, top:** Big 352 Packard V-8 was good for 275 bhp. **Center left:** Driving position is firm and upright. **Right:** Dash design is very pleasing to enthusiasts. **Bottom:** Doors open wide for good access to front and rear.*

Stude Golden Hawk

more economically with Studebaker V-8s, and with automatic transmissions from Borg-Warner or Detroit Gear.

Likewise, the new sedan-based hardtops would cost tooling dollars that the corporation didn't have. If Studebaker was to field a pillarless style-leader in '56, it would have to base it on the existing '53–55 coupe.

That lovely "Loewy Coupe" had been Studebaker's glory and, to some extent, its undoing. Bourke's group had developed it as a show car for Studebaker's centennial in '52, but management made an eleventh-hour decision to launch it as a limited-production model for 1953. Unfortunately, they also ordered Loewy to wring a bread-and-butter sedan out of the same styling theme. Not surprisingly, the long, slender, elegantly aerodynamic coupe translated into a high, narrow sedan with oddly sloped front and rear ends. Sales plunged when South Bend literally couldn't build the coupes fast enough—and couldn't give the sedans away.

Changes to both sedans and coupes had been minimal for '54 and then moderate for '55, when Sales chief Ken Elliott dictated a new and clumsily chromed front end—over the objections of both Bourke and Loewy. That January brought Studebaker's first wraparound windshield to sedans (and wagons) only. But it also brought a limited-edition flagship coupe called the President Speedster—trimmed inside like a custom hot-rod, with deep, diamond-shaped pleats in its leather upholstery and businesslike Stewart-Warner gauges set in an engine-turned panel. *Motor Life* found the Speedster "more like a sports car than any other hardtop." It set the tone for the Hawks to follow.

Now Nance asked Loewy's departing

designers to facelift the coupe on their way out the door, while sticking to a strict tooling budget that specified so many dollars per panel. Bourke nonetheless welcomed the chance to reverse some of the damage done in '55. A completely new front end, he decided, would give the biggest bang for the tooling buck, so he lifted the Mercedes-inspired snout virtually intact from the big sedan that was never to be. Then he squared up the coupe's sloping rear deck, while saving 80 percent of the inner deck stampings—which meant there was no real increase in trunk room. Still kibitzing, Elliott insisted on plenty of chrome doodads, but at least he let Bourke design them this time. Perhaps the result wasn't as pure as the

'53–54 coupe, but it looked enormously better than the '55, and was really quite handsome in its own right. And the Speedster-inspired dashboard was a revelation: a wall-to-wall spread of engine-turned metal housing handsome Stewart-Warner gauges.

Previously, Studebaker had called its pillared coupes Starlights, and pillarless models Starliners, and offered them in a range of price and trim that approximately covered the spread from a Chevrolet Two-Ten to an Olds 88. Nance heartily endorsed this strategy, which applied to Studebaker sedans as well. For '56, all the coupes became Hawks—although the origin of the name has not been recorded. At $1,986, the base-model, pillared-top Flight Hawk shared its 185-c.i.d., 101-bhp flathead six, as well as its level of trim, with the $1,946 Champion sedan. Next up came the $2,101 Power Hawk, still a pillared coupe but packing the 259-c.i.d., ohv V-8 from the equivalently trimmed Commander. This engine developed 170 bhp with a two-barrel carb, or 185 with a four-barrel and dual exhausts. Hardtop Sky Hawks, at $2,477, corresponded to President sedans, with a 210-bhp 289. Overdrive or a Borg-Warner automatic were optional on all three.

But the fanciest chick in the nest was the Golden Hawk, priced $100 over a Buick Century, and identifiable on the outside by an extra helping of chrome and what Bourke called "damnable plastic fins" grafted onto the same '53–55 quarter panel. (Years later, the

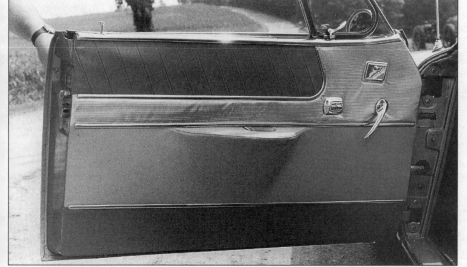

Stude Golden Hawk

designer wrote in *Automobile Quarterly* that he "kept those little fins at the rear of the Golden Hawk as restrained as I could and still please Sales.") Inside, Golden Hawks came with a tachometer (optional in lesser Hawks), a manifold-vacuum gauge, and rich cloth-and-vinyl upholstery.

But the Golden Hawk's most distinguishing feature was the Packard V-8 under the hood: not the Clipper 320, but the four-barrel 352 from the Clipper Custom, developing 275 bhp and bolted to a three-speed manual transmission with overdrive or to Packard's sophisticated Ultramatic (see sidebar, page 77). Oddly, the package did not include Packard's pioneering limited-slip differential. Still, the '56 Golden Hawk was the only model—ever—to combine a Studebaker badge and Packard power.

Sporty as they looked, the old coupes hadn't been known for their handling. The engineers, under Gene Hardig, addressed this problem with softer springs but firmer shocks for the Hawk. Golden Hawks and Sky Hawks featured finned-drum brakes, although the drum sizes—11 inches in front, 10 in the back—were the same as in any V-8 Stude sedan. For the Golden Hawk,

Studebaker advertising claimed not only the best power-to-weight ratio but also the best ratio of brake area to weight of any American car. "Engineered to out-handle and out-run sports cars costing thousands more," the Golden Hawk offered "sports performance [with] room for 5 and a full-size trunk!"

Far from out-handling sports cars, however, the Golden Hawk developed a reputation for nose-heavy understeer. Most contemporary road tests only hinted at the problem. The *Motor Trend* staff reveled in the stability and precise steering of their manually steered Golden Hawk, reporting severe understeer only in tight, low-speed turns. They found the Golden Hawk's brakes "adequate for a sports-*type* car" (their emphasis) and praised them for not fading away completely in hard use.

Auto Age called the Golden Hawk "one of the fastest and best-looking cars ever made on these shores...a car of prey... going out after the Thunderbird, Corvette, Chrysler '300' market with a vengeance"—and then gingerly danced around its chassis shortcomings: "The steering felt perhaps a trifle slow for so fast a car, but dead accurate and free from play, and there was a slight but pleasant degree of understeer.... If you have been wondering, by the way, what

Who Killed Studebaker?

The March 1964 edition of *Car and Driver* has achieved a certain notoriety for its controversial comparison of GTOs from both Pontiac and Ferrari. But the same issue might as well be remembered for an equally audacious article titled "Who Killed Studebaker?" The venerable old South Bend automaker had fled to Canada just months before, leaving some 6,000 Indianians unemployed.

C/D's answer to its own question is angry and unflattering, characterizing Studebaker as "a company doomed for years, finally dying by its own hand." The editors pointed to "dead-last engineering," soft labor policies, and stubborn, insular management as proof that "Studebaker deserved to fail."

Automobile Quarterly waited until 1972 to publish a somewhat more sympathetic postmortem. Veteran historian Maurice Hendry attacked the *C/D* article as the product of a "Europhile press... psychologically incapable of recognizing good sound engineering—if it happens to have 'made in the USA' on it." Hardly dead last, Hendry argued, Studebaker had "a modern short-stroke ohv V-8, independent front suspension, automatic overdrive and power steering either before, at the same time as, or shortly after any of the Big Three."

Special Interest Autos seems to have drawn from both of these sources when it presented its own, more even-handed analysis of "How Studebaker Came Not To Be" in 1974.

Two dozen years later, we still see some merit to both arguments.

As *C/D* alleged, the Studebaker V-8 was undeniably heavy for its displacement. Various sources cite weights of 625–682 pounds for an engine that couldn't grow beyond 289 cubic inches; Cadillac's 331-c.i.d. V-8 weighed only 699 pounds. On the other hand, as an independent with just a fraction of GM's resources, Studebaker deserves credit for developing a modern V-8 at all—only two years after Cadillac and Olds, at the same time as Chrysler, and a year ahead of Ford.

Studebakers had vacuum-assisted brakes and variable-ratio steering in the 1930s. Certainly, as *C/D* noted, Studebakers suffered from brake fade and slow steering. So did Buicks.

Yes, Studebaker's labor costs in the forties were the highest in the industry. According to Hendry, however, tough cuts in the period from 1954–59 brought them in line with the Big Three's. Maybe by then it was too late.

Hendry blamed Studebaker's demise on the same 1953–56 Ford vs. Chevy sales blitz that finished the other independents. But then even he admitted that Stude's dog-ugly '53 sedan had left South Bend's corporate pants around its ankles. *C/D* speculated that "had the sedans been offered in the 54-inch-high, 120-inch-wheelbase version that Loewy had in mind, Studebaker might still be building cars." Well, maybe. Obviously, a sedan that

shared external sheet metal with the coupe would have looked worlds better, and might have spared some of South Bend's dwindling resources. But it's hard to imagine how it could have offered adequate rear-seat room for the four-door family trade. On the other hand, GM had no trouble peddling stylish four-door hardtops with somewhat restricted rear compartments two years later.

The *C/D* article was particularly hard on Nance. True, he spent $74 million of Packard's money and had nothing to show for it but the Hawk and a sedan that was still narrow and unattractive. But this is the same James Nance who went on to manage Mercury, where he inspired class and subtlety in a division that was definitely headed the wrong way down Buck Rogers Boulevard.

Once Curtiss-Wright took over, it didn't matter anyway. Even *C/D* related how, by mid-'58, the Wall Street bankers were already casting lots for Studebaker's remains, anxiously coveting South Bend's $140 million in accumulated credits. When Harold Churchill, Nance's successor, actually made $28.5 million selling Larks, they maneuvered him out of the company.

Ultimately, Studebaker's fate was decided far from Indiana. Maybe an all-new car in '60, or '56, or even '53 wouldn't have made any difference anyway. But the people who put their hearts and sweat into designing and engineering and managing and assembling Studebakers deserved a better chance.

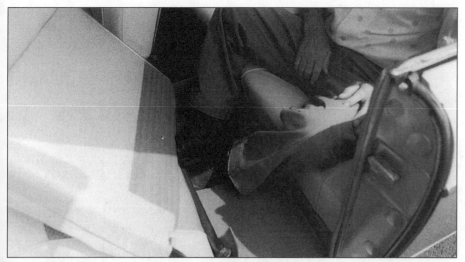

Facing page: Rear seats have gran turismo appearance thanks to center armrest. **Above:** *Deep footwells in rear for more leg room.* **Below:** *For a sporty car it has good trunk room.*

the heavier Packard engine has done to the balance of the Studebaker, let us say that the car does seem noticeably heavier at the front than last year's Speedster, but this works out seemingly to its advantage." Sure.

On assignment for *Speed Age*, Racer Bill Holland took a Golden Hawk around Packard's own 2.5-mile oval in Detroit on a rain-soaked day and still averaged 121.0 mph. He found the Golden Hawk's power steering "light in operation and not geared too fast for average reflexes," and its chassis "balanced properly so that it can still be controlled with the steering wheel while it is sliding."

Only *Car Life* openly criticized the Golden Hawk's handling: "Primarily the Hawk's trouble is weight distribution. The car is heavy on the front end, which results in a tendency for the rear wheels to slide on dry pavement.... The powerful, well-built engine on the Golden Hawk provides more power than the chassis design can properly handle. A full-throttle start in reduced 'D' range spins the rear wheels on dry pavement

and keeps the tires screaming on the concrete up to 25 mph.... These troubles could be remedied to some extent by filling the trunk with sand bags [but] perhaps the best solution is to buy the lower-priced Sky Hawk with its lighter-weight Studebaker V-8."

That said, *Car Life* still allowed that the Golden Hawk's overall roadability was "excellent when compared with other five- and six-passenger cars, but falls behind the two other semi-sports cars, Corvette and Thunderbird." And they thought the new front end, though "simple" and "pleasing," suggested a "South Bend Ferrari."

Studebaker sold just 82,000 cars in '56, but nearly one-quarter of them were Hawks. South Bend was on to something.

The big Packards were gone for '57, and with them their V-8 engine and Ultramatic transmission. The Hawk lineup was rationalized to just two models: the pillared Silver Hawk with six-cylinder or 259-c.i.d. V-8 power; and the hardtop Golden Hawk, now motivated by Studebaker's 289, but producing the

same 275 horses (at 4,800 rpm) thanks to a McCulloch centrifugal supercharger. Though the Stude V-8 weighed only 50–100 pounds less than the Packard mill, Hardig considered this a happier solution.

A column-shifter with overdrive was still standard, but the automatic option was now the three-speed, Borg-Warner-supplied "Flightomatic." The engineers even updated the Hawk chassis with variable-ratio steering and, finally, an optional "Twin Traction" limited-slip differential. Both Hawks now wore outward-curving fins, metal this time but still tacked on to those 1953-vintage fenders. *Sports Cars Illustrated* found the Golden Hawk's handling dramatically improved, while acceleration to 60 (despite a 14 percent reduction in peak torque) was quicker by a whisker.

The so-called "Packard Hawk" that joined the line in '58 was also powered by a supercharged Studebaker V-8.

Nance, meanwhile, had tried to borrow tooling dollars from the major New York insurance companies that held Studebaker stock. No deal. He proposed assembling cars for Ford or Chrysler, and even tried to convince GM to endorse a loan. Desperate for cash, Studebaker agreed to turn over its management to Curtiss-Wright in late '56. In return, the aerospace contractor bought up Studebaker's defense business and pre-paid a lease on two Studebaker plants. C-W president Roy Hurley planned to maintain South Bend at its break-even point for two years, write its losses off of C-W's taxes, then collect $40 million on a stock-option deal. Nance resigned before the ink was dry. So did Studebaker chairman Paul Hoffman. Studebaker's fate was sealed. ☙

Bibliography and Acknowledgments

Books: R.M. Clarke (editor), Studebaker Hawks & Larks 1956-1963 *(Brooklands Road Test Book); John A. Gunnell (editor),* Standard Catalog of American Cars 1946-1975; *Beverly Rae Kimes (editor),* Packard, a History of the Motorcar and the Company; *Richard M. Langworth,* Studebaker: The Postwar Years.

Periodicals: Robert E. Bourke, "The Starlight and the Starliner," Automobile Quarterly, *Vol 10, No 3; Maurice D. Hendry, "One Can Do a Lot of Remembering in South Bend," AQ, 10/3; Jim Lodge, "'56 Studebaker Golden Hawk Road Test,"* Motor Trend, *February 1956; Michael Richards, "The Life and Times of the Studebaker Hawk," AQ, 12/3; Rich Taylor, various articles in SIA #25; "Who Killed Studebaker?",* Car and Driver, *March 1964.*

Thanks to Kim M. Miller and Kathy Armstrong of the AACA Library and Research Center, Henry Siegle, and of course special thanks to Art Hettinger.

Comparison DriveReport of the
1956 Studebaker Sky Hawk
1958 Packard Hawk
1962 Gran Turismo Hawk

Originally published in Special Interest Autos #25, Nov.-Dec. 1974

Variations on a Soaring Theme

By Rich Taylor

Photography by Taylor-Constantine

The 1953 Studebaker Starliner has always seemed to me like the only American car that really, honestly, showed what Pininfarina and the "Italian style" were all about. And the Studebaker Hawk, while not as pretty, perhaps, was still awfully good. And it was a better car. It would go, and stop, and even—saints be praised—*handle*. Amazing. In my mind, the Studebaker Hawk was the first American GT car . . . lithe, stylish and powerful. It was a revelation in 1956.

Hawk development, once they got the basic concept down right, was primarily a matter of refinement. The last GT Hawks are superb cars . . . as well they should be after ten years of continuous development. But when we compared the Hawks side by side for this DriveReport, I was surprised to see how little difference there is between the first '56 and the last '64. The quantum leap forward obviously took place between the '53/'54 Starliner and the '56 Sky Hawk.

That's right, the Sky Hawk. Everybody remembers the Golden Hawk, but those Packard-engined beasties weren't really very good cars. They were a little heavy in the engine compartment, and a little short everywhere else. But the Sky Hawk is a solid, enjoyable machine, very much like the later Gran Turismo Hawks. It also has the cleanest styling of any from the Hawk line, closest to the '53 Starliner in concept and execution. So when we picked an early Hawk model for our tests, we decided we wanted a '56 Sky Hawk.

On the other hand, if you were going to pick a Hawk from the middle years, what could be better than The Last Of The Packards? The '58 Packard Hawk is basically the Sky Hawk . . . with Mylar fins, fiberglass grin and an outlandish McCulloch supercharger that turns it into a Land Speed Record car. Nowadays, the Packard is just about the rarest Hawk of all, probably because so few were built, and fewer still were treated with any sort of respect in their declining years. We decided the Packard Hawk was a perfect foil for the early and late Studebaker models we planned to assemble. All wrapped up in one admittedly eccentric car, we had part of the Studebaker Hawk's evolution as well as a sterile Packard mutant with no ancestors and no progeny.

Finally, of course, we had to examine the definitive Hawk. The general consensus was that Brooks Stevens' revamped Gran Turismo had it all over the others when it came to sophistication, performance and, well . . . elan. Visually understated and mechanically perfected, the GT Hawk is a mature car, created by mature men, for a mature enthusiast.

It doesn't have the naive beauty of the Sky Hawk nor the energetic exuberance of the Packard Hawk. It's just a timeless, styleless presence in consummate good taste.

Of course, at this point we'd given no thought to how we'd find three perfect Studebaker Hawks, assemble them all in one place, at one time . . . and convince their owners to let us thrash them around. It seemed like a gargantuan task . . . that was accomplished with one phone call. The east coast guru of the Studebaker Drivers Club, Herb Keller of Woodhaven, Queens, took care of the whole thing. All we were required to do was show up at the appointed place at the appointed hour, and be met by three cheery members of the SDC with three perfect Studebakers.

In the Sky Hawk was John Albert of Richmond Hill, who was subbing for his brother Joe, the owner of the car. Driving the Packard Hawk (one of fifteen Studebakers he owns) was Ernie Spicer of Ramsey, New Jersey. In the passenger seat was his super wife, Louise, who ended up serving as DriveReport coordinator, caterer and SIA den mother for the day. Their beautiful maroon and gold Packard Hawk, incidentally, is a former National First Prize winner. It's easily one of the cleanest Studebakers I've ever seen.

The cleanest belongs to John Mayer, the president of the Long Island chapter of the SDC. John drove his immaculate GT Hawk from Mamaroneck. It's also a National First Prize car, but it competes in the altered class, solely because of the little grilles John has installed in the two flanking Hawk nostrils. He bought two extra GT grilles when he got the car—brand new, by the way, in 1962—flattened them out, cut them up and installed the matching side grilles. If you notice in Brooks Stevens' design proposal for the GT on page 23, that's what he originally intended. But they were deleted by Studebaker president Sherwood Egbert to cut production costs. In any case, we decided John's car looks better that way, and more like the original Stevens design.

And just like that, thanks to Herb Keller and his friends from the Studebaker Drivers Club, we had our DriveReport . . . tested, tuned-up and ready to roll.

1956 SKY HAWK

Bob Bourke discusses the styling of the Sky Hawk on page 20, so I won't go into it any further here. Suffice to say, it seems taut, tight . . . and remarkably modern. It's also bigger than it looks. The Land Cruiser frame upon which all the Hawks perch has a wheelbase almost identical with that on a new full-size Chevy Impala. But in length, the Hawk is closer to the intermediate Chevelle. Which means it has surprisingly little overhang. Which in turn, contributes mightily to that delicate look. And though the roof seems low, it's actually 9 inches higher off the road than a Camaro. So although it looks and feels almost like a sporty car, the Sky Hawk is actually quite large. The only dimension that seems excessive is the width of the front seat, and it's really about the same as that on a compact Nova. The Sky Hawk does seat three across the front in comfort, though, and the transmission tunnel, particularly with Flightomatic, is unobtrusive. Stylish as it is, it's still as useful as a more mundane sedan, too.

As in all true sporty cars, the back seats are nearly impossible for anyone who comes equipped with a normal complement of legs and head. The roof dips way down in back, and though there is a footwell on each side of the driveshaft that drops below the level of the frame rails, they're only about a foot square. It's like sitting with your feet in a dishpan. Only

Continued on page 86

Joe Albert's Sky Hawk has accessory backing lights, otherwise it's stock. Black and white was a popular combination.

The Sky Hawk engine gives good performance and gas mileage from a mild state of tune. The missing air cleaner helps.

Sky Hawk interior shows two-tone trim and engine-turned dash. Dangerous and pesky seat belts fasten to the edge of the door.

Fluted decklid characterizes all Studebaker Hawks, but the chrome script and trim changed from model to model.

Ernie Spicer's Packard, maroon with gold Mylar fins, is a consistent concours winner. It's stock except for mud flaps.

John Mayer (president of the Long Island SDC) has given his white GT grilles at the front like Stevens' original sketch.

A McCulloch blower dominates the underhood view. Note the rubber belt drive and tension spring for the centrifugal clutch.

The GT engine has only a 2-barrel Carter, still, it provides plenty of snap even with an automatic. A 4-speed was a popular option.

Packard Hawk has a genuine leather interior, matching vinyl trim outside glass, padded dash and complete instrumentation.

Brooks Stevens gave the GT a "cockpit" with black on white gauges, bucket seats and a console over the driveshaft tunnel.

McRae's fiberglass grin adds no weight and little length to the Hawk; uses the same underlying structure that's on all.

The GT has luxurious reclining bucket seats in front and brushed aluminum door panels that match the dash.

HOW HAWKS CAME TO BE

If you think about it, you'll realize that the basic 1953/1954 Starliner shell . . . which Studebaker was forced to use on the Hawks . . . is a better body than anything that came out of Detroit in the Fifties. No matter what they did to it, then—and Studebaker design attempted some pretty awful things—the Starliner's innate class continued to shine through. If they could have afforded to design an all-new car, it's a pretty safe bet it would have been outrageously chromed and befinned . . . an instantly-forgotten copy of contemporary Chevys and Fords. Instead, the wonderfully sophisticated, perfectly subtle Starliner became the almost-as-pretty Hawk. From one point of view, then, it's a blessing Studebaker was broke.

When the 1956 Studebaker line was being planned, styling was handled by a group of roughly ten designers who worked for Raymond Loewy in South Bend. Loewy himself was under contract as a consultant . . . which meant he dropped by for three days a month to oversee his designers-in-residence, headed by Bob Bourke. It was Bourke who designed the '53/'54 Starliner . . . and the first Hawks as well.

When "Big Jim" Nance of Packard took over in October of 1954, he was already planning to get rid of Loewy. Loewy was Harold Vance's favorite, and he'd first come to Studebaker as a consultant in 1936, soon after Vance rose to power. By 1954, however, Loewy was an expensive luxury option that Studebaker could ill afford. In mid-1955, Loewy was asked to leave, and the Bourke styling group was disbanded as well. The 1956 Hawks were the last Studebaker models designed by Bourke. Nance's new designers, Bill Schmidt and Duncan McRae, started with the '57s. As you can tell from a glance at the Packard Hawk, McRae's ideas were slightly more, ah . . . flamboyant than Bourke's.

So were Ken Elliot's. Elliot was the vice-president in charge of Sales. In '55 and '56, he took over a fair portion of the design direction. The '53/'54 Starliner was an aesthetic triumph, but a financial disaster. And everyone knew it. So Sales helped style the chrome-plated '55s . . . an aesthetic and financial disaster. Still, Elliot kept at it. Bob Andrews, who was already working with Bourke in '55 says, "Sales really mapped out the Hawk line." Bourke was told to keep a full-length chrome spear along the lower body similar to that on the '55s, so that they could have spectacular two-tone paint schemes—like the famous lip-puckering lemon and lime, not to mention what Bourke calls "a particularly excruciating deep salmon

color." He was also told to provide plenty of other chrome, and that if he wanted to change the totally-chromed '55 snout, he'd have to replace it, in Andrews' phrase, "with something equally stunning."

In order to stay within his tiny budget, Bourke made only a few changes. He revamped the hood and the decklid, he put the parking lights up on the fenders, he devised the lightning strike chrome trim for the sides and changed the taillights. He also removed a chrome beltline molding that he'd originally had under the greenhouse on the Starliner, though it came back to stay in 1957, after he'd left. Finally, Bourke was forced to add "those damnable plastic fins"—kept as small as possible—to the top-of-the-line Golden Hawk. The interior—complete with simulated engine-turned aluminum on the dash—was lifted from the expensive and sporty President Speedster. Introduced in January of 1955, the Speedster was the forerunner of the Hawks in both conception and performance . . . though not in good looks.

The Golden Hawk was just too much of everything. The fins are bad enough. But the fake air vents where they meet the lightning strike are worse. Then there's that extra chrome wrap above the rear window, the chrome wheelwell moldings and the fluted rib along the rocker panels. But the worst extravagance of the '56 Golden Hawk lived in the engine compartment. The "horsepower race" required at least one model to compete with the high-performance Chrysler 300B and its ilk. Though the Studebaker staff offered token resistance, Nance had the 352 cubic inch, 275 horsepower Packard V-8 shoehorned into what Bourke calls the "rubber frame." The result was less than spectacular.

At the other end of the spectrum, there were two five-window coupes. Nance's desire to make Studebaker-Packard a full-line manufacturer meant they had to cover every market niche, however inadequately. The Flight Hawk was the bottom line. Powered, or rather underpowered, by an anemic 186 cubic inch, 101 horsepower version of Studebaker's antique L-head Six, it was hardly an enthusiast's car. The Power Hawk got a 259 cubic inch version of the fine—though conventional—overhead valve V-8 Studebaker introduced in 1951.

But there's another, often overlooked, model from 1956. The Sky Hawk avoided the fins, the extra chrome and the unnecessary bulk of the Packard boat anchor that ruined the Golden Hawk. With a 289 cubic inch, 210 horsepower Studebaker V-8, though, it was also twice the car of the underpowered coupes. The Sky Hawk is the best of the four, by far. And the 289 V-8 in a hardtop body was the definitive Hawk configuration from 1957 through 1964, the cost-cutting '59-'61 five-window coupes notwithstanding.

By the time Gene Hardig and Ed Reynolds got to work on engineering the '57 Hawks, Curtis-Wright had a controlling interest in Studebaker, Harold Churchill had replaced Jim Nance, and Duncan McRae was doing the styling. The Packard engine was scrapped, and replaced in the Golden Hawk by a "Jet-Stream" McCulloch-supercharged 289 Studebaker. The rated power output was the same, but with an optional 3-speed plus overdrive, Twin-Traction Spicer differential, variable ratio steering and weight distribution that approached a manageable 55/45, the new car was light years ahead.

Styling suffered in the transition. The chrome beltline trim returned, chrome teeth were added to the little side grilles, a huge scoop—complete with louvers but no air intake—was clapped onto the hood, and of course, there were bigger fins. McRae added fiberglass falsies over Bourke's rear fenders, using a chrome bead to hide the joint. It was a cheap and effective way to facelift a five-year-old design.

For 1958, only a few minor trim changes were made to the Golden Hawk. The Silver Hawk coupe that had replaced the separate Flight, Power and Sky Hawks in 1957 was continued as well, still fitted with either the L-head Six, the 259 or the 289. Total Hawk sales dropped over 50 percent in '58, a reaction to what was easily the most bizarre year for styling.

The most incredible was the limited-production Packard Hawk. The Last Of The Packards was a Studebaker Hawk . . . with some less than subtle additions. McRae replaced the squared-off Hawk decklid that Bourke had added with the original rounded trunk from the '53 Starliner . . . which Bourke had designed. On top of this, McRae glued a fiberglass fake spare tire cover. The fins were the same fiberglass caps that he had provided for 1957, now covered in waffle-pattern gold Mylar also used on Plymouth's Sport Fury.

At the front, McRae molded up a drooping fiberglass mouth influenced vaguely by the Maserati Allemano, with "Dagmar Bumpers" borrowed from the Cadillac of the previous season. A tall hood scoop helped to give the Packard Hawk even less grace. Real leather bucket seats added true style to the interior, however. This leather interior was first tried out in late '57 on the Hawk 400, a limited edition of 250 cars. It was the nicest interior package on any of the Hawks.

Churchill planned to push the Lark exclusively in 1959, and tried to torpedo the aging Hawk. Sales felt that the Hawk was needed as an exciting line leader for the utilitarian Larks, so an emasculated version of the Silver Hawk—complete with 259 economy V-8—became the top-of-the-line. The supercharged Golden Hawk, with its more expensive Starliner hardtop, disappeared forever. What took its place wasn't nearly as much automobile, though the price was considerably cheaper. In 1960, the 289 V-8 returned in the same car.

The next year, though, they built the most roadable Hawk of all. A 4-speed Borg-Warner transmission and 225 horsepower 289 V-8 went into the five-window coupe, and although the fins remained, McRae had stripped off the Mylar applique, the exotic paint and the extra chrome to expose the car's inherent good looks. The "one model" policy was so rigid that the new overhead valve Six never found its way into the Hawk, except in foreign markets. The dispirited old Hawk sold less than 4000 units in 1961, although it was really a damn nice car by then. It was clearly time for a change.

Sherwood Egbert was the major change; Brooks Stevens the minor chord. Stevens' masterful restyle of a ten-year-old body

into the stylish Gran Turismo Hawk on a miniscule budget is an industry legend. Borrowing elements from contemporary Lincolns, Thunderbirds and previous Hawks, he managed to give the effect of a complete restyle without changing any body panels except the top. The car took on a whole new feeling, despite the drawbacks of its aging chassis. Over the three years of GT Hawk production, it even learned to gracefully handle the 290 brutal horsepower of the supercharged R2 289 V-8 developed for the Avanti. It was a miracle of sorts that the '53 Starliner . . . a 120 horsepower, 95 mph car . . . could be transformed without apparent discomfort into a 290 horsepower, 140 mph Grand Tourer. As Stevens points out, though, "to Gene Hardig, nothing is impossible."

Keeping Studebaker-Worthington in the automobile business proved to a task beyond even his powers. Beyond anyone's powers. On miniscule budgets, with dwindling resources, the designers and engineers of Studebaker managed to make a stylish line-leader out of the same car for over a decade. In America, particularly in the "dynamic obsolesence" years of the Fifties, that was a miracle in itself. While five different presidents and numerous stockholders tried to untangle the web of Studebaker's incredible finances, the South Bend employees tried to make the best cars they could under the prevailing conditions. That the Hawk was as successful then . . . and as revered now . . . is due to them. They made some mistakes, sure. Some real lulus, to be honest. But the Hawks aren't among them.—*Moreford Pidgeon*

How Many Hawks Came To Be
Studebaker Hawk Production, 1956-1964

Year/Model	Engine Displacement (cubic inches)/ Horsepower (SAE gross)	Price (fob South Bend)	Total Production (worldwide)
1956			
Golden Hawk	352 V-8/275	$3061	4071
Sky Hawk	289 V-8/190-210	2477	3610
Power Hawk	259 V-8/170-185	2101 }	
Flight Hawk	186 In-6/101	1986 }	11484
1957			
Golden Hawk	289 V-8/275	$3182	4356
Silver Hawk 8	289 V-8/210-225	2263 }	
Silver Hawk 6	186 In-6/101	2142 }	14950
1958			
Packard Hawk	289 V-8/275	$3995	588
Golden Hawk	289 V-8/275	3282	878
Silver Hawk 8	289 V-8/210-225	2352 }	
Silver Hawk 6	186 In-6/101	2219 }	7294
1959			
Silver Hawk 8	259 V-8/180-195	$2495 }	
Silver Hawk 6	170 In-6/90	2360 }	7888
1960			
Hawk	289 V-8/210-225	$2650	4507
1961			
Hawk	289 V-8/210-225	$2650	3929
1962			
GT Hawk	289 V-8/210-225	$3095	9335
1963			
GT Hawk R2	289 V-8/290	$3675 }	
GT Hawk R1	289 V-8/240	3467 }	4634
GT Hawk	289 V-8/210-225	3095 }	
1964			
GT Hawk R2	289 V-8/290	$3538 }	
GT Hawk R1	289 V-8/240	3330 }	1767
GT Hawk	289 V-8/210-225	2958 }	

HOW STUDEBAKER CAME NOT TO BE

Exactly twenty years ago—October 1, 1954, to be precise—Studebaker and Packard officially merged. It was a heady moment. The potential of the giant corporation was unlimited. There were a few problems, to be sure, but everyone was certain things could be worked out. All you had to do was look at their recent successes to appreciate just what could be done.

In 1950, for example, more Studebakers were sold than ever before . . . some 268,229. Total sales were a healthy $268-million in 1947, but by 1953, president Harold Vance had driven Studebaker up to $594-million in sales . . . an incredible doubling of business in less than six years. It was a record to be proud of. From 1947 through 1953, Studebaker earned more than $108-million, after taxes. In 1949 alone, profits were nearly $30-million. Studebaker was one of the largest, solidest companies in America.

In the same seven years, Packard earned $48.5-million, a more than healthy profit for what was a much smaller firm. And if you considered the two companies together, they controlled over six percent of the total U.S. automobile market in 1948 and '49, and a solid 5.5 percent of the market from 1950 until 1953. Studebaker had substantial overseas sales, both companies were profiting from lucrative defense contracts growing out of the Korean War, and both got favorable allocations of scarce raw materials because they were government contractors. The future of the combine couldn't have been brighter.

What nobody mentioned . . . at least not loudly enough for anyone to hear . . . was another set of numbers. For instance, as early as June 22, 1954, when the two companies agreed to merge later that fall, Studebaker was losing money at the astounding rate of $2.5-million per month, and had already reported a first-quarter loss of $8.5-million. Packard on the other hand, was in much better shape. It only lost somewhere over $1.0-million in the same three months. Studebaker and Packard shares of the market, taken together, had dropped sickeningly to a mere 2.5 percent.

In 1955, Detroit had the best sales year in its history, pushing over seven million new cars out the doors. Studebaker-Packard withstood an unsuccessful strike by the UAW, and won an incredibly hardnosed settlement that saved the company $28-million in direct labor costs and $22-million in overhead. And yet in 1955, they managed to lose a spectacular $29.7-million on a market share of less than two percent.

What the hell happened? Well, lots of things. Studebaker-Packard got caught in a back alley with walls built out of its own ineptitude, some bad cars, the Korean War and an economic recession they should have seen coming, and, well . . . they got mugged by Henry Ford II. It's all there if you look. By the early Fifties, much of Studebaker's equipment was sadly out of date. The assembly lines were operating with tools and schedules that General Motors would have thrown out before World War II. Each car Studebaker made cost them hundreds of dollars more than a comparable Chevrolet. Studebakers sold at Buick prices. On a straight car for car comparison, however, Studebakers were so cheaply engineered that General Motors could have sold the same car for 25 percent less than it charged for Chevys . . . and still have made a handsome profit. Studebaker was also stuck with an antiquated dealer franchise system that they'd set up during the Depression, when the company would have *given* the cars away just to stay in business. Unfortunately, in the boom market of the late Forties and early Fifties, Studebaker was still giving cars away.

The cars themselves, largely because of consultant Raymond Loewy (and a staff of brilliant designers that included most of the significant stylists of the postwar period at one point or another), were the style leaders of the industry. Of course, the stylish 1950 "Torpedo" with the propeller nose was a dead horse on used car lots . . . and the "foreign style" 1953/1954 Starliner—certainly the most sophisticated design of any Fifties car—was a sales disaster. But Studebaker was still the most innovative automaker when it came to design. And although the L-head Six was a leftover from the Thirties—along with the infamous "rubber frame"—Studebaker did have a modern overhead valve V-8 by 1951 and a number of other engineering firsts. They just didn't have a reputation for decent engineering. And in the marketplace, they suffered because of it.

Then too, Studebaker and Packard were both heavily dependent upon government contracts. But when the Korean War glided to a standstill, Secretary of Defense Wilson withdrew a promised contract for $420-million worth of J-47 jet engines . . . just weeks before the two companies merged. The end of the Korean War had another marked effect, of course, and the prosperous seller's market of the war years turned into a recession . . . and a buyer's market. Studebaker-Packard lost substantially on all counts.

And then there was Henry Ford II. He decided for 1953 to head General Motors off once and for all. And so Ford dealers were shaving profits to the bone—perhaps making $50 or $100 on a car—at the same time that Studebaker-Packard was stuck overpaying dealers. General Motors eagerly joined the fray against Ford, and well into 1956, and even later, the two giants battled it out in the showrooms of America. Of course, when the elephants fight, the grass gets trampled—Hudson, Nash, Kaiser, Willys . . . Studebaker-Packard.

When Studebaker merged with Packard, the proxy statement claimed that the South Bend firm could break even on sales of 165,000 cars in 1954. After the October 1 incorporation, however, Walter Grant of Packard priced out Studebaker costs, and arrived at a break even point of 282,000 units. Of course, Studebaker failed to show a profit by even their own lenient standards. And 1955 was a worse year.

On January 15, 1956, "Big Jim" Nance, the former president of Packard who now headed up the combine, went to New York for a few meetings in high places. A number of big insurance companies owned large blocks of stock in Studebaker-Packard. What Nance had to say was simple: If you don't want your stock to become worthless when we go out of business, loan us $50-million now so we can tool up for an all-new line in 1957. He was turned down cold. For '57, Studebaker would be stuck with warmed over '56s, which were really warmed over '53s . . . which were the worst sales disaster in Studebaker history. Nance had to have the money.

With nowhere to turn—and only enough credit to keep operating until September of 1956—Nance reduced his request to a crisis level $35-million . . . and was turned down again. Desperate, he tried to interest Ford in producing their announced all-new car—which turned out to be the Edsel—in Studebaker factories. Ford declined. It was the best thing to happen to Studebaker in years. Some tentative talks were held at Chrysler, to no avail. And Nance even arranged a deal in which insurance companies would lend him the $50-million, but only if General Motors would endorse the loan. Albert Bradley, the financial wizard of GM, rightly figured that if Studebaker was successful, GM would be accused of monopoly; if Studebaker failed, GM would be the culprit.

Finally, Roy Hurley, the dynamic president of Curtis-Wright and a former automotive executive at Ford and Bendix, agreed to consider Studebaker-Packard as a $70-million tax loss that could be extended to a deficit $150-million with little trouble. In 1948, when Hurley took over Curtis-Wright, they had earned $5-million on $112-million in sales. In 1956, Curtis-Wright earned $35-million on $509-million in sales. At the time, Hurley seemed like a good bet to turn Studebaker-Packard around—an experienced car person with a proven track record and large assets behind him.

But Hurley had other plans. He recognized three major problems at Studebaker: The use of too much factory space for unprofitable production (meaning automobiles), an obvious shortage of capital, and production costs that were way out of line. Hurley may have been a car person, but more than that, he was a businessman. And keeping Studebaker-Packard in the car business was a losing proposition by 1956. Of course, what Curtis-Wright needed was a losing proposition. So in long range terms, Hurley needed Studebaker to lose a lot of money, and then get out of the car business. He was a better businessman than anybody else who'd run Studebaker . . . at least he steered the company in the direction he wanted.

Hurley declined a straight merger with Studebaker-Packard. What he got was a lease of the Utica, Michigan and Chippewa, Indiana manufacturing plants (Studebaker's two most efficient factories), for a prepaid rental of $25-million. He paid $10-million for what was left of Studebaker's defense business, he obtained a contract for Curtis-Wright to manage Studebaker-Packard on a cost basis for three years, and an option on five million shares of stock at less than market value. What he hoped to do was keep Studebaker at a roughly break even point for two years, write off its losses as a bad Curtis-Wright investment and then collect roughly $40-million (the difference between what he'd agreed to pay and the real selling price) on what would be 45 percent of Studebaker-Packard stock by the time he exercised his option.

Jim Nance resigned as soon as the contract was signed. So did Paul Hoffman, the Studebaker pioneer who had stayed on as Chairman. Harold Vance, the president of Studebaker during the years of its spectacular plunge into near bankruptcy, had already resigned his executive position in November, 1956 to join the Atomic Energy Commission.

Hurley brought up Harold Churchill to the presidency, juggled the accounting to reduce the company's net worth and show nominal profits, cancelled plans for the all-new 1957 line . . . and started the slow process of eventual diversification that ultimately saved Studebaker-Packard as a company, if not an automobile manufacturer. Churchill was a conscientious Studebaker long-timer, and he honestly wanted to save not only the company, but the car division as well. But only in 1959—largely because of the sales success of the compact Lark, which sold 138,000 units—was he able to show a profit.

Ironically, the $28.5-million that Studebaker made in 1959 helped stir up minority stockholders to investigate the internal management of the company. After a riotous 1960 annual meeting, Churchill was replaced by Sherwood Egbert, the charismatic executive vice-president of McCulloch Motors. An automotive equivalent of Jack Kennedy, he threw himself into the task of saving Studebaker. Egbert specialized in morale-boosting touches such as repainting the interior of the South Bend factory, dressing the foremen in spiffy white jackets, walking the assembly lines like a campaigning politician and converting a former clubhouse on the Studebaker proving grounds into his family home.

Egbert actually produced a slim profit in 1962, after $10-million in losses for 1961. There was even a point late in 1961 when Studebaker stock jumped more than 50 percent in very active trading, mostly because of confidence in Egbert and the enthusiastic public reception that Brooks Stevens' restyled Larks and Hawks had received. But it didn't last. Studebaker sold only 78,664 cars in 1961 (just 1.8 percent of the total market) and only 86,974 in 1962. The break even point was figured at roughly 120,000 units. In 1963, only 44,000 were sold, and production stopped permanently in November, 1963. Studebaker lost $20-million on the year, Egbert's health failed, and Byers Burlingame replaced him as president.

Everything done after production stopped at South Bend was a rather tawdry charade to keep Studebaker's franchise dealers from demanding compensation from funds the company didn't have. They temporarily produced sedans and wagons in Hamilton, Ontario . . . they built engines in South Bend . . . they even assembled Chevy-engined cars in Canada until March of 1966. The letter—if not the spirit—of the dealer contract was met. But there was no honest effort at true volume production.

In retrospect, Studebaker could have been saved. But in order to do that, the groundwork should have been done right after World War II, or even earlier. As late as 1951 or even 1952, there was still a chance. But after Harold Vance got into clearcut problems, it took Studebaker's board of directors over three years to find a solution—merger with Packard, which was a disasterous idea from the very beginning. For most of that time, Peter Peterson, the young executive vice-president, was thwarted at every turn. Peterson was a dynamic, hardnosed businessman . . . just what Studebaker needed. Frustrated, he left to take over Mack Trucks . . . an equally ailing company . . . which he turned around and made an industry success story. He might have done the same for Studebaker. As it was, by the time anyone with Peterson's business skills got into the presidency, the Studebaker coach had long since turned into a tax loss pumpkin.—*Rich Taylor*

How I made a few improvements to the Starliner and created the Studebaker Hawk ...By Bob Bourke

"At the time, we had in the neighborhood of forty men—clay modelers, woodworkers, designers. Our group was pretty independent . . . independent to the degree that we just had to keep our costs down. It was explained in meetings with management that they wanted to spend so many thousands of dollars in tooling for the hood, so much for the decklid, so much for trim, etc. We had to stay within those limits.

"Fundamentally, Studebaker wanted to get as different a car as they possibly could, with a minimum amount of tooling. The biggest single area we could change cheaply was the hood. And the grille, of course. Going from the sloped hood of the '53/'54 to a standup hood, that would immediately give it a distinguishing look.

"The next thing we wanted was to give a little foreign feel to the car, while also keeping it a fairly honest machine. We wanted to get that Mercedes feel at the front, while still retaining the split grilles at the sides. This car was done rather rapidly; we didn't get to make very many quarter-scale studies on it. But we did have some that I'd say were more radical—and better looking—than the Hawk . . . at least at the front end.

"The decklid that we made was a real hashup. We took the early '53 decklid—which was a very simple, rounded shape. When we tried to kick it as hard as we could, it came off as a very poorly-executed design for a kicked-up deck. But those horizontal ribs did help to identify the car immediately from the rear. We even saved about 80 percent of the inner decklid panel stamping dies. It didn't help increase the trunk capacity at all, of course, but it was a lot cheaper.

"Of course, it was given too much chrome and trim. Most of that left a bit to be desired. The Hawks weren't better than the '53s, certainly. The Sales division of management would pressure to get a different appearance. Whether you hung more trim on or cut some off, they didn't care. As long as it was different. And at that time, the more chrome you could get on, the better off you were. GM really showed a lot of chrome. Studebaker interpreted this to mean that the American public wanted so many square feet of chrome on a car. So we were pressed into over-decorating and over-identifying.

"After Studebaker and Packard got together, and Big Jim Nance took over—he was a great promoter, an electric personality—Harold Vance was ready to bow out. When Nance took over, he brought along his own group of whiz kids. They had already decided to phase Loewy out, because they couldn't afford him. His billings were about a million a year—this included a lot of woodworkers and clay modelers, too—and Loewy marked up everything. Salaries were marked up 100 percent. It was a great deal for Loewy, but the economics were unthinkable to the Packard people.

"When they phased out Loewy, I went sailing out the door, too. They brought in Bill Schmidt, and then he was replaced by Duncan McRae. They brought McRae down, and he was on the Studebaker payroll.

"It took Nance something like a year and a half to go through $64-million, and at the end of that, he had a couple of warmed-over versions of nothing. I'm not bitter, but you have to admit it was a tremendous loss to the company—done neatly and completely. It was absolutely pitiful."

Photos courtesy Richard Quinn Collection

Bob Bourke's '53 Starliner gave shape to the Hawks; a combination of innate quality and miniscule styling budgets kept the same body shell in production for over a decade.

Ken Elliot of Sales had a hand in styling the '55s; the abundance of chrome is one of his trademarks. The President Speedster appeared in January of 1955, a limited production, expensive and luxurious line leader. Diamond quilted seats, an engine-turned aluminum dash and unusual paint schemes helped distinguish it from more mundane Studebakers. Its success cleared the way for the Hawk line in 1956.

How I made a few improvements to the Starliner and created the Packard Hawk ...By Duncan McRae

"Soon after Nance took over, Bill Schmidt became director of design at Packard, and he took over at Studebaker, too. I was named chief designer at Studebaker, and Dick Teague took over at Packard. We came up with quite a few new prototypes for the two companies, with all-new sheetmetal.

"But finally it was realized that there just wasn't going to be enough money to do these new cars. The company at that point started to disintegrate. Bill Schmidt left to start his own company, and Dick Teague left with him.

Courtesy Fototecnica

Roy Hurley of Curtis-Wright liked the looks of the Maserati 3500 Gran Turismo Allemano, a $10,000 Italian sportster with a double overhead cam Straight Six. Duncan McRae's Packard Hawk borrowed this oval mouth and hood scoop; early prototypes even had the Maserati's fender louvers behind the front wheel. Taillights and roof are pretty similar, too. Hurley liked his one-off so much, it went into production.

The fake spare tire cover on the Packard trunk came from Chrysler's Imperial . . . but it first appeared on this 1955 Chrysler Flightsweep II idea car. Those slotted exhaust tips showed up on Steven's GT Hawk. The Chrysler's roof might have come from the '53 Starliner, though.

Courtesy Car and Driver

"So that left me with a whole bag of nothing. We didn't have any money, we were way behind for coming out with anything new, because we'd been planning on our new car that suddenly wasn't going to be produced. We did a facelift for the basic Studebaker that I'm not particularly pleased with. And we were forced to come up with some sort of Packard product . . . so the franchise dealers couldn't force Studebaker-Packard to buy back all their spare parts and tools. So we tried to make a Packard line out of the Studebakers.

"The Packard Hawk started out as a single vehicle for **Roy Hurley**, who'd come into Studebaker as a consultant from Curtis-Wright. After he came back from a European tour, where he'd seen a Maserati that he liked particularly well, he asked if we could build him a car something like that. After the first car was done, management decided to produce it.

"Hurley would stop in to look at the developing Hawk very infrequently. We had almost complete freedom to do what we wanted on it, because it was only intended as a single vehicle. There was no management interference at all. With the exception of not being able to spend any money on it, there was no problem from management.

"The Imperial at that time had a molded spare tire embossed in the decklid. We were looking for something to make the Studebaker deck look a little different. I don't know which one of us came up with that, it might have been . . . me. We built that on the old Starliner trunk. Since we wanted the Studebaker version and the Packard version to look different, we threw that spare tire thing on the old lid, and there it was. A different look. It wasn't a beauty.

"It had a very nice interior, though. A leather interior. That bit of interior that overflows on the doors to the exterior was supposed to be reminiscent of old aircraft. They always had a crashpad around the edge of the cockpit. For us, it was an attempt to make the interior appear to come outside the glass. Some of that sort of thing will be coming out of Detroit in a few years. I think you'll see it again. It wasn't very striking, but it did help to make the car look a little different. And that's what we were after.

"It's pretty difficult to take any car in isolation and critique it. You have to gather around it the competitors from that same year. I've seen lots of vehicles that look like hell, but when you realize they were competing against say, General Motors in 1958, they don't look so bad.

"The bullet bumpers on the Packard Hawk, for example, were contemporary with the same devices on the '57 Chevrolet and Cadillacs from those same years. You have to gather those other vehicles around to appreciate what was being attempted, even though it may not have come out all that well."

How I made a few improvements to the Starliner and created the Gran Turismo Hawk ... By Brooks Stevens

"I have to begin with Sherwood Egbert. I'd known him for years, because McCulloch/Paxton was one of my clients. We'd been involved together in the Paxton rear-engine steam car, and some other projects. So when Egbert went to Studebaker, he immediately called me, and I flew down to South Bend. He had inherited a design situation that he didn't like, and wanted to change.

"Studebaker was still in bed with Mercedes at that point, and that was a consideration. And Loewy was under contract again. So Egbert decided to put Loewy on to the sports car project that later became the Avanti, and gave me the Hawk to restyle. One of his considerations was that we take money out of it, not add expense. It had enough horrifying things—fins, geegaws, and chrome—appliqued all over it already. We wanted to clean it up and give it some sort of contemporary look. That was number one.

"And Egbert wanted to move fast. He had never been involved with automobiles before, so when you said it would take eighteen months to tool up for a new model, he didn't even hear you. The old manufacturing people would explain how complicated something was, and he'd say, 'But I'm not a car person. I don't know that you can't do it my way.'

"So for the Hawk, he started me on the project in May, I think it was. He wanted it as soon as possible. So I said I'd see what I could do. I was in such a hurry, I wanted something that I knew would sell, that the public would accept. Something that wouldn't have to be sold to them. Since the old Hawks had that look, we gave it a touch of the Mercedes grille. I'd always liked that anyway. We took out all the indentations in the doors and all that stuff left over from the '53 car—which would tell people it was a '53. I ripped off all the stuff from the fenders—the fins and all that—and brought it back to the basic '53 configuration. Which was very good. I changed the headlight cowls and created a new dashboard, and we put on wood-graining and other little touches that were being used at the time, to make it look contemporary.

"The greenhouse was inspired by the Thunderbird. We put on those slab-sided C-pillars, and a new recessed rear window. It was cheaper than a rounded or curved window, being flatter, but we didn't stress that point too much in our marketing, of course. I think we gave it a character of its own. The Lincoln Continental had those chrome moldings atop the fenders, so we borrowed those, since we had a potential problem with the fender seams, anyway. So out of all these things, we used a lot of popular concepts, which I think we merged together rather comfortably.

"Finally, in order to expedite things, we had a big meeting in Egbert's office; he, myself and Gene Hardig—the vice-president of engineering and the most wonderful of God's people who ever walked this earth. Gene was the savour of whatever we had left. He'd try anything. Nothing was impossible. He liked what he saw. And Egbert liked the fact that

I'd taken $28 per car out of that thing the minute I removed those stupid fins and the rest of the fiberglass.

"I went back to Milwaukee, had a car sent up the next day, we cut it apart and made a steel, handbuilt prototype. It was trimmed, painted, everything. We sent that to South Bend in early June. I went off to Le Mans. I got a telegram from Gene Hardig, saying, 'The board approved the Hawk. Not one change. We'll introduce it in September.'

"I thought that was fine. In a year and a half we'd see the new car. When I got back, I found out Egbert intended to introduce it to the dealers in Chicago that September. We only had four months! But Hardig said, 'Egbert doesn't know we can't do that.' So we did it. We had every little tool and die guy in the Midwest making some part of that automobile. But we made it on time.

"Of course, it didn't do any good. Egbert's health started to fail, the public lost confidence in the company, and it just went downhill. The Avanti was way behind, and the body had to be glued together from 300 parts or something. It was crazy. I started on a series of three prototypes for an all-new line . . . including an all-new Hawk. Where Detroit would have spent $200-million, we could spend $50-million. We were going to make a whole new car for what it cost to restyle a Plymouth doorhandle. Egbert expected to get the money from Wall Street, but in case that failed, we started facelifting and warming over what we had.

"We made up drawings and models and we went to Wall Street and made speeches and did everything under the sun to show them what we were going to do. And I'd have some one of these pompous bankers ask me 'Where's South Bend?' or some dumb thing.

"They didn't know or care. That was the end. Without additional money we couldn't do what we had to do. We went jumping from pillar to post, trying everything. Egbert was getting sicker by the day, and finally it just all fell apart."

Stevens styled the GT Hawk in less than a month—here's an early version. Corrugated cardboard makes a new roof line right over top of an early Sky Hawk body. The little fender caps, blades on front fenders and grille trim are done the same way. Notice the smoothed out ridges in the kicked-up decklid, the smoothed-out door and dechromed body . . . also the Principalite de Monaco license plates.

Along with his styling proposals, Stevens gave this exploded view to Egbert. It shows how few new parts were required to turn a Starliner into a GT Hawk . . . mostly just trim pieces, except for the roof assembly. Notice he intended grille mesh in the two side grilles as well as the center Mercedes grille, but production cars have open slots.

(Far right) For 1965, Stevens planned a revamp of the front end, retaining Mercedes touch, but cleaner and tighter. Ironically, this type of front end—complete with stand-up hood ornament—is now in style. Chevrolet's Monte Carlo, for example, looks very much like this sketch.

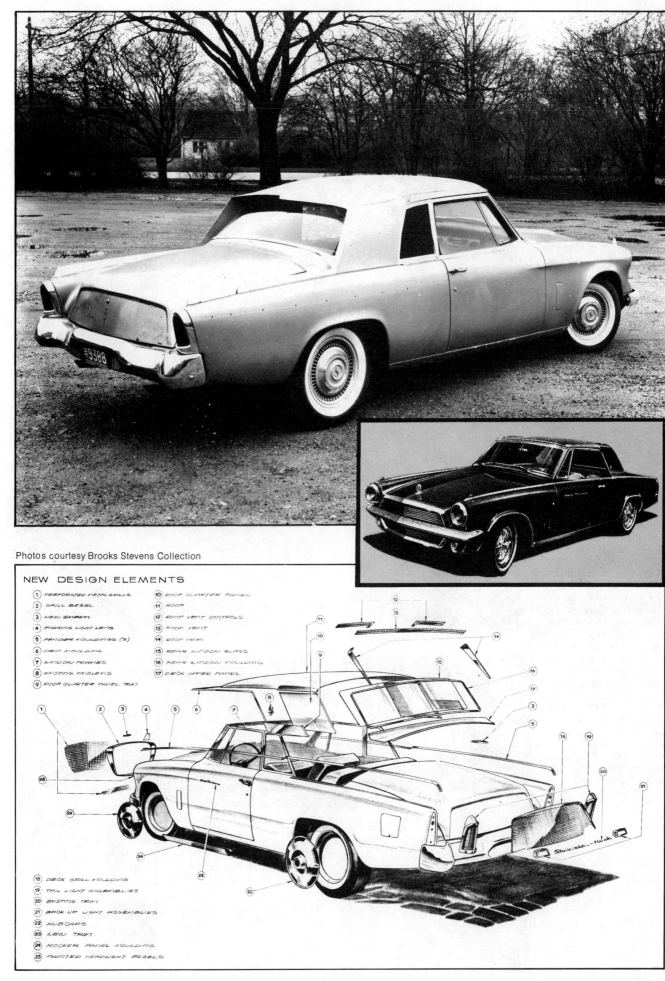

Photos courtesy Brooks Stevens Collection

NEW DESIGN ELEMENTS

1. PERFORATED METAL GRILLS
2. GRILL BEZEL
3. NEW EMBLEM
4. PARKING LIGHT LENS
5. FENDER MOULDINGS (2)
6. DRIP MOULDING
7. WINDOW FRAMES
8. EXISTING EMBLEMS
9. ROOF QUARTER PANEL TRIM
10. ROOF QUARTER PANEL
11. ROOF
12. ROOF VENT CONTROLS
13. ROOF VENT
14. ROOF TRIM
15. REAR WINDOW GLASS
16. REAR WINDOW MOULDING
17. DECK UPPER PANEL

18. DECK GRILL MOULDING
19. TAIL LIGHT ASSEMBLIES
20. EXISTING TRIM
21. BACK-UP LIGHT ASSEMBLIES
22. HUBCAPS
23. NEW TRIM
24. ROCKER PANEL MOULDING
25. PAINTED HEADLIGHT BEZELS

83

(Top) The Sky Hawk is surprisingly stable in low-speed corners, much better than the Starliner . . . but it's still no sports car. Final understeer and slow power steering combine to make it unnerving at high speeds. The taillights retain the simplicity of the original Starliner lens. The Golden Hawk added fins and chrome for a much busier look at the rear end.

(Center) The Packard Hawk handles better than the Sky Hawk since it has more power to get the tail out. The McCulloch blower has almost too much punch for the chassis, though, and the light tail wants to break away without warning. Extravagant styling includes fiberglass caps over the rear fenders. Underneath, they're just like the Sky Hawk.

(Bottom) Stevens gave the GT Hawk a majestic body, Gene Hardig supplied handling to match. Basic specifications hardly differ from the Sky Hawk, yet the result is a much steadier car that handles perfectly under all conditions. The mild engine is more tractable than that in the Packard Hawk, but an optional 290 hp R2 with blower provided even more power than previously, and gave a 140 mph top speed. Wider tires would help high speed handling, but they weren't available when the Hawks were new. The carefully designed taillights are indicative of Stevens' attention to detail. They bolt to '53 Starliner fenders without alterations, but provide an entirely different contour. Flattened exhaust tips are stock, nest right under the bumper.

(Far left) The Sky Hawk has the same rear seat as the Starliner. Headroom is limited by the stylishly low roof, legroom depends upon dishpan-shaped footwells angled toward the center. The armrest is fixed, so it's a space for just two uncomfortable people.

The Packard Hawk interior is exactly the same structurally, but luxurious natural-toned leather upholstery and thick carpets make it much plusher. It *looks* more comfortable, but isn't.

The GT Hawk makes better use of the same space —the higher roof gives decent headroom, the folding armrest accomodates three and individually adjustable front buckets allow you to have more legroom in the back, at least on one side.

(Left) The Sky Hawk still has the Starliner's molded flash in the door, high style in 1953, dated soon after. The other Hawks have smooth doors.

(Lower left) The Packard Hawk's fiberglass nose is bonded directly to the same steel fenders used on all the Hawks. Miraculously, only slight crazing marks the joint.

The GT Hawk has chrome trim covering the fender seams, highlighted by tiny lucite fins.

(Below) The Sky Hawk is distinguished by its "lightning strike," requested by management in order to form a line between the two-tone paint.

The GT grille bolts to the same hood that's interchangeable between all Hawks. Extra stainless steel rim is separate.

The Packard Hawk has anodized gold aluminum wings on its parking lights, matching the Mylar on the tailfins.

Continued from page 74

the most patient passengers can stand it for more than a few minutes at the most.

But the Sky Hawk driver can keep himself happy for hours. Vision is excellent in all directions, and even if the wheel sits a bit too close, and curiously low, it's no worse than in any other mid-Fifties car. The dashboard is filled with real instruments—no idiot lights—padded on the top and covered with imitation engine-turned aluminum that looks functional and racy. A useful touch are the vents which open directly from the fenders into the footwells—standard on all Studebakers, but a nice feature, nonetheless.

Driving fast in the Sky Hawk isn't particularly pleasant. There's a fair amount of body roll in high speed turns, with the inevitable tendency toward final understeer inherent in a front-heavy car. There's so little weight on the rear wheels, in fact, that traction was a chronic problem for hot rodders who tried to drag race Hawks. The rear end seems equally light when you're crowding into a turn. The slow steering doesn't help, and it has that annoying but typical Saginaw power steering numbness that masks most road feel.

If you drive it in a saner manner, however, the Sky Hawk seems perfectly contemporary, fairly economical—even with the optional 4-barrel Carter as fitted to Joe Albert's car—and surprisingly quiet, to boot. That stylish body is apparently as aerodynamic as it looks, something Bonneville speed record racers discovered years ago about the Starliner, too. The smooth flow of air over the Sky Hawk produces virtually no wind noise, even at high speeds. But that fits its nature perfectly. The Sky Hawk is a very low-key car.

1958 PACKARD HAWK

Ernie Spicer's Packard, on the other hand, is an incredible beast. The underhood view is completely dominated by the huge McCulloch blower, the interior sound level is defined by the supercharger's high speed whine and the driver's impressions rest solely on sensory inputs received when he mashes the throttle. The optional Twin-Traction differential helps some, but even with the standard equipment Flightomatic (Borg-Warner 3-speed automatic), the Packard Hawk can chirp the tires in any gear. It gathers speed with a dignified rush until the tach needle reaches 2500 rpm at full throttle. Then the blower boost pressure goes positive and the Hawk takes off. Mid-range acceleration is really impressive, among the quickest of all street cars in 1958 (the same is true for the '57/'58 Golden Hawks, of course, brothers under the skin). The top speed for a supercharged Hawk—as recorded by *Hot Rod* magazine at the time—was 122.7 mph at El Mirage dry lake . . . and Racer Brown figured the car would do 127 or more with a little fine tuning.

As ol' Racer pointed out, the nice thing about the McCulloch blower is that at cruising speeds it doesn't produce a positive manifold pressure. So in effect, most of the time you have an unsupercharged car breathing through an economical Carter 2-barrel (at only 7.8:1 compression ratio). So gas mileage isn't as bad as you'd expect, if you only take it easy. Which can be hard to do, because it's really *fun* to get on the gas and get supercar performance from a 17-year-old car.

Just driving around is almost as much fun, watching people watching you. Most pedestrians simply stare when they see the car go by. It's not that it's so exotic, it's just that they can't believe it looks the way it does. I'll not say a word, pro or con. I distinctly remember not liking the looks of the car at all in

---

Price when new: $2477.00 ($3995.00) [3095.00] fob South Bend
Current valuation: *Excellent;* $2000.00 ($4500.00) [$2500.00]

ENGINE

Type	90° V-8, overhead valves, watercooled, cast iron block and heads, 5 main bearings
Bore and stroke	3.56 x 3.63 in.
Displacement	289.0 cu. in.
Max. bhp @ rpm	210 @ 4500 (275 @ 4800) [210 @ 4500]
Max. torque @ rpm	292 @ 2800 (333 @ 3200) [300 @ 3000]
Compression ratio	8.3:1 (7.8:1) [8.5:1]
Induction system	4-bbl Carter downdraft carburetor (2-bbl Stromberg downdraft carburetor, McCulloch supercharger, centrifugal-type, variable rate, maximum boost: 5 psi [2-bbl Carter downdraft carburetor]
Exhaust system	Cast iron manifolds, dual exhausts
Electrical system	12 volt, 60 amp-hr battery, coil

TRANSMISSION

Type	Borg-Warner 3-speed automatic, column shift, maximum torque converter ratio: 2.15
Ratios	*1st:* 2.40 *2nd:* 1.47 *3rd:* 1.0 *Rev:* 2.0

DIFFERENTIAL

Type	Hypoid final drive, Spicer-Thornton limited-slip
Ratio	3.31:1
Drive axles	Semi-floating

STEERING

Type	Saginaw integral recirculating ball, power assist
Turns lock to lock	4.5
Ratio	18.2:1
Turn circle	41 feet

BRAKES

Type	Wagner four-wheel, hydraulically-operated cast iron drums, power assist
Diameter	F: 11.0 x 2.5 in.; R: 10.0 x 2.0 in.
Lining area	172.8 sq. in.

CHASSIS AND BODY

Frame	Box section steel, double-drop side rails, 5 cross members
Body construction	All steel
Body style	Two-door, 5-passenger front engine, rear-wheel-drive Hardtop

SUSPENSION

Front	Ind. unequal-length upper and lower control arms, coil springs, tubular hydraulic shock absorbers
Rear	Rigid axle, semi-elliptic leaf springs, tubular hydraulic shock absorbers
Tires	6.70 x 15 (8.00 x 14) [7.10 x 15], 4-ply
Wheels	5.0 x 15-in. (5.5 x 14-in.) stamped steel, 5-bolt

WEIGHTS AND MEASURES

Wheelbase	120.5 in.
Overall length	204.0 in. (205.2 in.) [204.0 in.]
Overall height	58.1 in. (54.6 in.) [55.0 in.]
Overall width	71.3 in.
Front tread	56.7 in. (56.7 in.) [57.3 in.]
Rear tread	55.7 in. (55.7 in.) [56.2 in.]
Ground clearance	6.5 in.
Dry weight	3230 lbs. (3470 lbs.) [3230 lbs.]

CAPACITIES

Crankcase	5 qts.
Cooling system	18 qts.
Fuel tank	18 gal.

PERFORMANCE

Acceleration:	
0-30 mph	4.2 (3.5) [4.0] sec.
0-40 mph	7.0 (5.0) [6.8] sec.
0-50 mph	9.2 (6.5) [9.0] sec.
0-60 mph	12.0 (8.8) [11.7] sec.
0-70 mph	15.5 (12.0) [15.3] sec.
0-80 mph	19.9 (16.0) [19.6] sec.
Standing ¼-mile	19.0 (16.7) [19.1] sec. at 76.0 (82.3) [78.0] mph
Top speed	110 mph (120 mph) [112 mph]

FUEL CONSUMPTION

City driving	14-16 mpg (11-13 mpg) [14-16 mpg]
Highway driving	20-22 mpg (19-21 mpg) [19-21 mpg]

(Note: Where specifications differ, Packard Hawk figures are given in parantheses, Gran Turismo Hawk figures in brackets. Otherwise, all specifications are identical for all three models.)

1956 Studebaker Sky Hawk 56H-K7
1958 Packard Hawk 58L-K9
1962 Studebaker Gran Turismo Hawk 62V-K6

RUSSELL VON SAUERS, The Graphic Automobile Studio

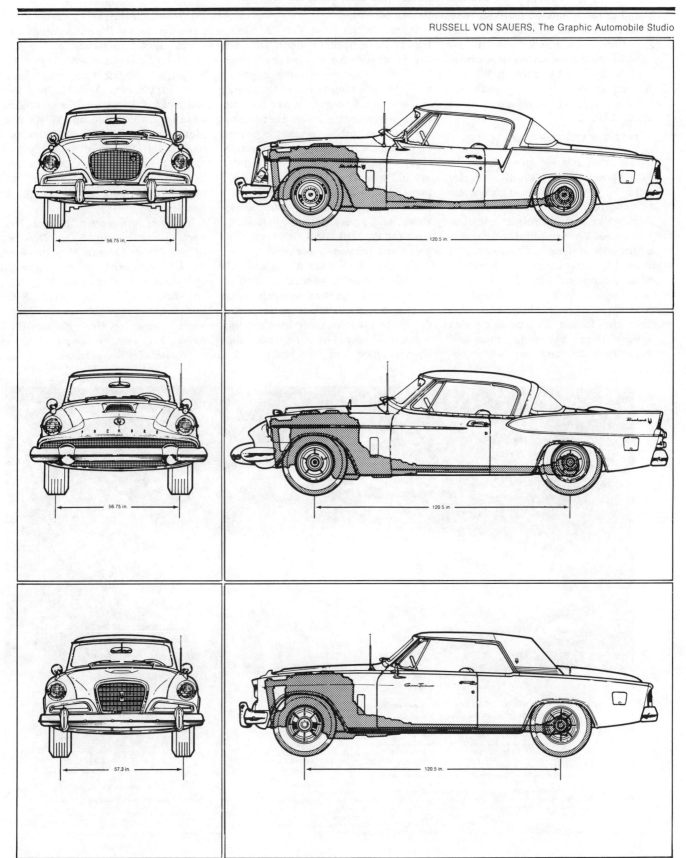

1958, but now its kooky grin seems kind of pleasant, somehow. Duncan McRae has his own opinions, of course, which he shares on page 21. Studebaker-Packard's advertising agency in 1958 was forced to reach into the universal copywriters' bag of stock superlatives to try and describe the Hawk. They called it "The Most Original Styling in America" and "Sculptured Elegance on Wheels." As they correctly pointed out though, "there's nothing on the road like a Packard Hawk."

1962 GRAN TURISMO HAWK

The most amazing thing about the Gran Turismo is that it's really so similar to the '56 Sky Hawk . . . and it's not *that* different from the '53 Starliner. And yet it feels like a much solider car. The power-assist Wagner finned brake drums are the same as those on all Hawks . . . as is the Flightomatic, the 289 V-8 with either 2-barrel or 4-barrel Carter, the total frame, the body shell and well . . . everything. The really big differences between the '56 and '62 have to do with invisible things like spring rates and shock absorbers, and the little differ-

ences with things like reclining front bucket seats instead of a bench, a better quality of trim and upholstery and a myriad—nay, seemingly endless—supply of little styling touches courtesy of Brooks Stevens.

Indeed, at this point, the '62/'64 GT Hawks have been so identified with Brooks Stevens that it's hard to approach the car without responding in preset ways. Stevens himself is so charismatic, it's hard to tell whether you're responding to Stevens or the Hawk. He tells how the GT was rushed together beginning on page 22, but he leaves out the totally engaging personality of the car, not unlike his own. The GT Hawk is smooth, polished, urbane . . . even witty. It has a much stronger personality than the Sky Hawk, and a very different personality from the Packard Hawk. It's cool, composed and somehow, just right.

Certainly, even when it was new, the GT Hawk strongly affected enthusiasts. They weren't impressed so much by the mechanical specifications of the car—though by 1963 you could have not only a Borg-Warner 4-speed manual and Twin-Traction, but disc brakes and a

290 horsepower McCulloch-supercharged R2 good for 140 mph—as they were by what you can only call the car's, well . . . character.

The whole country responded pretty much the same way. When the GT Hawk was introduced to the public, Studebaker shares jumped 50 percent on the stock exchange. And in *Motor Trend*, Jim Wright mirrored the public opinion of 1962. "It's a car," he said, "that feels and looks as if it's been engineered instead of just dreamed up . . . it's completely masculine in character, and reminiscent of some of the really great cars of the early Thirties. It looks, feels and drives like a *real* automobile." You might say that about all the Hawks. &

Our thanks to Robert E. Bourke, Westport, Conn.; Duncan McRae, Dearborn, Mich.; Brooks Stevens, Mequon, Wisc.; Dick Quinn, Mokena, Ill.; John and Joseph Albert, Richmond Hill, N.Y.; John Mayer, Mamaroneck, N.Y.; Ernest and Louise Spicer, Ramsey, N.J. Our special thanks to Herb Keller, Woodhaven, N.Y. and the Long Island chapter, Studebaker Drivers Club.

Courtesy of Ken McGee Auto Literature

From the Home of the Golden Hawks . . .

Packard Hawk

In the Finest Tradition of Packard Craftsmanship
. . . a Distinctive New, Full-Powered Sports-Styled Car

The newest member of a long line of distinguished motor cars . . . the power-equipped 1958 Packard Hawk combines for the first time famous Packard luxury and efficiency with dashing sports car styling. All the comfort and quality features that consumers have long associated with Packard automobiles are here . . . plus striking sports car design from the Continent with such exclusive new features as luxurious all-leather seats, weatherproof outside vinyl arm-rests, low slung European frontal styling. A sport-type simulated tire cover completes the picture of motion in action. And talk about performance! The all-new Packard Hawk is powered by a 275 horsepower V-8 engine . . . teamed with a self-lubricating, noiseless Jet-Stream Supercharger that provides quicksilver acceleration for unbeatable passing ability at highway cruising speeds. Yes, it's all here in one completely unique and authentic American sports car . . . superior roadability . . . prestige luxury . . . power brakes . . . ample seating room for an entire family. But above all, when you take the wheel of your new Packard Hawk, you can be certain you have made a sound investment in quality—the same quality that has proven itself through the years with satisfied Packard customers the world over.

That wonderful feel of real leather, the gleam of hand-polished surfaces, the array of sports car instruments . . . these are features you note and admire instantly when you see the Packard Hawk. Front seat is wide for three; the rear seat has a fold-away center arm rest for the comfort of both passengers. It is a luxurious interior of functional design, as befits a leading car of the Packard line.

In their fleet beauty, in their appropriateness to family use, these new Hawks strike a fresh note in beauty and performance. They set a revolutionary new trend in sports-inspired cars—cars fleet, mobile and entirely suited to the needs of the modern family.

SKY HAWK Powered by the Sweepstakes 289 210-hp V8.

POWER HAWK Powered by the 170-hp Sweepstakes 259 V8.

STUDEBAKER

invites your inspection

of a distinctive new family sports classic

The Gran Turismo

Hawk

designed and made in the meticulous tradition of

the great European road cars and offering

the comforts and conveniences

preferred by the discerning

American motorist

• The embodiment of roadability and driving ease from the gleaming expanse of hood through the smallest hand-crafted detail.

• Full 120″ wheelbase; Thunderbolt V-8 OHV engine; 3 speed synchromesh transmission standard. Optional floor-mounted 4-speed gear box or Automatic.

• Variable-rate front coil springs and anti-sway bar; asymmetrical rear springing; telescopic shock absorbers; finned-drum brakes.

• True Gran Turismo interiors; full five-passenger capacity; sports car type bucket seats forward, let-down arm rest in rear, optional reclining seats.

• Luxury-padded safety dash, recessed instrumentation. Rich, pleated vinyl upholstery, deep pile carpet. Exquisite detail in all appointments.

• The long list of Gran Turismo Hawk options include: Hill-Holder, limited slip differential, air conditioning.

by Ken Gross, *Feature Editor*

How Studebaker beat the Big Three to the compact punch....

1960 Lark Convertible

Above: Rear styling borrowed from Corvair, which Studebaker designers knew about before its introduction. Virgil Exner Jr. did the tail lamps. Right: Unlock two header latches and tickle the under-dash switch and the top disappears in 15 seconds flat. A neat boot hides it while it's down.

NINETEEN FIFTY-NINE was already too late, but you can't fault Studebaker president Harold E. Churchill for trying. The success of AMC's Rambler American seemed to point the way for an independent to survive. Studebaker saw daylight and rushed headlong toward the compact car.

Former Studebaker production chief Otto Klausmeyer recalls, "Harold Churchill was a fine gentleman—a great nut-and-bolt engineer—as honest as they make 'em. He was largely instrumental in starting the Lark.

"It was obvious that most of the rest of the industry was going for bigger, wider, faster, more powerful cars. By that time, Studebaker was in a position where they couldn't spend any money to develop big cars or for any kind of major redesign program. There was only one route to take, and anybody with an ounce of brains would have taken it. And that's just what he did. He shrunk the Champion down slightly—it was mostly a small car anyway—and deliberately made a compact out of it." [Note: All Studebakers had the same dimensions, body for body, after 1951.]

Certainly, Studebaker's new direction made good sense—so long as the Big Three stayed out of compacts. As it turned out, though, the Big Three didn't for long.

SIA covered Studebaker's decline and fall (see SIA #25, *How Studebaker Came Not To Be*). The Lark's short success story represented a ray of hope for people like Churchill, who sincerely believed the principal products from South Bend should always be automobiles.

We talked recently with Harold Churchill, plus former Studebaker styling chief Duncan McRae, designers Bob Doehler, Ted Pietsch, Virgil Exner, Jr., and engineering assistant E.T. Reynolds. From their recollections, we've put together this intriguing account of the Lark's birth.

In 1958, Studebaker was still trying to be price-competitive with the Big Three—a futile effort considering the company's antiquated tooling and small production runs. The marketing result, a barebones

Champion called the Scotsman, was a less-than-satisfactory solution that brought down Studebaker's already eroded image.

Harold Churchill remembers, "The Scotsman was a drab price leader—not another body like Packard's 110 had been. When you trimmed all the appointments down, you still hadn't changed the concept of the basic car. The Scotsman showed a full-sized competitive direction for us, but we knew it didn't go far enough.

"What strength we had was in offering something a bit different than the main market was offering. After all, that's true of American Motors today. I think our product-planning people had information

about the competitive compacts, but we took a chance because we thought we could move quicker than they did.

"There wasn't any difference of opinion between me and Studebaker's directors. That's a figment of somebody's imagination. The problem for Studebaker—and I recognized this—lay in comparing the cost benefits of an investment in tooling for a new car against what could be accomplished by broadening the industrial base of the corporation through diversifying."

Churchill won the first round when he convinced Studebaker's board that they could develop a new car inexpensively, in a crash program—a car aimed squarely at a market segment then occupied only by Rambler.

POPULAR SCIENCE'S auto editor and new-car sleuth, Devon Francis, inter-

viewed Harold Churchill prior to the Lark's debut. "We wanted to give the U.S. motorist what, to date, the industry has not supplied," said Churchill, "namely a smaller full-sized car to transport passengers at minimum cost consistent with maximum comfort and safety."

The term "smaller, full-sized car" is significant. It differentiated the Lark from AMC's American. Truth was, the concept originated in engineering—not from Studebaker's styling studios.

Virgil Exner Jr. remembers, "I came to South Bend in the fall of '57 and was there for six months. At approximately the first of the next year, we began making sketches and clays for a small car based on the Champion—but a little smaller. We thought at first it would be an all-new car; as designers we *always* hope for that. But Gene Hardig [Studebaker's chief engineer] brought in a prototype that they'd more or less been building on their own. It was sort of a neat cobbled-up job in metal. And it clearly showed what engineering was thinking of doing in terms of using existing components."

Duncan McRae comments: "We'd been discussing the possibility of a small car in our product-planning meetings. Mr. Churchill brought out some old films of the 1939 Champion. When that car was introduced, it instilled a lot of morale just when Studebaker needed it most [see *1939 Studebaker Champion drive Report*, SIA #35]. We all agreed we had to do *something* like that again. But we realized Studebaker couldn't afford an all-new car. We'd have to salvage a great deal from what went on before.

"Gene [Hardig] put his package together to give management a visual idea of what to expect. He wasn't competing with us. He simply wanted to show the size car we'd end up with. His prototype was a Champion, sawed off at both ends—just a seating buck, really—to show how much room there'd be for passengers and to illustrate minimum overall length.

"The center was an existing Champion body, originally designed for 1953. We also investigated the use of the old '47 Starlite body. Unfortunately, the beltline was too high. So we used the lower body which followed and designed a new front and a new rear end for it. First we introduced the hardtop coupe, 2- and 4-door sedans, and 2-door wagon. Later the 4-door wagon and convertible were developed for 1960.

"The short overhang resulted from using the Champion as the center section. We wanted a small car, so a lot had to be taken off ahead of the front wheels. I was directing styling at the time, but many other people were involved—Bill Bonner, Ray Everts, and Bob Doehler were some of them. We developed two full-sized clay models; Bill Bonner was in charge of one and Bob Doehler the other. When they were completed, I was pleased that the product-planning committee selected the model Bill Bonner had created."

Bob Doehler continues, "I think Duncan had a pre-set idea of what the new car was to look like. Hardig's prototype constituted the basic direction, and it defined the body package through the cowl and doors. We had only to design new fenders—and the front and rear ends. The car came off awfully well considering those ridiculous overhang dimensions. Not in the rear—I was all for that. But the front looked like one of those cross-country trucks with no meat ahead of the wheels. The Lark was skimpy in that respect."

Virgil Exner Jr. remembers, "McRae and the styling group were doing full-sized clays by Feb. 1958. Everything else was canceled out as far as new-car ideas were concerned. All I did on the Lark was a little bit on the rear quarter and tail-light area. Bonner pretty much did the entire front end—which was the most important part.

"I don't think the grille was influenced by Mercedes-Benz. I know Duncan was impressed by the Chrysler showcars, especially the DeSoto Adventurer (see *Thinking Ahead, The Ghia-Chrysler Showcars*, SIA #30). I remember him telling me that he really liked some of the front-end designs my father had been doing."

McRae confirmed that the Lark's grille was not influenced by Mercedes. "Actually," he told me, "it was more of a Lancia approach. Bob Bourke had designed the early Hawk, and we wanted to get the feel of that type of front end without copying it.

"Once the design direction had been established, it took only seven months from the time we started until the Lark hit the road. It was a fabulous effort by Gene Hardig. The car didn't cost much to build and was well received."

THE SECRET of the Lark's speedy development came by the clever use of old Studebaker bits and pieces. In addition to the '53 center section, Larks took their wraparound windshields from the '55½ Studebakers, their central glovebox from the '56s; the steering wheel came from the '57s; and the lowered roofline and hardtop doors were a legacy from the '58s.

Once the parts were sorted out, the tooling and changeover program went amaz-

ingly smoothly, according to Harold Churchill. "We put a lot of tooling into one die shop and had absolutely no problems as far as tryouts were concerned. If you spread out the contracts, you almost always have a few tryout problems. This time, when the dies came into the plant, everything went together as it should—not like the '53s, where there were a lot of problems [see *1953 Starliner driveReport*, SIA #13].

"We didn't use anywhere near the launching reserve that we'd provided for the Lark. When you start a new model, you always make a provision for downtime and that sort of thing as a result of something new going down the line. It went together well, I think, because of damn good planning. The Lark went together like a shoe that fit the foot. Nothing magic about it, just sound business practice. Budd supplied the big sheetmetal dies on time, and we easily met the target date for production."

Gene Hardig's contribution to the Lark didn't end with the body package. His engineering staff tore into the 20-year-old Champion engine to adapt the venerable little 6. Hardig told POPSCI's Francis he wanted "...a smaller, stiffer engine." A new crankshaft for the shorter stroke, with more overlap between mains, was a start. The Champion's stroke was reduced from 4.375 to four inches even. Displacement dropped from 185.6 to 169.6 cid, as in the 1941-54 Champ; horsepower went from 101 to 90, and torque dropped from 152 @ 1800 to 145 @ 2000. Hardig's engineers boosted the Lark's compression ratio from the Champion's 7.8:1 to 8.3:1.

The 259.2-cid V-8, which produced a healthy 180 bhp (195 with a 4-barrel carburetor and dual exhausts), was unchanged except for a redesigned intake manifold and compression ratio boost from 8.3:1 to 8.8:1.

Devon Francis chronicled the Lark's development, emphasizing the cleverness of the small Studebaker development team —restricted by available funds and, most importantly, *time* itself. "Working from the ladder-type Champion frame, the engineers retained its width, shortened it and added stiffeners. The gauge of the frame metal for the V-8 was increased. Torsional rigidity (resistance to twisting) shot up 24%, and beam rigidity (resistance to fore and aft bending) increased 23%.

"A series of foreign cars, meantime, began to cruise Studebaker's 3-mile test track. Churchill, Hardig, and R&D director Mike de Blumenthal wanted to find out what the imports had that they could use. One result of that was the design of a box section for the front of the car, made from a single metal stamping. This was also part of the stiffening process.

"While Duncan McRae, the company's chief stylist, went to work on appearance under an injunction from Churchill to keep it simple, work was started on the springing. This was tricky because the Lark was to be considerably lightened. Yet it had to have a feel of weight and stability if it was to appeal to motorists who would want to heavy-foot the gas pedal on cross-country trips.

"A handbuilt [Lark] was driven at varying speeds over the roughest roads on the proving ground *without* shock absorbers. The object was to mate the front and rear spring rates (the amount of deflection under load) and frequencies (the number of cycles per minute under shock).

"'We made it on our second try,' reported de Blumenthal, looking as though he had just seen a miracle.

"Overhangs, naturally, were razored down. Compared with the Champion's 35.6 inches in front, the Lark was fixed at 27.0 inches. The rear overhang was reduced from 50.3 inches to 39.5. An immediate result of the surgery in front, in which the engine was moved back, was a reduction in steering effort. Compared to the Champion, it requires 22% less pulling on the wheel to park the Lark with a V-8, 12% less with the Six.

"The Champion's brakes were adapted without change on the Lark 6, giving it one square inch of brake area for each 17.5 pounds of car. And the V-8—which comes with bigger brakes—has one square inch for every 17.1 pounds. These figures better the ones for Rambler *or* for Chevrolet, Ford or Plymouth.

"Once off the ground, the project moved fast. Sometimes, in a jam, the engineers worked around the clock. In a small company, changes don't have to await the approval of a 50-man committee.

"'Want to see what we've done to the manifolding on the 259-inch?' Hardig would telephone Churchill.

"'Yup,' would be Churchill's reply. He was there in five minutes."

CHURCHILL TOLD STUDEBAKER historian Fred K. Fox that the Lark name "...was selected from a large group of uncopyrighted names by the marketing department and D'Arcy, Studebaker's advertising agency. A professor of semantics from Northwestern concluded that the name *Lark* would be a successful companion to the existing Hawk."

The Lark was a well kept secret as far as the public was concerned. The launch, understandably, caused great excitement. Much of the hysteria began right at home in South Bend where 30,000 workers, knowing their jobs were on the line, rallied behind the stubby newcomer.

John Ragel, an official of South Bend's Association of Commerce, told *Wall Street Journal* reporter George Melloan, "Always at key points in Studebaker's history, they've come up with a lifesaver when they had to have it. They did it in 1939 with the Champion. I think they've done it again."

Studebaker was in dire straits at the 9-month mark in 1958—they'd already lost $22.5 million for that recession year, which saw all automakers down and the newborn Edsel already on its way out. Stude accountants hadn't used black ink since 1954—the year of the Packard merger. But Melloan was impressed with South Bend's support for Studebaker.

"One doesn't have to spend five minutes in this Indiana town," he wrote, "to feel the excitement generated by the new Lark.

Above: Mr. & Mrs. Ed Reynolds Jr. use their Lark convertible as daily transportation. *Below:* Radio antenna rolls up and down with this knob, similar to 1953 Studebaker's. This Lark has GM's Wonderbar radio, a Studebaker accessory dubbed "Signal Seeker."

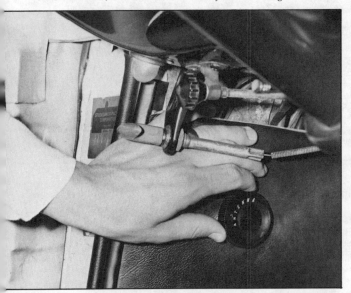

Later Larks could be ordered with Avanti R-1 to R-3 options, giving them tremendous performance. It's not bad, though, even with the base 180-bhp V-8.

Above: Split reclining seatbacks form bed, adjust to any position. Upholstery is red Naugahyde, and this is the original you see here. *Below:* Front seatback folds far forward to make entry into rear area easier. Driveshaft tunnel interferes relatively little with rear passengers.

For a stubby car, the Lark's trunk is nice-sized. Double walls prevent dings from interior. All the cargo, though, has to come out to get at the spare tire, and that's a mighty tall liftover sill.

DUNCAN MCRAE

Above: Studebaker's chief engineer, Eugene Hardig (left), and chief designer Duncan McRae unveil the first 1959 Lark in South Bend's old brick-floored plant. Right: Lark convertible, unlike coupes and sedans, uses an X-braced frame (other bodies use ladder type), with additional box sections in body sheetmetal.

THE 1960 COMPACT CHALLENGE

	Corvair	Falcon	Valiant	American	Lark VI	Lark VIII
Wheelbase	108.0	109.5	106.5	100.0	108.5	108.5
Weight	2340	2288	2705	2475	2577	2710
Tire size	6.50 x 13	6.00 x 13	6.50 x 13	5.90 x 15	5.90 x 15	6.40 x 15
Engine type	opp. a/c	in-line	in-line	in-line	in-line	v-type
Valves/cyls.	Ohv-6	Ohv-6	Ohv-6	L-head 6	L-head 6	Ohv-8
Bore/stroke, in.	3.38 x 2.60	3.50 x 2.50	3.40 x 3.12	3.18 x 4.75	3.00 x 4.00	3.56 x 3.25
Compression	8.0:1	8.7:1	8.5:1	8.0:1	8.3:1	8.8:1
Displacement	140.0	144.3	170.0	195.6	169.6	259.2
Horsepower	80@4400	90@4200	101@4400	90@3800	90@4000	180@4500
Torque	125@2400	138@2000	155@2400	150@1600	145@2000	260@2800
Mpg	17-22	22-27	18-23	22-27	18-23	14-18
0-60 acceleration	18.2 sec.	17.2 sec.	16.7 sec.	19.3 sec.	20.0 sec.	14.9 sec.
Base-priced 4-door sedan	$1860	$2053	$1912	$1835	$1793	$1911

1960 Lark driveReport

continued

Everywhere—on lamp posts, trucks, store counters—there are dozens of blue signs, 'South Bend goes up with Studebaker' or 'Buy the Lark.' Printed by a local group, the posters were put up by firemen and other city employees.

"Studebaker-Packard has dropped nearly all its traditional motorcars...to bet its future on the Lark. And the jobs of nearly a fifth of South Bend's manufacturing force depend upon the outcome."

The motoring press, often critical, gave the Lark a quick once-over and came up mostly with accolades. The irrepressible Tom McCahill of MECHANIX ILLUSTRATED summed up the prevailing attitude.

"In America, the birth of a new car is like the birth of a first male heir to the throne in a monarchy—all economists wish it success and so do all the guys in my business. Studebaker introduced a small car a year or two ago called the Scotsman, which went over like girlie pictures in a nudist camp.

"To say Studebaker was not in the healthiest of conditions would be like walking through a morgue and wondering what vitamins might do for the inmates. With the introduction of the 1959 Lark, everyone from the Wall Street Journal to the Department of Commerce wished Studebaker luck. So did I and many MI readers who have written me. It would appear to be a last-ditch stand, similar to Custer's when he found he had one bullet left—so let's take a look at the bullet."

Uncle Tom examined the bullet in his usual objective way. "To boil it all down," he wrote, "these Larks are interesting cars, but I'm sorry to say not too exciting when such things are considered as price, performance, and even economy of operation....Both Larks I tested offered good, honest transportation. I've driven better, but I've driven a lot worse. If you buy one because it fits your needs, the chances are that both you and Studebaker will be very happy about the whole thing."

ROAD & TRACK, in its more sober fashion, commented, "The Studebaker Lark, a less insolent chariot, presents a bland face to the world. This sort of simplicity in an age of baubles, bangles and beads, is a rare sight indeed...the body design is not up to American standards—it is restrained, it is readily identifiable, and many people will like it. However, some of the old tools and dies had to be used and the result is a vehicle which, to us, seems extraordinarily high and overall a trifle stubby looking." Still R&T's hard-to-please editors confidently predicted the Lark would outsell the more utilitarian Volkswagen. (It came close in 1959, but after that VW's sales kept going up while Studebaker's went down.)

While the press ranged from encouraging to cautious, the public's reaction was nothing short of ravenous by Studebaker standards. The first Lark went on sale on Nov. 8, 1958. Within two months, S-P recorded its first profit in five long years. Stude even had 30,000 advance orders!

Studebaker's midyear 1959 press releases showed some rather sensational numbers. First, Lark sales made for a 381% increase in production. Studebaker's

market share nearly trebled—from 0.95% to 2.52%. Over 1000 new dealers were attracted by the Lark. Studebaker dealer working capital doubled, and their profits averaged 2.4% of sales—compared with an industry average of 2.0%. Studebaker-Packard's retail sales at midyear were still running 250% higher than the first six months of 1958. Studebaker ended 1959 with 131,508 sales, compared with 49,770 in 1958.

Significantly, 70% of the cars traded in on new Larks were competitive makes. Studebaker wasn't cannibalizing itself—the Lark was attracting new customers. Of course, while Studebaker was fighting for its life, the Big Three were watching closely. Harold Churchill's gamble had won the South Bend independent a year's head-start. It proved to be precious little time.

When the Lark bowed, GM, Ford, and Chrysler were finalizing the Corvair, Falcon, and Valiant. Foreign car sales, approaching 5% of the market, now had to be taken seriously. The "captive imports," like Opel, Vauxhall, Simca, and Anglia, hadn't begun to stem the tide. Detroit knew that the public wanted red-white-and-blue little cars. After all, they were already showing this in Kenosha and South Bend.

We asked Virgil Exner Jr., whose father was Chrysler's styling v.p., how much Studebaker's designers knew about the competitive small cars. He replied, "I didn't see the Valiant until after I left Studebaker, but I knew generally what was going on. There was no intrigue as far as that was concerned. We designers were influenced by the Corvair type of styling. We

Everything's in ovals on and under the instrument panel, with deep padding on top. Lark's centered glovebox gives right oval to radio speaker.

knew GM would go for that and that Ford would have a typical lumpy little car."

FOR 1960, THE BATTLE LINES were redrawn with five American small cars competing. Studebaker still had a marketing edge. The Lark, with its big-car center section, offered more comfort and a greater range of body styles than competitors.

But the revamped, short-stroke Champion 6 proved to be a gas guzzler. Studebaker's accountants forced engineering to swap a Carter AS for the Champ's original Carter WE carburetor. The sad result found the V-8 out-ton-miling its kid brother in the Mobilgas Economy Run. Hardig and his men worked on a sidedraft as a replacement; eventually they ended up modifying the Lark's carburetor substantially.

Understandably, despite the Big Three's new cars, S-P management hesitated tampering with what seemed like 1959's winning combination. Harold Churchill's policy on changing the Lark was rigid. "There will be improvements in the products," he stated, "but there will be permanence of design."

For 1960, AUTOMOBILE TOPICS quoted Studebaker's president as saying, "The Lark has been designed deliberately to stay in style indefinitely—buyers resent their new car being made obsolete by each ensuing year's new model." For this reason, you really have to be an expert to tell a '60 Lark from a '59. A 4-door station wagon and a convertible were added to the model lineup for 1960, though.

Duncan McRae and his design team were pleased with the Lark's success but felt it was just the beginning. "It proved to us," McRae told me in Australia, "that we should build an all-new small car to follow the Lark. But some of Studebaker's management felt that we had a Volkswagen on our hands—that we would *never* have to change it.

"I disagreed, and we started two clay models. Mr. Churchill came by one day and wondered what we were doing. I said, 'This will be the followup for the Lark.' He said, 'You don't need it.' That left us without a project. All of us felt that the Lark was a good interim car but that it wouldn't last forever. Shortly after that, I left the company."

When McRae left, Gene Hardig and new styling director Randal (Randy) Faurot, formerly of AMC, began planning the Lark's successors in earnest. Apparently, Churchill sized up the competition, saw the impact from the Big Three's entries, and reversed his never-change-the-Lark policy. He encouraged the development of two new light cars—on 100- and 108-inch wheelbases (see *More Stude Studies*, SIA #7). After $4 million went into a massive design program, the board of directors rejected the prototype, and the project died.

The 1961 Larks emerged with only minor detail changes. Gene Hardig's engineers finally converted the long-suffering Champion 6 to overhead valves. Although the revised engine was more powerful (112-bhp vs. 90), it tended to suffer from cracks that developed between the valve seats—a problem never satisfactorily solved.

Detroit, for 1961, brought forth four *additional* compacts—the Dodge Lancer, Pontiac Tempest, Buick Special, and Olds F-85. Studebaker's directors had additional changes planned for the new model year, too. After seeing their $28.5 million 1959 profit melt to less than $708,850 in 1960, they had no further use for Harold Churchill.

The Lark's windfall profits had been used for diversification. Churchill's plans to aggressively continue marketing automobiles made him expendable. Strangely, though, the board opted for Sherwood Egbert as a replacement. Egbert turned out to be nearly as committed as his predecessor to the proposition of building automobiles to save Studebaker.

Churchill told SIA, "They were looking for fresh blood. He had a good record at McCulloch in chainsaws. I took early retirement and became a consultant to the board."

Former Studebaker engineering assistant Ed Reynolds elaborates, "The board of directors had *no* interest in automobiles. All they were interested in was the big tax loss carried forward from all the tax losses over the years. To be brutally frank, they were just interested in seeing the company either merged into a conglomerate or purchased by somebody.

"Church, with his interest and love of Studebaker, fought that approach. There was a collision of ideologies and personalities and everything else. Finally, they practically booted him upstairs—he became a sort of consultant but he never was directly active after that.

"Church's trademark was that he always wore suspenders. It'd be warm and he'd have his coat off—and you could tell him a mile away with those suspenders. Every-

1960 Lark driveReport

body in the plant called him Church. He didn't object to being called by his nickname. He was very different from Egbert in that respect. *He* was Mr. Egbert—you didn't call *him* Sherwood. Egbert wasn't universally liked, you know. But Church *was* liked and highly respected in the plant."

EGBERT MANAGED to keep Studebaker's directors happy while he actively diversified the corporation's interests. Yet he pinned his hopes of saving the automotive side of the business on the brilliant Loewy-designed Avanti (see *Six-Week Wonder, SIA #32*). Egbert also got some help from Brooks Stevens, who redesigned the company's bread-and-butter Larks and also created the Gran Turismo Hawks. For a short time, confidence meant smiles in South Bend.

The restyled '62 Larks sold 93,052 units, up nearly 30,000 cars from 1961. Thereafter, it was all downhill. For 1963, despite an innovative sliding-roof station wagon and the powerful punch of the R-1, R-2, and R-3 Avanti V-8s, Lark sales fell to 75,377. In 1964, the Lark name was dropped on the Cruiser and Daytona models, retained on the Challenger and Commander, and sales dribbled to 44,232.

South Bend was shut down in Dec. 1963 and production increased at Hamilton, Ont. Studebakers, no longer called Larks, still trickled off the lines for two more

years: 17,078 in 1965 and 8864 cars in the final year, 1966.

Studebaker thus produced 563,960 "Larks" in eight model years—in an effort that was doomed from the outset. The realities of automotive marketing guaranteed that *even* if poor Studebaker *had* found an opportunity, as soon as volume warranted, the Big-Three could exploit the new direction and drive South Bend's share back down. The Lark's initial success only served to encourage Detroit to forge ahead with its compact plans.

"Harold Churchill knew it was only a question of time before Detroit would begin building compacts," Ed Reynolds points out, "but he felt that if we could just get our feet on the ground, Studebaker could withstand the impact. The thing that really hurt us was that Studebaker had a lot of dual dealerships with Ford, GM, and Chrysler. When the Big Three launched their small cars for 1960, they forced those dual dealers to give up Studebaker. It really hurt us to lose those stores."

Paradoxically, the Lark *saved* Studebaker as a corporation. All that cash from the Lark's tremendously successful first year paved the way for diversification. Studebaker survives today as Studebaker-Worthington, a producer of aerospace equipment, garden tractors, compressors, generators, and refrigeration units.

The old South Bend plant is abandoned now. When its doors closed, one out of every five people in the city became unemployed. South Bend has recovered, but the ghostly, deserted buildings bear mute testimony to the industrial might that once was Studebaker.

ED REYNOLDS JR., son of former Studebaker engineering assistant E.T. Reynolds, owns the 1960 Lark convertible we borrowed for this driveReport. It's equipped with nearly every conceivable Lark convenience accessory and makes, overall, a tremendously good impression.

It's ironic, with all the downsizing going on in Detroit these days, that the Lark's dimensions are very much what all U.S. automakers are now trying to get into their intermediates. GM's 1978 crop of A-bodied specialty coupes (Monte Carlo, Grand Prix, Buick Regal, and Cutlass Supreme) uses the same 108-inch wheelbase as the Lark. Externally, though, GM's cars are longer, and internally there's not so much seating space.

The Lark V-8's performance beats most new cars in every way, and this is with the 2-barrel, 180-bhp version. The Borg-Warner 3-speed automatic takes a while to get wound up—it's smooth and quiet, but it seems to take its sweet time getting power from the engine to the rear tires. With stick and overdrive, this ragtop would be a real screamer. Later in the Lark's career, of course, the various Avanti 289s became available, with and without McCulloch blowers. Avanti disc brakes also made later Larks among the earliest U.S. production cars to quit front drums (although the Lark's drum brakes are more than adequate for general driving).

The seats, beautifully pleated and with reclining backs, stand comfortably high up off the floor. They're a bit close to the steering wheel, however, and the gas pedal ought to be nearer the transmission tunnel for more foot support.

Workmanship inside and out are excellent in this 1960 model—better than most U.S. cars of that era. The power steering centers itself well and gives good road feel despite being a trifle slow (4.5 turns lock to lock).

Cornering brings out some body lean, but the car sticks well to the road. Normal weight distribution with the V-8 is 57/43, but when you put four people in the car it balances out to a more stable 51/49. The Lark VI (6), since its engine weighs about half as much as the V-8, has more neutral handling even without the extra passengers.

All in all, the Lark does very much what it's supposed to do. It's a sensible-sized car both inside and out. The reason Studebaker failed as an automaker had nothing to do with its cars. □

Our thanks to Harold Churchill, Bremen, Ind.; Otto Klausmeyer, South Bend, Ind.; Ed Reynolds Jr., Pomona, Calif.; E.T. Reynolds, Ponchatoula, La.; Duncan Mc-Rae, Apollo Bay, Victoria, Australia; Ted Pietsch, North Hollywood, Calif.; Bob Doehler, Milwaukee, Wisc.; Virgil Exner Jr., Grosse Ile, Mich.; Eugene Hardig, Naples, Fla.; James J. Bradley, National Automotive History Collection, Detroit Public Library, Detroit; Fred K. Fox, Dick Quinn, and Carl Thompson of the Studebaker Drivers Club, Inc., Box 791, Oswego, Ill. 60543.

Studebaker returned to the 259 V-8 (from 289 previously) in 1959. It put out 180 or 195 bhp, depending on carb and exhaust. Owner Reynolds has installed a later-model air conditioner.

specifications

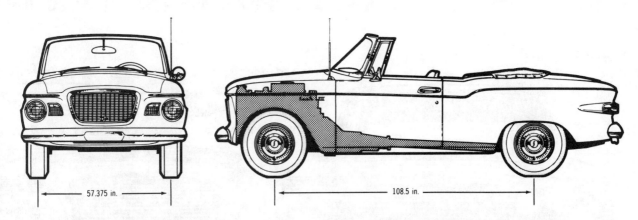

57.375 in.

108.5 in.

1960 Studebaker Lark Regal VIII Convertible

Price when new . . . . $2756 f.o.b. South Bend (1960).

Options . . . . .Flightomatic, air conditioning, Signal Seeker radio, heater, imitation leather, reclining seats with headrests, heavy-duty suspension, oil filter.

ENGINE
Type . . . . .Ohv V-8, cast-iron block, water cooled, 5 mains, full pressure lubrication.
Bore & stroke . . . . 3.56 x 3.25 in.
Displacement . . . . 259.2 cid.
Max. bhp @ rpm . . . . .180 @ 4500.
Max. torque @ rpm . . . . .260 @ 2800.
Compression ratio . . . . 8.8:1.
Induction system . . . . . . .Single 2-bbl downdraft carburetor.
Exhaust system . . . . .Cast-iron manifolds, single muffler.
Electrical system . . . . .12-volt battery/coil.

CLUTCH
Type . . . . None.

TRANSMISSION
Type . . . . .Flightomatic 3-speed automatic torque converter with planetary gears.
Ratios: 1st . . . . 2.40:1.
2nd . . . . 1.47:1.
3rd . . . . 1.00:1.
Reverse . . . . 2.00:1.

DIFFERENTIAL
Type .Hypoid, Hotchkiss drive.
Ratio. . . . . 3.07:1.
Drive axles . . . . Semi-floating.

STEERING
Type . . . . .Cam and single roller stud.
Turns lock to lock . . . . .4.5.
Ratio . . . . .Variable, 24.5:1 av.
Turn circle . . . . 40.0 ft.

BRAKES
Type . . . . .4-wheel hydraulic drums, international expanding.
Drum diameter . . . . .11-in. front, 10-in. rear.
Total lining swept area . . . . 172.8 sq. in.

CHASSIS & BODY
Frame. . . . . .Box-section steel, central X-member, 4 crossmembers.
Body construction . . . . All steel.
Body style . . . . .2-door, 5-passenger convertible.

SUSPENSION
Front . . . . .Unequal-length A-arms, coil springs, tubular hydraulic shock absorbers, link stabilizer bar.
Rear . . . . .Rigid axle, semi-elliptic leaf springs, tubular hydraulic shock absorbers.
Tires . . . . .6.40 x 15, tube type, 4-ply.
Wheels . . . . .Pressed steel, drop-center rims, lug-bolted to brake drum.

WEIGHTS & MEASURES
Wheelbase . . . . .108.5 in.
Overall length . . . . .175.0 in.
Overall height . . . . 57.5 in.
Overall width . . . . 71.38 in.
Front tread . . . . .57.375 in.
Rear tread. . . . . .56.562 in.
Ground clearance . . . . 8.5 in.
Curb weight . . . . 3492 lb.

CAPACITIES
Crankcase. . . . . .5.0 qt. (add 1 qt. for filter)
Cooling system . . . . .17.0 qt. (add 1 qt. for heater)
Fuel tank . . . . 18.0 gal.

FUEL CONSUMPTION
Best . . . . 18-20 mpg.
Average . . . . 14-16 mpg.

PERFORMANCE (from Motor Trend, 6/60, test of Lark conv. with optl. 195-bhp V-8):
0-30 mph . . . . 4.5 sec.
0-40 mph . . . . 8.5 sec.
0-50 mph . . . . 13.0 sec.
0-60 mph . . . . 14.7 sec.
0-70 mph . . . . 20.3 sec.
Standing ¼ mile . . . . .20.6 sec. & 71.0 mph.
Top speed (av.) . . . . .106.0 mph.

With its minimal front and rear overhang, Lark constitutes a compact with a full-sized interior. Upper series has chrome surrounding its grille.

1959-1966 Lark Spotter's Guide

by Jeff Godshall

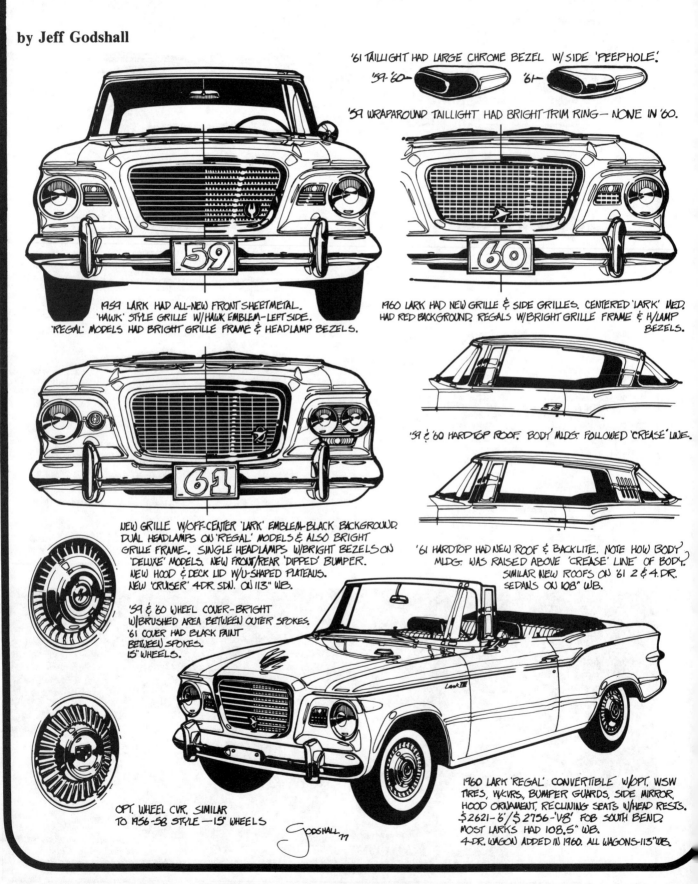

'61 TAILLIGHT HAD LARGE CHROME BEZEL W/SIDE 'PEEPHOLE'.

'59-'60 — '61 —

'59 WRAPAROUND TAILLIGHT HAD BRIGHT TRIM RING—NONE IN '60.

1959 LARK HAD ALL-NEW FRONT SHEETMETAL. 'HAWK' STYLE GRILLE W/HAWK EMBLEM—LEFT SIDE. 'REGAL' MODELS HAD BRIGHT GRILLE FRAME & HEADLAMP BEZELS.

1960 LARK HAD NEW GRILLE & SIDE GRILLES. CENTERED 'LARK' MED. HAD RED BACKGROUND. REGALS W/BRIGHT GRILLE FRAME & H/LAMP BEZELS.

'59 & '60 HARDTOP ROOF. BODY' MLDG. FOLLOWED 'CREASE' LINE.

'61 HARDTOP HAD NEW ROOF & BACKLITE. NOTE HOW BODY' MLDG. WAS RAISED ABOVE 'CREASE' LINE OF BODY. SIMILAR NEW ROOFS ON '61 2 & 4-DR. SEDANS ON 108" WB.

NEW GRILLE W/OFF-CENTER 'LARK' EMBLEM—BLACK BACKGROUND. DUAL HEADLAMPS ON 'REGAL' MODELS & ALSO BRIGHT GRILLE FRAME. SINGLE HEADLAMPS W/BRIGHT BEZELS ON 'DELUXE' MODELS. NEW FRONT/REAR 'DIPPED' BUMPER. NEW HOOD & DECK LID W/U-SHAPED PLATEAUS. NEW 'CRUISER' 4-DR. SDN. ON 113" WB.

'59 & '60 WHEEL COVER-BRIGHT W/BRUSHED AREA BETWEEN OUTER SPOKES. '61 COVER HAD BLACK PAINT BETWEEN SPOKES. 15" WHEELS.

OPT. WHEEL CVR. SIMILAR TO 1956-58 STYLE—15" WHEELS

Godshall '77

1960 LARK 'REGAL' CONVERTIBLE W/OPT. WSW TIRES, W/CVRS, BUMPER GUARDS, SIDE MIRROR, HOOD ORNAMENT, RECLINING SEATS W/HEAD RESTS. $2621-'6'/$2756-'V8' FOB SOUTH BEND? MOST LARKS HAD 108.5" WB. 4-DR. WAGON ADDED IN 1960. ALL WAGONS-113"WB.

Originally published in Special Interest Autos #42, Nov.-Dec. 1977

LARK

BEGINNING 1962 ALL SDNS. & WAGONS ON 113" WB.; ALL 2-DR. CARS ON 109" WB. 4 SERIES— DELUXE, REGAL, DAYTONA, & CRUISER (V-8 ONLY).
ALL MODELS HAD DUAL HEADLAMPS. 'DAYTONA' SERIES HDTP. & CONVERTIBLE HAD BUCKET SEATS & CONSOLE & SPL. BODY SIDE MLDG. W/DAYTONA SCRIPT. OTHER MODELS HAD 'DIPPED' MLDG. 2-DR. WAGON DROPPED.

NEW GRILLE W/MERCEDES-STYLING. TWO PROMINENT HORIZONTAL BARS OVERLAY THREE VERTICAL BARS. NEW HOOD & FRONT SHEETMETAL. NEW OPT. BUMPER GUARDS. GOLD 'LARK' EMBLEM @ LOWER LEFT. FINE MESH TEXTURE BEHIND BARS.

ALL MODELS HAD 'LARK' LETTERS ON FRONT FNDR. USE OF 'VIII' (8) & 'VI' (6) EMBLEMS DISCONTINUED. SIDE MLDGS. MOVED BACK TO BODY 'CREASE' LINE.

CAR MADE LONGER IN A MOVE AWAY FROM COMPACT LOOK. SOME MODELS OVER 13" LONGER.

ALL-NEW REAR END W/NEW QTR. PNLS., DECK LID. & LOWER DECK PNL. GAS FILLER MOVED FROM RIGHT QTR. TO ABOVE BUMPER ON ALL BUT WAGONS. NEW ROUND TAILLIGHTS W/INNER CHROME RING. NEW OVAL BACK-UP LAMPS. NEW REAR WINDOW ON SDNS. & HDTPS. NEW QTR. PNLS. & TAILLIGHTS ON WAGON. NEW 'V-8' EMBLEM FOR DECK LID.

1962 'CRUISER' SDN. HAD VENT WINDOWS IN REAR DOORS. $2493–V-8 ONLY.

1962 WHEEL COVER— SAME AS 1961 EXCEPT W/RED CENTER & WHITE PAINT BETWEEN OUTER SPOKES.

Godshall '77

1962 'DAYTONA' HDTP.— $2308: V-8-ADD $135. 'LARK' EMBLEM ON 'C' PILLAR.

NEW HOOD ORNAMENT.

NEW OPT. VERTICAL BUMPER GUARDS — & 'WINGUARD' BUMPER EXTENSIONS. STD. ON 'CRUISER' SDN.

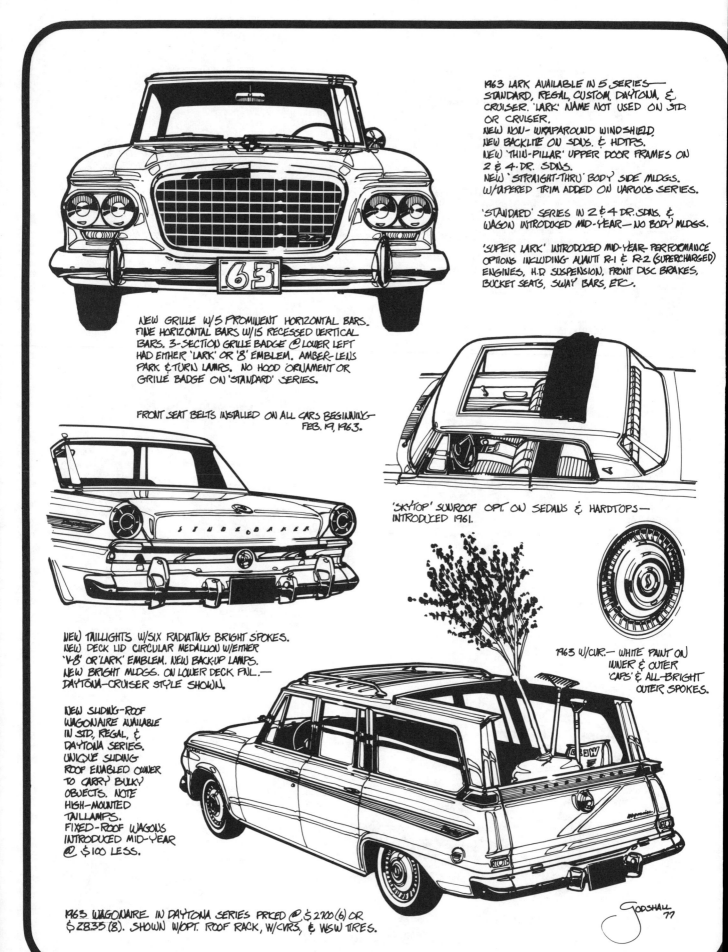

1963 LARK AVAILABLE IN 5 SERIES—
STANDARD, REGAL, CUSTOM DAYTONA, &
CRUISER. 'LARK' NAME NOT USED ON STD.
OR CRUISER.
NEW NON-WRAPAROUND WINDSHIELD.
NEW BACKLITE ON SDNS. & HDTPS.
NEW 'THIN-PILLAR' UPPER DOOR FRAMES ON
2 & 4-DR. SDNS.
NEW 'STRAIGHT-THRU' BODY SIDE MLDGS.
W/TAPERED TRIM ADDED ON VARIOUS SERIES.

'STANDARD' SERIES IN 2 & 4 DR. SDNS. &
WAGON INTRODUCED MID-YEAR— NO BODY MLDGS.

'SUPER LARK' INTRODUCED MID-YEAR-PERFORMANCE
OPTIONS INCLUDING AVANTI R-1 & R-2 (SUPERCHARGED)
ENGINES, H.D. SUSPENSION, FRONT DISC BRAKES,
BUCKET SEATS, SWAY BARS, ETC.

NEW GRILLE W/5 PROMINENT HORIZONTAL BARS.
FINE HORIZONTAL BARS W/15 RECESSED VERTICAL
BARS. 3-SECTION GRILLE BADGE @ LOWER LEFT
HAD EITHER 'LARK' OR '8' EMBLEM. AMBER-LENS
PARK & TURN LAMPS. NO HOOD ORNAMENT OR
GRILLE BADGE ON 'STANDARD' SERIES.

FRONT SEAT BELTS INSTALLED ON ALL CARS BEGINNING-
FEB. 19, 1963.

'SKYTOP' SUNROOF OPT. ON SEDANS & HARDTOPS—
INTRODUCED 1961.

NEW TAILLIGHTS W/SIX RADIATING BRIGHT SPOKES.
NEW DECK LID CIRCULAR MEDALLION W/EITHER
'V-8' OR 'LARK' EMBLEM. NEW BACK-UP LAMPS.
NEW BRIGHT MLDGS. ON LOWER DECK PNL.—
DAYTONA-CRUISER STYLE SHOWN.

1963 W/CVR.— WHITE PAINT ON
INNER & OUTER
'CAPS' & ALL-BRIGHT
OUTER SPOKES.

NEW SLIDING-ROOF
WAGONAIRE AVAILABLE
IN STD, REGAL, &
DAYTONA SERIES.
UNIQUE SLIDING
ROOF ENABLED OWNER
TO CARRY BULKY
OBJECTS. NOTE
HIGH-MOUNTED
TAILLAMPS.
FIXED-ROOF WAGONS
INTRODUCED MID-YEAR
@ $100 LESS.

1963 WAGONAIRE IN DAYTONA SERIES PRICED @ $2700 (6) OR
$2835 (8). SHOWN W/OPT. ROOF RACK, W/CVRS, & WSW TIRES.

GODSHALL
77

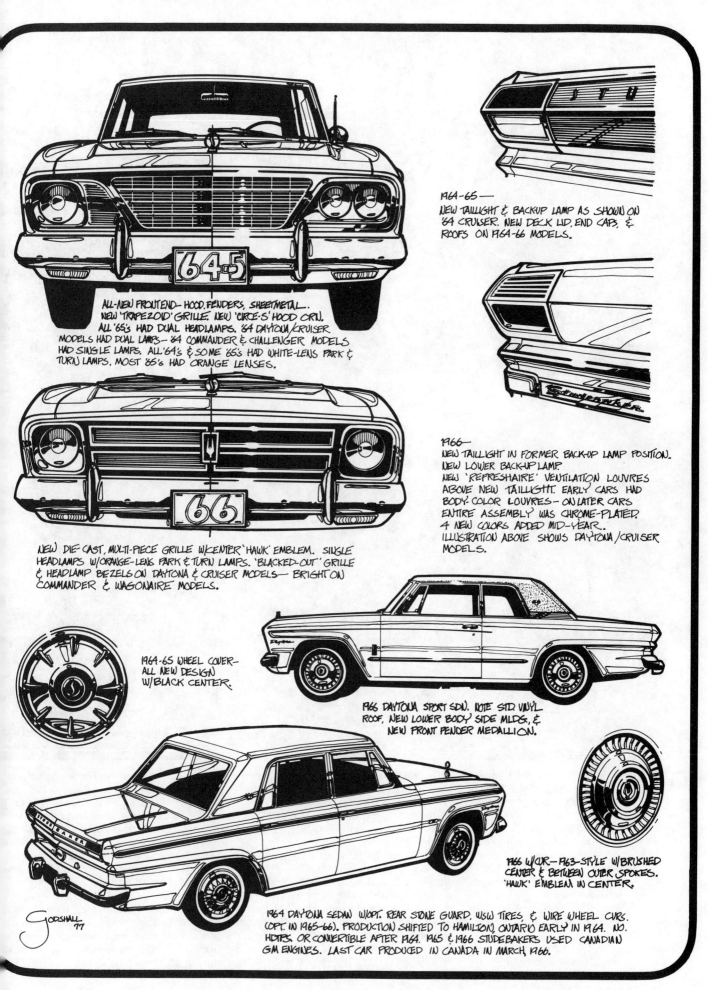

64-5

ALL-NEW FRONT END—HOOD, FENDERS, SHEETMETAL.
NEW 'TRAPEZOID' GRILLE. NEW 'CIRCLE-S' HOOD ORN.
ALL '65'S HAD DUAL HEADLAMPS. '64 DAYTONA/CRUISER
MODELS HAD DUAL LAMPS—'64 COMMANDER & CHALLENGER MODELS
HAD SINGLE LAMPS. ALL '64'S & SOME '65'S HAD WHITE-LENS PARK &
TURN LAMPS. MOST '65'S HAD ORANGE LENSES.

66

NEW DIE-CAST, MULTI-PIECE GRILLE W/CENTER 'HAWK' EMBLEM. SINGLE
HEADLAMPS W/ORANGE-LENS PARK & TURN LAMPS. 'BLACKED-OUT' GRILLE
& HEADLAMP BEZELS ON DAYTONA & CRUISER MODELS—BRIGHT ON
COMMANDER & WAGONAIRE MODELS.

1964-65—
NEW TAILLIGHT & BACKUP LAMP AS SHOWN ON
'64 CRUISER. NEW DECK LID, END CAPS, &
ROOFS ON 1964-66 MODELS.

1966—
NEW TAILLIGHT IN FORMER BACK-UP LAMP POSITION.
NEW LOWER BACK-UP LAMP.
NEW 'REFRESHAIRE' VENTILATION LOUVRES
ABOVE NEW TAILLIGHT. EARLY CARS HAD
BODY-COLOR LOUVRES—ON LATER CARS
ENTIRE ASSEMBLY WAS CHROME-PLATED.
4 NEW COLORS ADDED MID-YEAR.
ILLUSTRATION ABOVE SHOWS DAYTONA/CRUISER
MODELS.

1964-65 WHEEL COVER—
ALL NEW DESIGN
W/BLACK CENTER.

1966 DAYTONA SPORT SDN. NOTE STD VINYL
ROOF, NEW LOWER BODY SIDE MLDG., &
NEW FRONT FENDER MEDALLION.

1966 W/CVR—1963-STYLE W/BRUSHED
CENTER & BETWEEN OUTER SPOKES.
'HAWK' EMBLEM IN CENTER.

GODSHALL
'77

1964 DAYTONA SEDAN W/OPT. REAR STONE GUARD, WSW TIRES, & WIRE WHEEL CVRS.
(OPT. IN 1965-66). PRODUCTION SHIFTED TO HAMILTON, ONTARIO EARLY IN 1964. NO.
HDTPS. OR CONVERTIBLE AFTER 1964. 1965 & 1966 STUDEBAKERS USED CANADIAN
GM ENGINES. LAST CAR PRODUCED IN CANADA IN MARCH, 1966.

Convertible Wagon

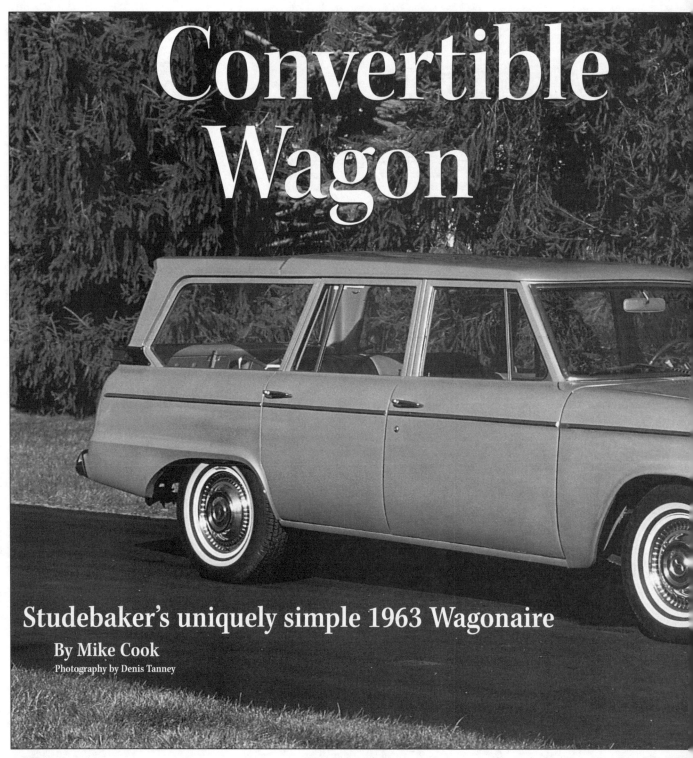

Studebaker's uniquely simple 1963 Wagonaire

By Mike Cook

Photography by Denis Tanney

With its responsive 259 small-block V-8 spinning out 180 hp at 4,500 rpm and a rear sliding roof that opens to the sky above, the 1963 Studebaker Wagonaire is one of the most distinctive station wagons ever created.

Ten years newer than the Willys wagon featured in *SIA* #165, the Wagonaire was no less unique—a station wagon with a rear roof section that could slide forward to accommodate tall loads. Conceived by designer Brooks Stevens, the roof feature made the car into what one Studebaker brochure

calls the "world's only wagon-convertible." It was an idea exclusive to Studebaker, one of the innovations the struggling manufacturer came up with as it tried to attract customers in its last years.

One of my friends, an industrial film producer, quickly saw the merit in the sliding roof and bought a Wagonaire as a camera car! I have vivid memories of that car rolling through New York on a shoot, with a cameraman standing up in the back filming away with his Arriflex on a tripod. Now, my nostalgia was rewarded by the sight of our feature '63

Wagonaire in its smooth coat of metallic Rose Mist paint, gassed and ready to go.

Owner Ward Ruoff had spent several days freeing the wagon from its winter storage cocoon of blankets and making it ready for the road as he had not driven it much since completing the restoration. The fuel system was cleared, the battery charged and the 259-cubic-inch V-8 was idling smoothly. Unfortunately, his test drive that morning turned up a leaking brake wheel cylinder which made pumping the brakes a necessity and they were erratic enough to prevent daring to do any highway driving. My

Originally published in Special Interest Autos #176, Mar.-Apr. 2000

plenty of go. The ride was firm but not bouncy. Without a seatbelt, I slid around on the vinyl, but that's the way cars were. The brake and accelerator pedal positions were good and I was relaxed, elbow out the window, and checking out stations on the vintage push-button AM radio.

Instruments and controls were all concentrated in front of me in the padded dashboard. Fuel, temperature, oil pressure and battery charge gauges were in the left of three round dials. The center one had the Studebaker "Lazy S" logo but could have contained either a clock or tachometer. The speedometer was on the right. White letters on charcoal instrument faces made for good visibility. Identical levers flanked the instruments, defrost on the left, heat on the right. The ignition switch and toggle switches for lights, interior light, fan and wipers were in a row below the instruments. A "T" handle for hood release, a small panel with the instrument dimmer and electric tailgate window switch, two vent control knobs and the cane-type handbrake were located below the dash. The large, two-spoked steering wheel had a Lark logo in the center and a chrome half-horn ring below the spokes.

The glove box had the word "Vanity" in script on the door. When opened, it revealed a vanity mirror à la Jaguar XJ sedan and a flip-up arrangement incorporating cup sockets and a storage box. Cup holders, no less; way ahead of its time!

I drove a few blocks, pumped the brakes, slowed with no problem and made a U-turn. Starting back, I was impressed again with the acceleration from the combination of Studebaker's overweight 259 and the old three-speed Borg Warner automatic, called "Flightomatic" by Studebaker. This unit was used by many of the world's car makers and catalogs show parts common to everything from Studebakers to Jaguars. I had no doubt that the car would cruise the highway at good speed.

Ward's Wagonaire was comfortable and solid with adequate power and plenty of room, but it was easy to see why Studebaker's 1963 literature dwelt on sturdy construction, durability, low purchase price and operating cost, styling, horsepower, ride; anything but handling and roadability. Even at 40 mph, this was an old-fashioned feeling car to drive. Studebaker grafted the new Raymond Loewy-styled bodies on to their vintage chassis in 1953 and, though styling changed drastically over the next thirteen years, the underpinnings didn't. Popular and profitable, the Lark kept Studebaker in business for a while, but cars from the Big Three had more modern suspensions and handled far better. The Studebaker front end had

driving impressions would have to be at 40 mph, max.

Despite a history of driving sports cars, I enjoy sitting high in a car. Entering the Studebaker was easy through the wide and tall door opening, and the seating position was fine. I sat erect, delighted to find that the top of the steering wheel was at my chin level, allowing excellent visibility through the deep windshield. The bench seat was adjustable fore and aft only but the seatback angle and padding suited my spine and I was immediately comfortable. The pedals were in easy reach and

the car has a wide brake pedal to allow left foot braking.

The glass area on the Studebaker was outstanding and there were no blind spots as I backed out into the street, noting that the turning circle was pretty large. I had to wind the wheel like raising an anchor to get around tight corners, but that's typical of some older domestic cars on which the manufacturer made no effort to improve the steering ratio despite power assist. Finding Drive on the old P-N-D-L-R quadrant, I pressed the gas pedal and the Wagonaire stepped right off with

quite ordinary independent suspension with coil springs and tube shocks. The rear had a straight axle with leaf springs and nothing else to locate it. Even the futuristic Avanti, launched in 1963, had the same suspension with traction bars and a rear anti-roll bar added as standard equipment.

Contemporary road tests bear out my opinion of the handling. In January 1962, *Motor Trend* tested a Studebaker Lark Daytona hardtop with mechanical specifications identical to our test Wagonaire. Though they liked the Daytona, *MT*'s editors said: "cornering ability is not as good as it could be" and referred to the springs being the only locators for the rear axle. In October of '62,

Road & Track tested a supercharged Avanti and downgraded it for handling despite the added axle locators, saying: "...the car does not get a very impressive grip on the road surface." They also commented that having 59 percent of the weight in the front caused marked initial understeer. Then, lack of rear traction caused it to swing out abruptly if power was applied too hard.

Half an hour in the car had given me a good overall impression, and I pulled back into Ward's driveway, noting that all gauges read normal. With the brakes fixed, this wagon would be ready to travel! It was time to check out how well it would handle loads for a trip. I pressed the toggle switch to lower the tailgate window and got out to study the car's unique roof. Interestingly, although the tailgate window could be electric, the sliding roof is manual. Operation is easy.

With the tailgate window lowered, I reached in and turned a large recessed central handle to unlock the sliding portion. Then I simply pushed it forward. It was certainly a good idea, well executed in terms of operation, but no attempt was made to conceal the workings. Ward says all of the wagons had the interior channels, etc., whether the sliding option was installed or not. He also says that they generally leak—the locking device also forces the section up against gaskets but the arrangement doesn't seal very well. Though it was certainly

Optional wheel covers liven up this Wagonaire.

Side markings include Lark fender lettering.

PROS & CONS

Pros
Affordable
Unique design
Great photographer's car

Con
Low status
Trim hard to find
Uninspired handling

Lark-embossings embellish the door panels.

Left: When it comes to hauling large parcels, the sky really is the limit. Above: A 1963 ad illustrates the Wagonaire in action.

Tailgate glass is electrically operated.

Two-spoke wheel permits superb visibility to all instruments.

the most interesting feature, the sliding rear roof was not standard on wagons in 1963. Studebaker literature shows an economy Wagonaire with a fixed steel top; evidently the sliding roof fixed in place without the hardware needed to open it.

In the tailgate, which drops down even with the interior floor, there is a recess for another option, a folding ladder that flipped over to rest on the ground to allow stepping up onto the tailgate and into the rear of the car. Friends in the Studebaker club warned Ward about installing and using it because the tailgate is a bit flimsy, not reinforced from the original, which was designed before the roof feature and step were conceived.

The cargo area is roomy. It had a very strong cargo floor of three-quarter-inch plywood and, with the roof open, could hold, for example, a refrigerator or a good-sized tree with root ball. No provision for a third seat was visible, but it was available and could be folded away into the rear floor where the spare tire normally resided. In the brochure, it notes that four "Captive-air, puncture-proof" tires were supplied when the rear-facing third seat was fitted.

This is a full six-passenger car (eight with the optional third seat) and the wide, high seats are like sitting on a firm sofa. The original upholstery had vinyl sides with cloth inserts that were very worn, so Ward replaced it with all vinyl in two-tone light rose and maroon. The light portion is a perfect match for the Rose paint. A factory all-vinyl interior

AT LAST GASP BUT STILL TRYING

By 1963, Studebaker was operating on a desperation basis—losing money and unable to sell enough cars to keep production home in South Bend, Indiana. There would be only three more years of production, the last two in Canada. But 1964 would be the last year for Studebaker engines. Cars built in Hamilton, Ontario, used Chevrolet sixes and eights. Yet, in those last years, Studebaker engineers and stylists hung in there, creatively restyling ten-year-old bodies and trying to attract buyers with innovations like the Wagonaire sliding roof and a broad range of power options.

How many other domestic cars offered a sun-roof as Studebaker did on the Lark Daytona? Beginning in 1963, disc brakes were a Studebaker option as well, something the foundering company might have skipped. Most manufacturers offered at least one model with four-speed stick, but Studebaker had it available on all V-8 models. There was a choice of six axle ratios available with limited slip differential. Even more impressive were the power options.

Beginning in 1951, as a 232.6-c.i.d. developing 102 horsepower, the Studebaker V-8 was soon standardized at 259 cubic inches. It was later punched out to 289, the "Thunderbolt" version. The base engines were rated at 180 and 210 hp with the standard two-barrel carburetor and dual exhaust. However, Jet Thrust versions, as used in Avantis, had higher compression and a Carter four-barrel while the Super Jet Thrust added a Paxton supercharg-

er. Jet Thrust horsepower was quoted at 225. Paxton blown figures were not released by the factory, but, in his *Studebaker Buyers Guide*, Dick Langworth quotes 290 hp for the production blown unit. Contrary to industry practice of offering the hottest engines only in fully loaded models, Studebaker would sell you a Jet Thrust in a basic "Standard" two-door.

Studebaker had been known for offering quality, low-priced cars and their market timing had sometimes been excellent. Witness the Lark which hit the market in 1959, a recession year, just in time to attract buyers with flatter-than-usual pocketbooks. They tried again in 1963 with a full range called "Standard," The brochure, headlined "From the Advanced Thinking of Studebaker," lists two- and four-door sedans and Wagonaires, all with vinyl upholstery and a minimum of chrome. The illustrations show no hood ornaments or wheel covers. Window trim is painted and tires are black-walls. The text spends a lot of space touting the Skybolt straight-six but the options list goes right up through the 4-barrel carb V-8 engine.

Other 1963 accessories included the push-button radio, bumper guards, the famous "Hill-holder" which kept manual shift cars from rolling back on hills, luggage racks and a hang-on, under-dash air conditioner. Even in 1966, the final year, there was a new grille treatment and added flow-through ventilation. Whatever the economic situation, Studebaker was still trying to offer a full range of products and options until the very end.

Decade-old chassis design gives the Wagonaire a dated ride, even for 1963.

was offered in '63, so his work is appropriate and a very professional looking job it is! He also changed the headliner to a perforated fabric type. The tattered original was molded fiber—Ward calls it "cardboard"—and was simply not available.

Originally, the windlace sealing the doors was the "fuzzy" type. Though it was available, he replaced it with handmade vinyl-covered seals for durability. The door panels are original with the attractive Lark emblem embossed in the upper section, but the bottom sections were recovered in black carpet over the original scruffy-looking black vinyl. He can't confirm if Larks came with carpet on the door panel bottom but some Hawk models had it.

When purchased, the car needed some bodywork, and it was soon apparent that the body differs quite a bit from the sedan. Once you get past the A-post, the roof seems to be completely different—not just an altered sedan roof. The entire upper structure looks different from the sedan, including the windows. Ward replaced the rear quarter panels with NOS parts and the rear doors with good used doors from a sedan. He had to use the original window frames on the rear doors because the wagon windows were a different shape. The tailgate required work, as the bottom was rusted out. He repainted the car in his garage and it is an excellent job.

The chrome on the taillight housings was bad. They are very difficult to find, being unique to the Wagonaire, so he

OWNER'S OUTLOOK

Ward Ruoff, an electronics engineer for a sizable computer firm, may have gained the prerequisite restoration knowledge at a small shop he once worked for, but the passion he has for Studebakers came from his dad. "I was 15 when my father bought me my first car, a 1963 Hawk," Ward vividly recollects. Like most enthusiasts he's been hooked on the marque he was first introduced to ever since.

"In 1988, one of my friends told me that he was going to sell his daily-driven Wagonaire," Ward continues. "I always liked the quirkiness and originality of the wagon's folding roof and distinctive Rose Mist paint, so I bought it from him. At first I was just going to liven it up with a new coat of paint and some interior work." Ward quickly fell under the mesmerizing restoration spell and wound up redoing the entire car.

"The Wagonaire went from a whole car, to being apart in my garage, to becoming a mess. When that finally happened, I found it difficult to stay interested," Ward confides. Wanting the car back to being whole again and tired of having his garage under siege, Ward arduously pressed on with the restoration.

He did every part of the refurbishment himself except for welding on the two new rear quarter panels. "While I was refinishing the Wagonaire, one of my friends was restoring a 1952 Chevy. We wound up bartering our services with each other. I reupholstered his interior and he welded on my quarter panels. It worked out great for both of us."

Now that the Wagonaire is whole again Ward takes great pride driving and showing it. "It's not simply another everyday car," Ward proudly explains. "With its sliding rear roof section and unique color, it's even unusual for a Studebaker."

The Wagonaire may not get the same 30 mpg as his commuter-conscious Honda, but the Studebaker's durable V-8 returns a very satisfying 20 mpg. "That's better than most 1960s cars," Ward proudly informs us. "Behind the wheel, the seating is very upright and visibility is at a premium. And because it has manual steering and brakes it doesn't drive like my everyday Honda, but it's not really supposed to either."

specifications

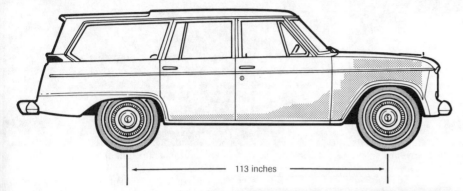

113 inches

57.375 inches

1963 Studebaker Wagonaire

ENGINE

Type	Water cooled V-8, overhead valve, cast iron block and heads, 5 main bearings
Bore x stroke	3.56 inches x 3.25 inches
Displacement	259 cubic inches
Compression ratio	8.5:1
Firing order	1, 8, 4, 3, 6, 5, 7, 2
Horsepower @ rpm	180 @ 4,500
Torque @ rpm	260 @ 2,800
Factory redline	4,800 rpm
Fuel system	Stromberg 2-barrel carburetor, Carter mechanical fuel pump
Electrical system	12-volt system with 35-amp alternator, negative ground

TRANSMISSION

Type	Optional 3-speed "Flightomatic," column shift with PNDLR quadrant
Ratios	1st: 2.40:1; 2nd: 1.47:1; 3rd: 1.00:1; Reverse: 2.00:1
Rear axle	3.31:1

STEERING

Type	Saginaw recirculating ball. Optional power steering on test car
Ratio	24:1
Turns lock-to-lock	4.4 (with power)
Steering wheel	17 inches

BRAKES

Type	4-wheel, cast-iron drums, hydraulically actuated
Front drums	11 x 2 inches
Rear drums	10 x 2 inches
Total braking area	172.8 square inches
Parking brake	Pedal type

CHASSIS & BODY

Construction	Box section, double drop construction, all-steel ladder chassis with 4 top cross-members and central X-member. All body panels stamped steel

SUSPENSION

Front	Independent with upper and lower control arms, coil springs and telescopic shock absorbers. Stabilizer bar fitted to all V-8 powered models
Rear	Straight axle with 4 leaf springs. Frame mounted telescopic shock absorbers
Tires	6.50 x 15 inch 2-ply
Wheels	15-inch steel disc with 4.5-inch rims

WEIGHTS AND MEASURES

Wheelbase	113 inches
Overall length	190.1875 inches
Overall width	71.25 inches
Overall height	57 inches
Front track	57.375 inches
Rear track	56.5625 inches
Ground clearance	7.6875 inches
Curb weight	3,435 pounds
Turning circle	30 feet

CAPACITIES

Engine oil	5 quarts
Cooling system	17 quarts, 18 with Climatizer system
Fuel tank	18 gallons
Auto. transmission	18 pints
Rear axle	2.5 pints

PERFORMANCE

Acceleration 0-30	5.0 seconds
0-60	14.3 seconds
Standing 1/4 mile	21.2 seconds
Top speed	Est. 90-95 mph
Fuel consumption	14-17 miles per US gallon

(From *Motor Trend* test of 1962 Lark Daytona Convertible with same engine and transmission. The convertible was 130 pounds lighter but carried a passenger.)

---

painted them satin black. The attractive result looks like molded black polycarbonate. He later found good chromed housings but likes the black. The bumpers were replaced with NOS while still available.

I liked the shape of the Wagonaire. There are no lines out of place and the trim is extremely simple. The grille is very Mercedes-like (remember that

Reasonable power comes from the optional 359 V-8 engine.

107

Prop-up mirror stows beneath the "Vanity"-inscribed glovebox cover.

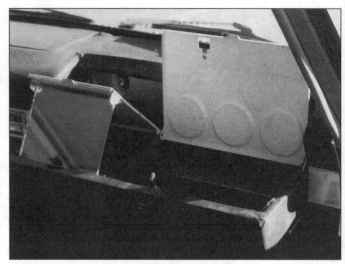
Separate compartment contains cup socket and storage box.

SPECIALISTS & RESTORERS

Kelley's Korner
22 14th St.
Dept. SIA-176
Bristol, TN 37620
423-968-5583
Engine rebuilds, brake, suspension, and electrical service

Royal Gorge Studebaker
109 West Front St.
Dept. SIA-176
Florence, CO 81226
719-784-4169
Complete restoration service

Steve's Studebaker-Packard
P.O. Box 6914
Dept. SIA-176
Napa, CA 94581
707-255-8945
Suspension rebuilding

Studebakers West
335A Convention Way
Dept. SIA-176
Redwood City, CA 94063
650-366-8787
Mechanical, chassis, engine, transmission, and electrical work.

PARTS SUPPLIERS

Egge Machine Company
11707 Slauson Ave., Dept. SIA-176
Santa Fe Springs, CA 90670
800-866-EGGE
E-mail: info@egge.com
Full line of bearings, valve train, and internal engine parts.

Kelley's Korner
22 14th St., Dept. SIA-176
Bristol, TN 37620
423-968-5583
Mechanical and electrical parts

L&L Antique Auto Trim
403 Spruce
Box 177, Dept. SIA-176
Pierce City, MO 65723
417-476-2871
Running boards and moldings

Phil's Studebaker
11250 Harrison Rd., Dept. SIA-176
Osceola, IN 46561-9375
219-674-0084
NOS, reproduction and used parts

Royal Gorge Studebaker
109 West Front St., Dept. SIA-176

Florence, CO 81226
719-784-4169
Extensive line of mechanical, electrical, and trim parts

Steve's Studebaker-Packard
P.O. Box 6914, Dept. SIA-176
Napa, CA 94581
707-255-8945
Suspension and mechanical parts

Studebaker of California
1400 Santa Fe Ave., Dept. SIA-176
Long Beach, CA 90813
562-435-0157
Reproduction and NOS parts for 1945-up cars

Studebaker Parts & Locations
228 Marquiss Cir., Dept. SIA-176
Clinton, TN 37716
615-457-3002
Parts and parts locator for 1939 and up

Studebakers West
335A Convention Way, Dept. SIA-176
Redwood City, CA 94063
650-366-8787
Mechanical, engine, electrical, and chassis parts

Studebaker was the US distributor for Mercedes until mid-1965) with a chrome surround and a grid pattern with polished horizontal bars. Atop the grille stands a small Lazy S in a chrome frame. Chrome housings holding paired headlights and rectangular parking lights flank the grille.

Side identification consists of "Lark" lettering on the forward end of the front fenders and the Lazy S in the center of the very shiny, red-rimmed chrome wheel covers. Studebaker is lettered across the top of the tailgate door and Wagonaire, in script, is at lower right. Some brochure photos show small bumper guards, front and rear, but this Wagonaire did not have them. Viewing from the rear, I noted that the high-mounted taillights anticipated later safety trends.

Ward Ruoff already had several Studebakers but "wanted a wagon." He purchased his for $250 from another Studebaker fan in Philadelphia who used it as his business vehicle. He was a piano tuner, but presumably even the Wagonaire roof couldn't accommodate a piano! Ward set out to put the car in good condition as a regular driver. He did not want a restoration, just a good looking, good running car, but got into the spirit of the thing and went through the entire car, doing all the work himself. Despite his desire for a driver, it has accumulated virtually no miles in 12 years of ownership and shows 98,568—probably original. Having gotten it running for our photo and test session, he resolved to take it out on the road this year.

Ward came by his Studebaker enthusiasm from his father who drove them regularly and wore out one '63 Lark driving back and forth to Brooklyn from their home in Buffalo. Dad gave the Lark to Ward and bought a Daytona. Starting with that Lark when he was fifteen, Ward has accumulated five other South Bend products in addition to the Wagonaire. They are a 1963 Lark two-door, 1950 Champion four-door bullet nose, 1950

Champion business coupe, 1956 pickup, and 1957 supercharged Golden Hawk.

Until a year or so ago, all of these resided in Buffalo, but they are now stored on his property in New Jersey, save for the Champion business coupe, which is being restored in Buffalo. Often acquired at very reasonable prices, some of the cars are in decent shape, some pretty far gone, but all represent an enthusiasm that developed as he grew up. He comments that most are worth very little. The Golden Hawk is the most valuable. It is worth at least twice as much as the Wagonaire but, as cars go, collecting Studebakers is economical.

The Studebaker Wagonaire was a simple, honest car. Its straight-line styling is actually rather handsome. Built to haul people and cargo with a minimum of problems, it had few features and no plethora of "systems." As a special interest car, it offers only the unique roof—the rest is Plain Jane South Bend. By 1963, US manufacturers had recovered from the excess slathers and chrome of the 1950s, but the Wagonaire still stands out with minimal trim—chrome side strip, simple chrome bumpers usable at either end of the car, chrome quad light housings and chrome grille. It is almost European looking—the grille adapted from Mercedes adds to the impression.

Ruoff's lovingly restored Wagonaire is not in demand as a collectible, even though only 11,915 were built in 1963. That doesn't matter; it isn't for sale. He owns and works on other cars—there's an Austin-Healey Sprite "in the process" in his garage right now, but he just likes Studebakers and he will go on liking them and that's that! ೞ

WHAT TO PAY

Model	Low	Avg.	High
Lark 4-dr. Wagon	$2,000	$3,500	$5,000
Lark Daytona			
4-dr. Wagon	$2,500	$4,000	$5,800
Lark Regal			
4-dr. Wagon	$2,300	$3,500	$5,000
Air conditioning			
add	$500	$800	$1,000

MUSEUM

Studebaker National Museum
525 South Main St.
South Bend, IN 45501
888-391-5600
Regalia and research

PARTS PRICES

Carpet set	$190.00
Clutch	$89.00
Driveshaft rebuild kit	$90.00
Engine gasket set (V-8)	$120.00
Ignition switch	$85.00
Master cylinder repair kit	$40.00
Power steering repair kit	$160.00
Relined brake shoes (front)	$40.00
Windshield seal	$70.00
Wire harness (dashboard forward)	$275.00

PRODUCTION

1963 Wagonaire 10,487

MURDER OR SUICIDE?

The Studebaker marque died a controversial death in another country. Automotive historians and car nuts have been discussing the circumstances of its demise ever since and the opinions are both strong and varied.

Dick Langworth, in *The Illustrated Studebaker Buyer's Guide*, says: "Studebaker has had a bum rap." He goes on to talk about the brillance of Studebaker design and the frequent successes the company had before World War II. *Car And Driver's* editorial staff, writing in their March 1964 issue, describes Studebaker as a company that had never known failure, then pillories Albert R. Erskine, who became president of a highly profitable Studebaker in the late 1920s and left in 1933, having bankrupted the company. *Car And Driver's* thesis is that despite lasting thirty more years, the company never recovered.

Sales were back up by WWII, due to the very nice-looking and good-performing Champion, styled by Raymond Loewy. Well supplied with cash from wartime contracts building trucks and aircraft engines, Studebaker scored first in the post-war design race, launching the first modern car design as a 1947. This was the car that suffered endless jokes about being doubled-ended and how it was impossible to tell if it was coming or going, but people liked it. So successful were these new, fenderless models that the company came close to five percent of the car market, selling over 268,000 in 1950. Though volume dropped off in the next few years, the company was making lots of money and they had vision enough to commission Loewy to do another complete re-design for 1953.

Certainly the best-looking new design of the 1950s, the new Starliner hardtop and Starlight coupe won instant public accep-

tance. However, stodgy Studebaker sales people demanded that Loewy's sedan design depart from the coupe's low European look. The result was a tall, dumpy-looking car with only a hint of the coupe's grace. Completing the debacle, Studebaker had scheduled only 20 percent coupes for 1953 production and 80 percent sedans. Public demand was the reverse.

Losing money, Studebaker merged with Packard, strictly to get tax-loss credits, according to *Car And Driver*. Packard died in 1958. A new working arrangement with Curtiss-Wright, which needed manufacturing facilities, provided the cash to develop and launch the Lark, leading to a 1959 profit. The Board did not see fit to invest the profit in tooling needed to keep the Lark competitive against the 1960 compacts coming from the Big Three and the final downward slide began.

This was a company that made over a million dollars in 1878 building horse-drawn wagons. This was the car-maker in fifth place overall in the USA in the mid-twenties. It was a company that was bankrupt in 1933 and made a profit in 1935! It was also the firm whose sales people thought that their product line of Champion, Commander and President should be topped by a luxury model called Dictator! When profits were made, time after time, Studebaker directors refused to invest to stay competitive in the market.

Public preferences and Big Three competition were major factors, but erratic Studebaker management really toppled the company. John M. Studebaker built the company to a peak in the 1920s and Albert Erskine put it in receivership. Paul G. Hoffman took over and made it profitable again. When he left in 1948, Harold Vance couldn't maintain the pace.

James Nance, who came in with the Packard merger lost $74 million in two years. The Lark was developed under Harold Churchill who, despite making a profit, was ousted by the company's banker/receivers, who wanted to dump the car business and concentrate on the corporation's profitable subsidiaries.

While the car business was floundering, the company had invested in other industries. The *Canadian Financial Post* for February 13, 1965, a year after Studebaker production was moved to Hamilton, Ontario, stated that while Studebaker Corporation lost $17 million in 1963, all of the subsidiaries, such as Onan Generators and Gravely Tractors, made money. Subsidiary profits actually put Studebaker in the black in 1964 despite a drastic drop in car sales. No wonder Wall Street wanted Studebaker out of the car business. Churchill was dumped, replaced as CEO by Clarence Francis who stayed only long enough to hire Sherwood Egbert from McCullough. Egbert revamped the dealer organization and tried hard to energize South Bend, but he also conceived the Avanti which, despite its futuristic image, merely drained money from the dying car company. Egbert's replacement, Byers Burlingame, conducted the funeral.

A 1958 quote from General Motors Chairman, Frederic Donner, appears in both Langworth's book and *Car And Driver*. Asked in 1958 if GM was trying to drive the small automakers out of business, he said: "And when did you stop beating your wife? If you are thinking of Studebaker-Packard, did you ever stop to wonder what they did with the profits of the lush war years? Did they reinvest them in the business? We didn't drive them to their present condition. They drove themselves there." What more can we add?

STUDEBAKER R3 AVANTI

by Fred K. Fox
photos by George Krem, Jr.
and George Krem, Sr.

I N the fall of 1963, any adventurous American car buyer who had about $6,000 to spare, could walk into his local Studebaker dealership and place an order for an R3 Studebaker Avanti with a 2.87:1 rear axle ratio, four-speed transmission and dual valve springs. If all went well, in about a month our adventurous buyer would receive delivery of the fastest — up to that time — purely stock car ever built in America. If he could find a straightaway long enough — and had the nerve — his new Avanti could propel him up to 170 mph. This could be done immediately since all R3 engines were thoroughly broken in before being installed in Avanti chassis.

Sadly, no buyer ever ordered exactly the car described above. Although never ordered, such a car was not some secret offering known only to the Bonneville Salt Flat crowd. The R3 performance package and 2.87:1 axle were clearly listed in Studebaker literature which included the full line "Different...by

Design" showroom display book. The optional dual valve springs were also no secret. Detailed information on the special valve springs was given in the standard "AMA Specifications" forms issued in August 1963. The performance of such a car was clearly described in major articles in *Hot Rod, Motor Trend* and other enthusiasts' magazines. In September 1963, Andy Granatelli drove "#9" Avanti, an R3 production prototype with specifications just like our "adventurer's" car, to a two-way United States Auto Club timed flying mile record of 170.75 mph. The previous top speed for an American production car was the 153 mph attained by Mickey Thompson in a Pontiac Catalina.

Although a 170 mph Avanti was never sold through a Studebaker dealer, nine production R3 Avantis with more manageable rear axle ratios found their way out of dealership doors and into private garages. Though extremely rare, these nine cars were definitely production model vehicles, although their production heritage was far from ordinary.

The general story of the Studebaker Avanti was detailed in *SIA #32*. Briefly, the Avanti project was instigated in March 1961 by Sherwood Egbert, Studebaker-Packard's dynamic new

six-foot four-inch, 40-year-old president. Egbert had previously been executive vice president of California's profitable McCulloch Corporation. His official hiring at Studebaker in February 1961 caused quite a storm. Many executives and old-time employees were very displeased about having a California hot shot take over the venerable old Indiana firm.

Egbert and Raymond Loewy got together and started laying out the plans for the Avanti project. Loewy and three other designers locked themselves in a rented home in Palm Springs, California, and in just over two weeks they had a ⅛-scale clay model and detailed drawings completed. The model and drawings were handed over to Studebaker designer Robert Doehler, and by April 27, 1961, Bob and his clay modelers had a full-sized Avanti clay finished. It was one of the fastest styling developments in the history of automobile production.

Egbert showed the full-sized clay to the board and convinced them that the Avanti was the way to go. The board gave the OK for the Avanti to be put into production. Not much money was available, so it was decided to make the Avanti body out of fiberglass and mount it on a slightly modified Lark V-8 convertible chassis. Fiberglass body construction reduced initial tooling costs and allowed some styling techniques that could not easily be achieved with metal.

The Avanti body styling created by Loewy's group and Bob Doehler gave

Egbert the "advanced styling" he was looking for. Next he turned his attention to performance. There was absolutely no money for developing a new suspension system or engine, so he was forced to use the V-8 engine and suspension components that Studebaker had first introduced in 1951. Both had been upgraded through the years, but by 1961 they certainly were not on the leading edge of technology. Working with Studebaker's engineering boss, Gene Hardig, Egbert had the Lark suspension beefed up by adding a rear sway bar and rear radius rods. For roll-over protection, a roll bar was fastened to the frame. Outside of engine modifications, the most dynamic chassis development was the adoption of front disc brakes. The disc brakes were built by Bendix under license from Dunlop and were essentially the same as those used by Jaguar. The Avanti was the first full-sized American car to use caliper-type disc brakes. The final non-engine chassis development was in the transmission area. A three-speed transmission with floor shift lever was standard. Optional was a four-speed or a "Power-shift" automatic. Studebaker had introduced a four-speed on its 1961 Hawk, but the Power-shift was new for the Avanti. Essentially, the Power-shift was a modification of Studebaker's Borg-Warner Flightomatic. The Power-shift was operated by a console lever and could be manually shifted from first to second to third or just put in drive. If desired, it could be held in first or

second. In drive, it started in second and then shifted to third. This was a short-coming, and many Avanti owners eventually modified their automatics so that they would start in first when placed in drive.

Egbert's final challenge was to get some road-burning performance out of Studebaker's small V-8. When introduced in 1951, it displaced 232.6 cubic inches and produced only 120 horsepower. By 1961, it was being marketed as a 259 and a 289. The 289-cubic-inch version with a four-barrel carburetor produced 225 horsepower. Two hundred and twenty-five horsepower was adequate for most of Studebaker's applications, but it certainly wouldn't make the Avanti famous for high-speed performance. To partially solve the problem, Hardig directed the development of two new versions of the 289 engine. The first, labeled the R1, was a normally aspirated engine with 10.25:1 compression ratio and a new camshaft. The higher compression ratio (the regular 289 was 8.5:1) and slightly wilder cam increased the horsepower to 240. The second version was fitted with a Paxton Model SN supercharger. Studebaker had used superchargers in 1957-58, so their application was nothing new to Hardig. The supercharged version was labeled the R2. It used the new cam, a 9.0:1 compression ratio to allow for use of the blower, and a sealed Carter AFB four-barrel carburetor (the 1957-58 supercharged models had used a two-barrel carburetor). The R2 was rated at 289 horsepower. Today, 240 and 289 horsepower sounds pretty impressive, but these are old gross-horsepower ratings; also in 1962, many engines produced considerably more horsepower. For instance, Chevrolet's famous 409 was good for one horsepower per cubic inch. Realizing that trying to compete with Detroit's horsepower ratings was impossible, Egbert chose not to advertise horsepower figures for the R series engines. Although not in the 300 plus horsepower bracket, the R1 and R2 engines did quite well when installed in the new Avanti. Lightweight fiberglass construction and a very slippery body allowed the Avanti to turn in some pretty impressive performance figures. A stock R2-powered Avanti topped 158 mph at Bonneville, and *Road & Track* tested an R2 Avanti with four-speed that did 0-60 in 7.3 seconds. Many contemporary cars with much more power could not do as well, but Egbert was not satisfied. Enter Anthony Granatelli.

Andy Granatelli was born on March 18, 1923, in Dallas, Texas, but he grew up in Chicago with grease under his fingernails and gas fumes in his lungs. Along with brothers Vince and Joe, Andy loved nothing better than driving and building high-speed cars. By the late fifties he had developed quite a rep-

AMERICA'S FASTEST STOCK CAR?

R3 AVANTI
continued

utation for his hot-rodding abilities and his Grancor line of speed equipment. His achievements were well known to Egbert. Actually, Egbert was personally acquainted with Granatelli. They had met in 1958 when Granatelli purchased the Paxton Products division from the McCulloch Corporation, Egbert's former employer. The name Paxton came from Robert P. Mc-Culloch's middle name. In 1958, Paxton's main product was belt-driven McCulloch superchargers, most of which were sold to

Studebaker. After Granatelli took over, the superchargers were made more reliable and renamed Paxton instead of McCulloch. In the late fifties and early sixties, the Granatellis were putting Paxton superchargers on all kinds of cars and dragging them out to Bonneville to see how fast they would go. Andy and his brothers got a Corvair to do 128 mph; a six-cylinder Falcon Ranchero topped 144 mph, and a Paxton supercharged Chrysler 300F did the flying mile at 166 mph.

Egbert was convinced that Andy Granatelli was the man he needed to give the Avanti *real* performance image. Since the R2 Avanti was scheduled to

use Paxton superchargers, and Studebaker was still looking for profitable subsidiaries, Egbert approached Granatelli about buying Paxton Products. Of course, Egbert wanted Andy and his brothers to be included in the package deal. In March 1962, just one month before the Avanti was publicly unveiled, the Studebaker-Packard Corporation (renamed the Studebaker Corporation on July 2, 1962) purchased Paxton Products and appointed Andy Granatelli as head of the division. There was no secret about why Granatelli had been brought on board. In a report to the shareholders at the annual meeting on April 26, 1962 (the day the Avanti was first publicly shown), Egbert noted that "Andy Granatelli...will assist in developing a performance image for our Studebaker Automotive Division...."

Egbert's fast moving style kept Andy on his toes. The *very* next day after the Paxton sale contract was signed, Egbert called Andy in Santa Monica, California, at 4.00 AM and laid out what he wanted achieved before the annual meeting. A prototype Avanti was secretly shipped to Santa Monica in March 1962. Egbert instructed the Granatellis to hop-up the R2 engine so it could produce some

What Makes an R3 an R3?

Exactly what did the Granatellis do to the old Studebaker V-8 to make it capable of propelling an Avanti up to 170 mph? The metamorphosis was pretty standard in racing circles, but it was something completely out of the ordinary for a production automobile. As mentioned, V-8 engine components were shipped from Studebaker's plant in South Bend, Indiana, to the Paxton Products facility in Santa Monica, California. The process involved numerous modifications, blueprinting and meticulous assembly. First the bare blocks were carefully checked and machined if necessary to make certain the cylinder decks were exactly parallel to crankshaft and at right angles to the cylinder bores. Next, the cylinders were bored out 3/32 of an inch to give a bore of 3 21/32 inches. The 289 stroke of 3⅝ inches was retained. The increased bore raised the displacement to 304.5 cubic inches (a few early R3 prototype engines displaced 299.4 cubic inches). At 304.5 cubic inches (4,991 cubic centimeters), the R3 engine was just within the five-liter (305 cubic inch) limit of the National and International Class C designation.

Heads with larger ports were specially cast for the R3 engine. These heads were fitted with much larger valves (1⅞-inch intake and 1⅝-inch exhaust) than used on R1 and R2 engines. Valves were undercut and polished. The heads were carefully machined and polished so that all eight combustion chambers had exactly the same volume. Single valve springs were standard, but Iskenderian dual valve springs were an option. Maximum rpm with the single springs was about 6,000, but with duals, the engine could be pushed to 8,000 rpm.

A slightly wilder 276° cam was fitted in the block, and a 288° cam was optional (dual valve springs were required with the 288° cam). Both were acceptable for street use and neither was as wild as the 300° cams used on some of the big block super stock engines of the era. The standard forged steel 289 crank was used, but with heavy-duty bearings and extra bearing

clearances to reduce friction. Stock connecting rod forgings were machined to take a press fit wrist pin. This eliminated the need for slotting the rod and using a clamp bolt. Special flat top, tin-plated forged aluminum pistons were purchased from Forgedtrue. The top edges of the cylinder bores were chamfered to match the cylinder head combustion chambers and allow clearance for the larger valves. Before assembly, the completed block was dye-checked to make sure it was perfect. Major moving parts were balanced and magnafluxed.

Regular R2 engines used a sealed Carter AFB carburetor with the blower feeding into the top. On the R3, as on earlier 1957-58 supercharged Studebaker engines, the carburetor was put inside a cast-aluminum pressure box. Unlike the earlier style, a four-barrel instead of a two-barrel carburetor was used. The pressure box was fitted with a flapper valve at the top that only closed when there was boost pressure. The open valve allowed venting of gas vapors and improved hot starting. On R3s, the carburetor was bolted to a special-made aluminum intake manifold. Because of the aluminum intake manifold, no heat riser valve was used, and the passage that allowed the exhaust heat to pass through the intake manifold was limited to about ⅜-inch diameter by a special threaded plug. People who have added a heat riser and removed the plug soon discover that they have burned out the intake manifold. R3s weren't engineered for quick short trips in cold weather. Custom exhaust headers were also used on R3 engines. As on all R series engines, a dual point Prestolite distributor was used, but on R3s a Prestolite transistor ignition system and special steel/silicone ignition wiring was added as standard equipment. On R3s, the distributor had no vacuum advance, only mechanical. R3s also had an oversize pan, a high capacity oil pump and extra breather caps. To keep the fan belt from jumping off, the alternator pulley was increased to 4¼ inches in diameter.

After very careful assembly, every R3 engine was attached to a dynamometer and run through a pre-selected cycle of different rpm ranges and water temperatures. During the three-hour break-in period, the oil was changed, the head bolts re-torqued, the valve clearances reset and the engine re-timed for maximum output. Every engine had to produce a minimum of 335 horsepower @ 5,350 rpm before it was approved for shipment to South Bend. According to Vincent Granatelli, R3 engines fitted with an optional high-output pulley set would produce 400 horsepower at 6,000 rpm. Remember, this was when the old gross-horsepower system was used. But even by today's standards, a high-performance R3 engine would probably exceed 300 SAE net horsepower. Compare that to the 200-250 horsepower ratings of today's "supercars" and you can better understand why an R3 Avanti can blow the doors off any stock domestic production car sold in America in 1986.

After final testing, the completed engines were boxed and shipped to South Bend for installation. Each engine was stamped with a special Paxton Products "B--" serial number. The engines were easy to recognize because the blocks were painted red. All other 1964 Studebaker blocks — except the R4 — were painted black. The later-developed R4 was a very high compression ratio (12:1) version of the R3 with two normally aspirated four-barrel AFB carburetors. Very few of the 280 horsepower R4s were built and only one was put in a production Studebaker, a Daytona hardtop special built for *Car Life* magazine. An experimental "R5" model with dual carbs, dual superchargers and Bendix fuel injection turned 196.62 mph at Bonneville, but this model — tagged the "Due Cento" — was never considered for regular production. R3s had a 9.75:1 compression ratio, but of course the supercharger, when at full boost, helped produce combustion chamber pressures closely equivalent to those of the R4. Both required ultra high octane fuel.

eally remarkable speed records. Working at a feverish pace — standard modus operandi for the Avanti project — the Granatellis performed some remarkable surgery on the old Studebaker engine. Eugene Hardig later told Andy that he had learned in 40 days more about performance shortcuts than he had gained in his 40 years of engineering experience.

On Friday, April 13, 1962, the hopped-up Avanti was taken to Jean, Nevada (about 30 miles southwest of Las Vegas), and put through its paces. During one run, it reached a timed top speed of 171.10 mph! The speed was verified by Thomas Bryant, president of the Southern California Timing Association. The speed was not an official two-way flying mile average and, of course, the car was not a production model. Some magazines, such as Car and Driver in its July 1962 issue, incorrectly reported that the speed was set by a production R2 model. Car and Driver went so far as to say that the new Avanti was "indisputably the fastest genuine production car in America, if not the world." Egbert created this misconception at the April 26 meeting when he proclaimed that the new Avanti was "the world's fastest production car." Egbert would have undoubtedly admitted that he was a little premature with his statement, but he certainly had no idea that it would be almost a year and a half before Andy Granatelli's creation would be offered for sale.

Both Egbert and Granatelli hoped that the hot engine — dubbed the R3 — could be quickly put into production. R3 engine specifications were established and sent in to the Automobile Manufacturers Association in July 1962. Information sent to dealers in May 1962 included mention of an optional "Studebaker Paxton Modified Engine," but it was noted that orders for such a powerplant would delay shipment. The plan called for engine assemblies to be sent to Santa Monica, modified and assembled by the Granatellis and then shipped back to South Bend where they would be installed in production Avantis. The plan sounded great, except for one problem: There were no Avantis to install them in! Egbert hoped to produce 1,000 Avantis per month. Instead, assembly difficulties held production down to only 24 cars in June and a lowly 14 in July. Egbert called the situation "organized chaos." All efforts were put into getting the assembly problems solved, and therefore the R3 engine was put on the back burner. The Avanti had been enthusiastically received by the press and buying public, but the lack of available cars was causing many cancelled orders and a widespread loss of confidence in the car. Added to all this, Egbert had cancer. In July 1961 he underwent

cancer surgery, and although he appeared to be making a remarkable recovery, he was not a well man.

All the problems in South Bend did not stop Andy Granatelli from continuing his research and development on the R3 engine. Actually the slowdown gave him time to catch his breath and iron out some problems that would have plagued production models had R3 Avantis been introduced in the summer of 1962. It also gave him time to dream up another engine variation, the R4 (see sidebar, page 112).

Besides all the effort and time put into each R3 engine, R3 chassis and bodies were also modified. Chassis were fitted with heavy-duty springs and heavy-duty control arm bushings with Zerk grease fittings. Heavy-duty flanged rear axles were used. Bodies were shimmed in the front so that they sat about one inch higher than R1-R2 Avantis. This provided room for the carburetor pressure box. The body was modified so the air cleaner and a supercharger air

intake tube could be placed forward of the radiator. Cooler outside air fed to the engine helped reduce pre-detonation.

The blueprinted engine, plus the body and chassis alterations, added $1,031 to the Avanti's $4,445 base price. Today that sounds like a great bargain, but remember in late 1963 a new Volkswagen Beetle listed for only $1,595. Our driveReport R3 Avanti listed for just under $6,000, which in December 1963 was enough to buy a new Cadillac DeVille convertible with all the trimmings.

Avanti fiberglass body panels were fabricated by the Molded Fiberglass Products Company of Ashtabula, Ohio, the same company that had the Corvette contract. At first the bodies were assembled in Ohio, but numerous quality control and dimensional problems convinced Studebaker to move assembly to South Bend. The early problems and the relocation of the assembly point were the main reasons for Avanti

Facing page: Only nine cars ever wore this badge. This page, top: The car is probably faster than the plane! Left and above: Avanti's rear-end styling is quite distinctive; features huge window and shape and details that look thoroughly up to date 23 years later.

R3 AVANTI

production being so delayed during the first few months. When the problems were finally sorted out, demand for the Avanti — as mentioned — had fallen way off. Egbert still felt the super performance R3 Avanti would help sales, so information on its availability was included in the 1964 sales literature that was first distributed in September 1963. The Granatellis, who had run a 299-cubic-inch R3 at Bonneville in August 1962 (two-way flying mile at 168.15 mph), were instructed to take a whole fleet of Studebakers to Bonneville in early September 1963 and see what they could do. The runs were timed to coincide with the introduction of the 1964 models. Before rains forced them to quit, Granatelli's team had set 72 USAC records with cars ranging from a six-cylinder Lark to the mighty #9 R3 Avanti that did the two-way flying mile

This page, above: Even today the Avanti is like no other shape on the road. Right: There's access to trunk from inside car. Facing page, clockwise from top left: Readable, balanced instrument package faces driver. Small round-headed levers are for heater and vent controls. Vanity tray was standard on all Studebaker Avantis. Gas filler pipe intrudes into rear shelf area.

Driving

It would be easy to assume that all the super performance Avanti R3s would have been beat to death during their first few years of use. This was true for some of them, but surprisingly, at least two have survived in basically original condition. One of the two is our driveReport car.

This car, serial number R5642, was ordered by Mr. Leo Linnabary from the Silvis, Illinois, Studebaker dealership in late July 1963. An official Studebaker *Sales Letter* sent to dealers on June 10, 1963, indicated that "The Avanti R3 ultra-high performance engine will be available on about August 1, 1963." Mr. Linnabary's order was prepared so that Studebaker would have it by August 1. The production order form, as mentioned earlier, was dated August 1, 1963. Undoubtedly, dealers had tried to order R3s for customers in mid-1962, but none of the early orders were fulfilled. Mr. Linnabary's order was the second R3 order accepted and processed by Studebaker.

Such prompt action by Leo Linnabary and his dealer gives the impression that Leo was dying to get his hands on an R3 and see what it could do. Actually, the main reason for the Avanti's purchase had little to do with the car's performance potential. It turns out that Leo's nephew ran the Studebaker dealership in Silvis. Leo had sunk $40,000 into the dealership, and one way he saw to recoup some of his investment was to order an expensive car. At the time, the R3 Avanti was the most expensive automobile offered by Studebaker (later in the year when the R4 was introduced, it became the most expensive if ordered with air conditioning — air conditioning was not available on supercharged models).

Evidently, neither Leo nor his nephew

put much pressure on Studebaker to rush the order along. In the end, it was almost five months before the car came down the assembly line in South Bend. Its final assembly date was December 26, 1963, 17 days after Studebaker had announced it was phasing out production in the United States. It was not shipped until January 14, 1964. It turned out that Leo's Avanti was the next to the last one produced by Studebaker. The last one, also an R3, was finished on the same day.

After Linnabary received shipment of his R3, he treated it with great care. During his ownership, he had it repainted its original Avanti White color, but beyond that he maintained the car in excellent original condition. The only notable change he made was the replacement of the seven-inch cast iron crankshaft pulley set with an optional high-performance eight-inch aluminum set.

In 1982, after a considerable amount of arm twisting, Leo agreed to trade his Avanti to George Krem, Jr. At that time, the car had only about 40,000 miles on the odometer. George Krem is one of the country's leading Avanti specialists. George, who grew up in South Bend, Indiana, has been an Avanti enthusiast ever since the day they were introduced. As a young man in 1962, he gave preview Avanti test rides at a Studebaker dealership in Roselle, Illinois. Since then he and his father have owned several Avantis. Besides the driveReport car, which is now owned jointly with his father, he currently owns R5546, the fifth R3 Avanti built, on which he recently completed an exacting restoration. George is well known in Studebaker circles and was national president of the 10,000-member Studebaker Drivers Club in 1982-84.

Since purchasing the driveReport car on December 20, 1982, George has maintained it with meticulous care. There was no need to restore the car, so all George has done is give it a good detailing and add two original Studebaker options, namely an AM-FM radio and a 14-inch fan (the 14-inch fan was listed as standard equipment for R3s in the June 1963 *Sales Letter*, but evidently all R3s were shipped with the standard 17-inch Avanti fan). George now lives in Iowa City, Iowa, but our test drive was made in South Bend, Indiana, Studebaker's old home town.

Anyone familiar with Studebaker Avantis would immediately notice something odd when approaching an R3 Avanti. The raised front end makes it sit almost level, quite a contrast from the rake of standard Studebaker Avantis. Avanti IIs have an almost level stance, but they have the front wheel-well opening reduced in size to compensate for the raised front. R3s use standard Studebaker Avanti front fender sections, so the raised front leaves a lot of room around the front tires.

Sliding behind the wheel is essentially the same as getting into any Studebaker Avanti. The only major difference is the R3's 8,000-rpm tachometer. Regular Avantis have a 6,000-rpm tach. Woodgrain on the steering wheel, around the instruments and on the console is a feature introduced near the end of the 1963 model run. George's Avanti has Metallic Red upholstery, a color that was supposed to have been discontinued on October 1, 1963. But, as mentioned, the production order was written up on August 1, 1963. In December, when the car was assembled, some thoughtful employee went to the trouble to locate the ordered upholstery instead of substituting the newer Claret Red material. Studebaker's history is filled at an average speed of 170.75 mph (170.78 for the flying kilometer). Newspapers from New York to California printed stories about the records. Every speed enthusiast in the country knew about the R3 Avanti and what it could do. They also knew Studebaker was offering the R3 and R4 engines in Studebaker Hawks and most Lark-type compacts. Company executives in South Bend and Studebaker dealers all across America sat back and waited for the flood of new-car orders. Besides selling a lot of the hot ones, they were certain all the performance publicity would increase sales of Studebaker's entire 1964 line. Egbert predicted a big rush for the R3 Avanti. As mentioned, the R3 had been dangled before the buying public since April 1962. Certainly hundreds of people were anxiously awaiting the time when they could have the first R3 Avanti in their town. In the June 1963 issue of *Car Life*, it was reported that Andy Granatelli had said the "R3 (engine) production...had not kept pace with orders." Well, either Andy

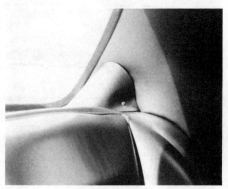

Impressions

with cases of automobiles being built with special-ordered features not listed in sales literature. Such a policy is a good way to satisfy customers, but not a profitable way to run a business.

Sitting behind the wheel of a Studebaker Avanti is like sitting in no other car of the 1963-64 era. Before you is a *full* set of round white on black instruments, including a manifold pressure gauge. On the console is the Power-shift lever and five small round-topped (flat on most '63s) levers that control venting and the Climatizer heater-defroster operation. Above the windshield in the center are six rocker switches that control the lights and the Climatizer fan. At night the instruments are lighted with a soft red glow. The overall effect is to give one the impression of sitting in an airplane cockpit, not an automobile. This is just the feeling Sherwood Egbert wanted. Looking down the hood, you see an asymmetric hood bulge that is an extension of the raised section of the instrument panel. Fit and finish on the inside are excellent. Window posts and other sections are protected with stitched vinyl with foam backing — no molded plastic here. The roll bar, which passes over just behind the driver's head, is also protected with a padded covering.

Head room is more than sufficient and the steering wheel position is quite natural. A tilt wheel was available, but not ordered on this model. The Avanti has true bucket seats, something few American car companies offered in 1964, but they are a little narrow and they are limited to forward and aft movement. Recaros they are not.

The ignition switch is located on the instrument panel just to the right of the steering column. It is a little awkward to get at, but not as bad as many of the steering column situated ones used on modern cars. A quick turn of the key and the R3 comes to life. Where is the vibration? Everyone knows that an idling supercar is like a nervous thoroughbred at the starting gate. Not this one. The standard 276° cam is mild enough to give a nice smooth idle. Put it in drive and look around. Front visibility is good, but my God, the small inside rearview mirror is almost useless. Driving this car is going to be like the neck-twisting days before Ray Harroun stuck a rearview mirror on his winning Marmon Wasp at the first Indy 500 in 1911. Foot off the brake, give it a little gas and off we go — no fuss, no vibration. Turn left, whoops, what's wrong? George's Avanti has the optional fast steering with no power assist. At low speeds, it takes some muscle to get it going where you wish. Once under way, it feels fine. Moving along easily at 30 miles per hour, the manifold pressure gauge indicates a vacuum of about 15 inches of mercury (HG) and the tachometer shows 1,400 rpm. The supercharger is just loafing. There is not the slightest impression that you are behind the wheel of one of the hottest cars ever built in America. The straight-through mufflers add a little rumble, but at 30 mph, in high gear, you feel like you are driving a family sedan down to the grocery store. *Hot Rod's* Ray Brock called it "surprisingly docile."

"Punch it," said George.

"Okay," was my reply. As the tachometer quickly moved up to and past 3,000 rpm, the car's character completely changed. I have driven some R2-powered Studebakers in the past (see *SIA* #57), but this was a whole new experience. The much better breathing engine, faster turning supercharger and other Granatelli alterations make the R3 turn into a real screamer once it climbs up past 3,000 rpm. The manifold pressure gauge slides over to the positive side and you feel your body pushed back into the seat. *Motor Trend's* August 1963 R3 production prototype did 0-60 in 6.7 seconds using the same Powershift automatic as in our driveReport car. Of course, manual four-speeds were quicker. Driving around South Bend did not give us a chance to come anywhere near testing the car's maximum performance, but short bursts of acceleration were an exciting experience. Fast corners indicated a tendency of the Avanti to oversteer, but the handling, although not in the class with a 1986 Corvette, is superior to most all domestic models of 22 years ago. The stiff suspension, anti-roll bars and radius rods help a lot. The lightweight fiberglass body also helps by lowering the center of gravity. The big drawback is the narrow 6.70x15 tires. George has a set of Halibrand mag wheels — a Studebaker option for 1964 — fitted with wide, low-profile tires. He reports that these greatly improve road adhesion, both in straightaway acceleration and cornering.

George's R3 has a final drive ratio of 3.54:1, so it is not capable of approaching 171 mph. During our test, we tried no high-speed runs, but on occasion George has taken it up to 120 mph. At that speed, the tach is registering 5,500 rpm and the manifold pressure gauge — at wide open throttle — is indicating eight pounds of supercharger boost. With a 3.54:1 ratio, a wide open throttle can only be maintained for a short time before the 6,000-rpm red line is exceeded. George has no desire to switch differential gears to match those of the record-setting Granatelli car. First, he wants to keep his car original and, second, people in Iowa don't exactly approve of land machines moving at three times the national speed limit.

specifications

Illustrations by Russell von Sauers, The Graphic Automobile Studio

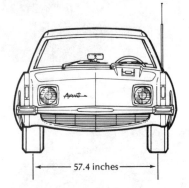

© copyright 1986, Special Interest Autos

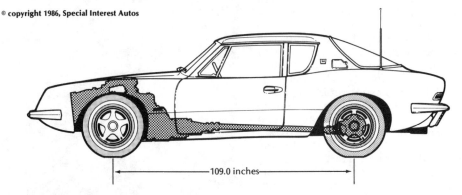

57.4 inches

109.0 inches

1964 Studebaker R3 Avanti

Base price	$4,445 (for R1)
Price as tested	$5,980 plus tax, license and delivery charges
Options	R3 performance package (includes heavy duty springs, flanged rear axle, aluminum intake manifold, exhaust headers, transistor ignition, 8,000-rpm tach), Power-shift automatic transmission, manual 16:1 steering, whitewall nylon tires, electric windshield washer, push button AM-FM radio, rear seat speaker, Twin Traction limited slip differential, front seat belts, 14-inch fan, high output aluminum crankshaft pulley)

ENGINE
Type	Overhead valve 90° V-8, cast-iron block and heads, five main bearings, solid valve lifters
Bore & stroke	3.656 inches x 3.625 inches
Displacement	304.5 cubic inches (4,991 cc)
Max bhp @ rpm	Rated 335 @ 5,350; actual 400 @ 6,000
Max torque @ rpm	Rated 320 @ 4,000
Compression ratio	9.75:1
Induction system	Paxton SN belt driven supercharger connected to a pressure box that houses a Carter AFB-3808S 4-bbl downdraft carburetor. Six pounds of boost at 5,200 rpm
Exhaust system	Cast-iron headers with dual mufflers and tailpipes
Electrical system	12-volt, negative ground, Prestolite dual point distributor, Prestolite transistor ignition system, Prestolite 40-amp alternator

TRANSMISSION
Type	3-speed Power-shift Warner AS2-10 automatic
Actuation	Console-mounted shift lever
Ratios: 1st	Torque converter x 2.40
2nd	Torque converter x 1.47
3rd	Torque converter x 1.00
Reverse	Torque converter x 2.00

DIFFERENTIAL
Type	Spicer Hypoid Twin Traction
Ratio	3.54:1
Drive axle	Semi-floating with safety flanges

STEERING
Type	Ross cam and single lever roller stud with variable ratio. No power assist
Ratios	16:1 gear, 18:1 to 22:1 overall
Turns lock to lock	3.5
Turning circle	37 feet

BRAKES
Front	Hydraulic Dunlop-style Bendix gray iron 11½-inch disc
Rear	Hydraulic 11-inch x 2-inch Budd finned drum
Assist	Bendix Master-Vac power assist
Total swept area	377 square inches

CHASSIS & BODY
Frame	Double-drop steel box section side rails, four cross member ladder-type with X member
Body construction	Reinforced fiberglass with steel roll bar
Body style	4-passenger, 2-door sport coupe
Configuration	Front engine, rear wheel drive

SUSPENSION
Front	Independent, coil springs with upper and lower unequal length A-arms, direct-acting tubular hydraulic shocks, and anti-roll bar
Rear	Solid axle, 6-leaf semi-elliptic springs, direct-acting tubular hydraulic shocks, radius rods and anti-roll bar. Hotchkiss drive
Wheels	Five-lug, 15-inch x 5-inch Budd steel disc
Tires	Nylon tubeless bias ply 6.70 x 15

WEIGHTS AND MEASURES
Wheelbase	109 inches
Overall length	192.4 inches
Overall height	53.8 inches
Overall width	70.3 inches
Front tread	57.4 inches
Rear tread	56.6 inches
Frontal area	21.1 square feet
Ground clearance	7.0 inches
Shipping weight	3,195 pounds
Curb weight	3,441 pounds
Weight distribution	59% front, 41% rear

CAPACITIES
Crankcase	6 quarts (7 with filter change)
Cooling system	18 quarts (with standard heater)
Fuel tank	21 gallons
Transmission	18 pints

PERFORMANCE
Maximum speed	171 mph
Acceleration	0-60 mph: 5.8 seconds
Standing start quarter mile	110 mph and 13.2 seconds

(with various final drive ratios and a 4-speed transmission)

R3 AVANTI

was pulling somebody's leg, or his production rate was limited to filling orders for prototypes. Except for one lone order written up in June 1963, dealers did not start placing any R3 orders until August 1963. The production order for the second R3 Avanti was written on August 1, 1963. This particular car, which is our driveReport car, was not completed until December 26, 1963! Production orders for three more R3 Avantis were written up in August, one in September and three in October, and that was it! A grand total of nine. The third one ordered was the first one finished, on October 17, 1963. The last one built was ordered on October 7, 1963, came off the line on December 26, 1963, and was shipped on January 10, 1964.

What happened? Sadly, Egbert had misjudged the buying public, especially current Studebaker owners. Although

Studebaker had produced some dramatic stylings in the past, its overall image was one of conservatism. The R3 Avanti, and all other Avantis for that matter, did not fit in with Studebaker's image. Getting Big Three buyers to switch to Studebaker had always been difficult, and very few long-time Studebaker owners were attracted to the Avanti. And finally, the $1,031 premium for the R3 was more than all but nine people were willing to pay.

Thus, in the end, the high-performance Bonneville runs did almost nothing to help Avanti or Studebaker sales. The whole survival of the automobile division depended on successful sales of the 1964 models. 1964 production had been started at 60 vehicles per hour, but by late October it was down to 35 per hour and 2,450 employees had been laid off. Then on November 5, 1963, Egbert had more cancer surgery and was given an indefinite leave of absence. Byers A. Burlingame took over, and shortly afterwards it was decided to stop Studebaker production in South Bend. The closure announcement was made public on December 9, 1963. Lark-type vehicle production was to be continued in Canada, but all Avanti, Hawk and truck production was terminated. R series engines were also discontinued. A little over two years later, the Candian plant was closed. In 1965, the Avanti Motor Corporation started producing 1966 model Avanti IIs, but they were powered by Chevrolet engines, not R series Studebaker engines.

Certainly more R3 Avantis would have been sold if Studebaker had continued in the American automobile business, but it is highly unlikely that they would have ever been a big success. Fortunately for enthusiasts, Studebaker did get a handful built before they closed their doors. □

Acknowledgements and Bibliography
They Call Me Mister 500 *by Anthony Granatelli*; Studebaker, The Complete Story *by William A. Cannon and Fred K. Fox*; Studebaker, Less Than They Promised *by Beatty, Furlong and Pennington*; Industrial Design *by Raymond Loewy*; Original Studebaker sales literature and dealer communiques; AMA Special Equipment Specifications *for 1963 and 1964 Avantis*; Contemporary articles from various car magazines; Original factory production, price and specification data from the collections of George Krem, Jr. and the author.
Our thanks to George Krem, Sr., and George Krem, Jr., owners of this article's feature car. Further thanks to George Krem, Jr. and Bob Palma for previewing the manuscript. Thanks also to James Talbot for providing information on high-speed automobile records.

Facing page: Spare lies in recessed well to allow flat floor. **This page, left:** *Chromed valve covers and extra breather caps were standard equipment.* **Below:** *From any angle it's a striking car.*

Raymond Loewy
1893-1986

Just as the author of this article was preparing to mail his manuscript to *SIA*, he learned of the death of Raymond Loewy, one of the world's most famous industrial designers and the leader of the team that designed the Avanti back in 1961.

Loewy was born in Paris on November 5, 1893. He came to the United States in 1919, became an American citizen in 1938 and passed away in Monaco on July 14, 1986. He and the design studios he owned styled thousands of products ranging from Lucky Strike packages to the interior design of Air Force One.

In the automobile field, Loewy first worked with Hupmobile and then in 1936 he signed a contract to design the 1938 Studebakers. His contracts with Studebaker lasted until the mid-1950s. The 1956 Studebaker Hawks were the last Studebakers his company styled before he took on the Avanti assignment in 1961.

Most of Loewy's designs were actually created by his subordinates. For instance, the famous 1953 Studebaker Starliner and Starlight "Loewy Coupes" were designed by Robert Bourke, Loewy's South Bend styling chief. Loewy's real talent was his ability to sell his studio's design ideas to hundreds of different companies. Only on a rare occasion did he ever actively get involved in designing one of his products. The Avanti was one of those rare occasions. He worked side by side with the other three stylists who developed the ⅛-scale clay Avanti model in Palm Springs. Loewy considered the Avanti one of the major hallmarks of his career. In his 1979 book, *Industrial Design*, the Avanti is given more exposure than any other of the thousands of products that were styled by his studios. He was also an Avanti owner. He owned a Studebaker Avanti at first and later acquired an Avanti II, which he still owned at the time of his death.

Raymond Loewy, Frank Lloyd Wright, Norman Bel Geddes, and a handful of other designers were responsible for creating the golden era of commercial design. Their efforts made our world a much more beautiful place in which to live.

photo courtesy of the author

Raymond Loewy, left, and Sherwood Egbert admire '62 prototype.

Studebaker Clubs and Parts Suppliers

These clubs and resources listings were compiled in July 2000. For the most up-to-date information, consult the latest issue of *Hemmings' Vintage Auto Almanac* and the Hemmings web site at www.hemmings.com.

CLUBS

Antique Studebaker Club Inc.
P.O. Box 28845
Dallas, TX 75228-0845
800-527-3452
Dues: $23/year
Membership: 1,300

Studebaker Drivers Club
P.O. Box 28788
Dallas, TX
800-527-3452
Dues: $27.50
Membership: 13,000

1956 Studebaker Golden Hawk Registry
31700 Wikiva River Rd.
Sorrento, FL 32776-9233
Dues: None

PARTS SUPPLIERS

Dakota Studebaker Parts
RR 1, Box 103A
Armour, SD 57313
605-724-2527
Large supply of sheetmetal and trim parts for 1936-1964 Studebakers

Dennis DuPont
77 Island Pond Rd.
Derry, NH 03038
603-434-9290
Extensive selection of NOS and used parts for 1930-1966 Studebakers

Kelly's Korner
22 14th St.
Bristol, TN 37620
423-968-5583
Substantial assortment of mechanical and body parts for 1925-1966 Studebaker cars and trucks

Loga Enterprises
5399 Old Town Hall Rd.
Eau Claire, MO 657232
715-832-7302
Full line of interior parts and trim for 1937-1966 Studebakers

Phil's Studebaker
11250 Harrison Rd.
Osceola, IN 46561-9375
219-674-0084
Wide range of NOS and reproduction body and trim parts for 1947-1966 Studebakers

Charles Schnetlage
22136 Roscoe Blvd.
Canoga Park, CA 91304
818-347-0334
Vast assortment of reproduction rubber products and brake parts for 1928-1957 Studebakers

Steve's Studebaker-Packard
P.O. Box 6914
Napa, CA 94581
707-255-8945
Large range of body, interior and suspension parts for 1953-1966 Studebakers

Studebaker of California
1400 Santa Fe Ave.
Long Beach, CA 90813
562-435-0157
Full stock of reproduction and NOS parts for 1946-1966 Studebakers

Studebaker Parts & Locations
228 Marquiss Cir.
Clinton, TN 37716
615-457-3002
Sizable assortment of new and used body and mechanical parts for 1939-1966 Studebakers and Avantis

Studebakers West
335A Convention Way
Redwood City, CA 94063
650-366-8787
Thousands of new and used mechanical, chassis, interior and electrical parts for most any Studebaker

NOTES

NOTES